Business, Politics, and Society

Business, Politics, and Society

An Anglo-American Comparison

Michael Moran

OXFORD
UNIVERSITY PRESS

OXFORD
UNIVERSITY PRESS

Great Clarendon Street, Oxford OX2 6DP

Oxford University Press is a department of the University of Oxford.
It furthers the University's objective of excellence in research, scholarship,
and education by publishing worldwide in

Oxford New York

Auckland Cape Town Dar es Salaam Hong Kong Karachi
Kuala Lumpur Madrid Melbourne Mexico City Nairobi
New Delhi Shanghai Taipei Toronto

With offices in

Argentina Austria Brazil Chile Czech Republic France Greece
Guatemala Hungary Italy Japan Poland Portugal Singapore
South Korea Switzerland Thailand Turkey Ukraine Vietnam

Oxford is a registered trade mark of Oxford University Press
in the UK and in certain other countries

Published in the United States
by Oxford University Press Inc., New York

British Library Cataloguing in Publication Data
Data available

Library of Congress Cataloging in Publication Data
Data available

Typeset by SPI Publisher Services, Pondicherry, India
Printed in Great Britain
on acid-free paper by the
MPG Books Group, Bodmin and Kings Lynn

ISBN 978–0–19–920255–3 (Hbk.)
       978–0–19–920256–0 (Pbk.)

1 3 5 7 9 10 8 6 4 2

CONTENTS

LIST OF BOXES   vii
LIST OF ABBREVIATIONS   ix
PREFACE   xi
ACKNOWLEDGEMENTS   xv

1 Studying Business and Politics   1

Comparing business politics   1
Business power and democratic politics   3
Models of capitalism and business power   7
Policy issues and the power of business   11
Capitalism, democracy, and the power of business   16

2 The History of Business and Politics   18

Paths to the present   18
The United Kingdom: business, oligarchies, and democracy   20
The United States: business, Populism, and democracy   28
Varieties of capitalism and varieties of democracy   37

3 Organizing Business   40

Business collective action and the politics of the firm   40
The United Kingdom: fragmentation and firm autonomy   42
The United States: organizing business under decentralized government   50
Business lobbying and the crisis of the business system   59

4 Politics and the Giant Multinational Corporation   61

Why giant firms matter politically   61
The giant firm and politics in the United Kingdom: the transformation of a private political world   63
The giant firm and American politics: great strengths and great weaknesses   70
The giant firm and global economic lobbying: the problem of strategic cohesion   77
The essentially political character of the giant corporation   82

5 Small Business and Politics 83

Small business, collective action, and political innovation 83
Small-business politics in the United Kingdom: decline and revival? 86
The United States: small business in a benign environment? 95
Political innovation and political weakness in the small-business sector 104

6 Business Politics and Party Politics 106

Business, parties, and democracy 106
Business and party politics in the United Kingdom: the rise of a
business-friendly party system 108
The United States: regulating the party–business connection 117
The travails of business-friendly parties 127

7 Business, Politics, and Society 129

Understanding the cultural setting of business 129
The United Kingdom: the transformation of a hegemonic order 132
The United States: between Gramsci and Schumpeter 140
From hegemony to pluralism 149

8 Restless Democracy and Restless Capitalism 151

Economic change and the politics of business representation 151
Restless democracy and business politics 153
Restless capitalism and business politics 159
Business, democracy, and legitimacy 164
Business power and the Anglo-American model of capitalism 169

BIBLIOGRAPHY 173
INDEX 191

☐ LIST OF BOXES

2.1 Politics and market building: the case of the EU   19

2.2 The changing history of the developmental state and big business:
the case of South Korea   27

2.3 An industrial statesman and politics: Henry Ford and 'Fordism'   36

3.1 The evolution of business lobbying in the EU   41

3.2 How the French business elite organizes itself politically   49

3.3 The Transatlantic Business Dialogue at work: the EU–US
summit of June 2008   58

4.1 The European Round Table of Industrialists: a voice of the
European business elite   62

4.2 Big business and politics in Russia   69

4.3 An American multinational enters UK supermarket politics:
the case of Wal-Mart   76

5.1 What does business do when it lobbies? The case of the
UK Federation of Small Businesses in Brussels   85

5.2 Small business and politics: the case of Japanese farmers   94

5.3 The organization of the small-business lobby: the UK FSB
and the US NFIB compared   103

6.1 Influencing the mood music in the European Parliament:
the European Business and Parliament scheme   107

6.2 'Clientelism' and party–business relations in Ireland:
Charlie Haughey loots business and the public purse   116

6.3 Regulating business money in the parties: a study in
contrasting national regulatory styles   126

7.1 Civil society groups and the regulation of business lobbyists in the EU   131

7.2 Lobbying a corporation about its marketing practices in the
developing world: Nestlé and the baby milk campaigns   139

7.3 How an Anglo-American giant responds to the challenge from
civil society groups: the case of BAT   148

8.1 Representing business in the EU: two strategies for collective
     action – Round Tables versus Grand Confederations   152

8.2 The World Economic Forum: transnational planning body
     or the world's most lavish cocktail party?   158

8.3 How the great financial crisis of 2007–9 changed business
     and politics in Anglo-America   168

LIST OF ABBREVIATIONS

ALTER-EU	Alliance for Lobbying Transparency and Ethics Regulation
BAT	British American Tobacco
CBI	Confederation of British Industry
CIFE	*Conseil des Fédérations Industrielles d'Europe*
CORE	Corporate Responsibility Coalition
ECSC	European Coal and Steel Community
ERT	European Round Table
ESBA	European Small Business Alliance
EU	European Union
FBI	Federation of British Industries
FEC	Federal Election Commission
FSB	Federation of Small Businesses
INFACT	Infant Formula Action Coalition
ITGA	International Tobacco Growers' Association
NAFTA	North American Free Trade Agreement
NAM	National Association of Manufacturers
NFIB	National Federation of Independent Business
NGOs	Non-governmental organizations
OFT	Office of Fair Trading
PACs	Political Action Committees
RNIB	Royal National Institute for the Blind
RUIE	Russian Union of Industrialists and Entrepreneurs
TABD	Transatlantic Business Dialogue
TEC	Transatlantic Economic Council
UNICE	*Union des Industries de la Communauté européenne*
WEF	World Economic Forum
WHO	World Health Organization

☐ PREFACE

Why write a textbook about business and politics? Why write a comparative text? And why frame the comparison in Anglo-American terms? I answer these questions here.

There now exists a rich research literature on business and politics. That literature provides the foundations for any textbook, including this one. I aim to write informed by the latest research. Some readers will have a good undergraduate grounding in political science. But the themes of the book – the political and social setting of business – are increasingly important on business studies courses, including those taught on Master's degrees. I have borne these latter students in mind, and one important consequence is that, while the book draws on the research literature, I have tried as far as possible to avoid the specialized language of professional political science. In any case, much valuable literature on this subject is not created by political science at all, but comes from sister disciplines – notably business and management itself, business history, sociology, and political economy. My aim is to synthesize as clearly and economically as possible what we know on the subject.

I have chosen to frame the material comparatively for very well-established reasons. In part, they are analytic: there is an important sense in which all serious social explanation is comparative. At the back of most single country studies lie implicit assumptions about what makes that case special. It is best to make those assumptions explicit, and the most effective way to do this is to frame any discussion of a single country comparatively.

The decision to frame the book comparatively was therefore easy to make. The size of that frame was quite another matter. I have here been obliged to make compromises. The United States is the leading capitalist democratic nation on earth and it is hard to imagine discussing business and politics without making the American case central. The United Kingdom has a substantive importance – as the fourth or fifth (depending on measurements) largest national economy on earth. As the first industrial society, it was also the pioneer of many important features of the connections between business and politics, especially business and the state. In recent years, the two national systems have occupied an important place in what is usually called the 'varieties of capitalism' literature. The United States and United Kingdom have often being assimilated to a common model of 'Anglo-American capitalism' (see, for instance, Albert 1993; Hutton 1995; Hall and Soskice 2001). The book is not a systematic test of the thesis that the United Kingdom and the United States do indeed conform to a common model. We will, though, see some striking differences in political patterns that might make us doubt that we are indeed looking at a single model of capitalist democracy.

Deciding to include the United States and the United Kingdom in the account posed no problems. Deciding to leave out others has been more difficult. In part, the book has to be shaped by a familiar trade off: focusing on the United Kingdom and the United States narrows the comparative range; but to encompass the other leading capitalist democracies, let alone the wider, expanding world of capitalism would demand a textbook unmanageable in size, and probably beyond the capacity of any single author. Concentrating on the United Kingdom and the United States creates two particularly serious gaps. First, it marginalizes an important system of business politics, organized in the European Union (EU), that has been created in the last generation. That European system is marginalized in these pages because, while I often discuss the EU, it is usually viewed through the lens of national systems – mostly the UK systems. (I use the plural because we shall see that an important sub-theme of the description of the United Kingdom is the emergence of distinctive national patterns in Scotland and Wales.) Second, the text also omits some of the most distinctive national worlds of capitalism, systems that are central to the 'varieties of capitalism' literature: the kind exemplified, for instance, by Germany and Japan.

Fully remedying these omissions would either demand a hugely expanded text or an even more schematic approach than is used in these pages. I have nevertheless tried to alleviate the problems by complementing the text with boxed features. There are three kinds of boxes in every chapter except Chapter 1 (which sets out the analytical frame of the book). One kind of box takes a single theme of the chapter and analyses the EU in terms of that theme, thus putting it centre stage. A second takes the theme of each chapter and illustrates it with an example from beyond the national worlds of American and British capitalism; its purpose is to expand the range of the discussion and to remind us that there are spheres of capitalist democracy beyond the United States and the United Kingdom. A third kind of box focuses comparatively on a single Anglo-American case relevant to the theme of the chapter. I do this because within each chapter the material is naturally dominated by accounts that focus on each country in turn. While I draw themes together comparatively in the conclusion to each chapter, the additional case boxes provide an extra way of sharpening the comparative focus of the book. All three kinds of boxes are 'cases' in the widest sense of that word. Sometimes, they are indeed narratives of particularly illuminating episodes in business politics; but in all instances they are designed to provide illustrations that give a particular life to the general features that dominate the description in the text of chapters.

Concentrating on the two cases of the United Kingdom and the United States therefore imposes limits, but it also opens up possibilities – and these possibilities provide important themes in the chapters that follow. Even a reader entirely new to the study of business systems and political systems will already recognize an important common feature of our two cases: they are not just varieties of capitalism, but also varieties of *capitalist democracy*. Their examination thus allows us to explore one of the most important political formations on earth today: that formation which tries to unite an economy based on principles of market allocation and private property (capitalism) with a political system based on principles of popular competition for political influence and leadership (democracy). The United States is not only the most important national economy on earth, but it is also the most powerful national system that claims to practise democratic politics. The 'varieties of capitalism' literature has attuned us to the notion that capitalism can take many different national and regional forms. But democratic politics also varies, and we shall see that democracy in Britain often means something very different from democracy in America. Nor is variation across country the only important difference. Democratic politics are no more fixed historically than are capitalist economies. The changing face of democratic politics over time can have big consequences for the way business functions politically.

This consideration – that democracy varies across space and across time – helps explain the organization of the book. In a capitalist democracy, the most obvious questions to ask are as follows: what does the fact of democracy do to the way business operates; and what does the fact of private property and a market economy do to the way democratic politics functions? Social scientists have argued long and hard about these general questions, and before we turn to the particular national cases we need to examine those arguments: that is the purpose of Chapter 1. Chapter 2 exists because democratic systems, and business systems, change over time. The way they change is deeply influenced by their origins. To make sense of business politics now, we need to know how it arrived at its present condition in our two countries. Once again, the variety of capitalism literature has attuned us to the importance of the different trajectories taken by national business systems; but we will see that the distinctive trajectories taken by national democratic systems are also critical for the way business operates politically.

Chapters 3 through 6 spring from a simple but vital observation: the essence of democratic politics is competition – for votes, for office, and for influence over policy decisions. Business has to organize to succeed in this competition. Chapters 3 through 5 examine the forms this organization takes. Chapters 3 and 4 can be considered twins. Chapter 3 examines collective action by business, notably in trade associations and 'peak' associations: the former are linked to particular industries and sectors, the latter (like the Confederation of British Industry in the

United Kingdom and the US Chamber of Commerce) claim to speak as the voice of business generally. The relationship between representative associations and the individual firms can, we shall see, be problematic. Firms can choose to plough their own political furrow, and if they are giant firms they will have resources to do this. That is why Chapter 4 looks in particular at the political role of the giant firm. Since most giant enterprises are also multinational in their reach, this chapter also gives us the opportunity to examine one of the most hotly debated issues in modern business politics: the political role of business in an age of globalization. One of the themes that will emerge from both Chapters 3 and 4 is that understanding the political significance and role of business demands sensitivity to differences between sectors, and between individual enterprises. Chapter 5 looks at a particularly important example of this: the distinctive political position of small business. Politicians have to organize to compete effectively; and business has to organize to influence politicians and other policy makers in this competitive environment. Chapter 6 focuses on the most elementary form of democratic competition: that organized by political parties competing for votes and, through votes, for public office. It is elementary but also fundamental. Business always has to have some answer to the question: what kind of relationship should it create with political parties?

Recall that the headline title of this book is 'Business, Politics, *and Society*'. It signals that the impact of cultural and social change beyond the formally organized business system and the formally organized political system is to be a recurrent theme. Chapter 7, however, takes this as its main focus. Chapter 8 does more than sum up. It does indeed recall some of the opening themes, but it also develops a particular argument: that the political position of business changes not just because of developments in the business system, but also because of the changing nature of democratic politics. This concluding chapter thus recalls us to one of the main features of the book: it is a study of the politics of business under capitalist *democracy*.

Michael Moran

University of Manchester
5 December 2008

ACKNOWLEDGEMENTS

I have as usual pestered colleagues, friends, and even family with earlier drafts of this book, and it is a pleasure to acknowledge their help. I benefited greatly from comments on all or part of the manuscript from David Coates, Wyn Grant, Douglas Jaenicke, Tim May, John McHugh, Joe Moran, Inderjeet Parmar, and Graham Wilson. I also received invaluable comments on an earlier draft from an anonymous reviewer for Oxford University Press. I thank Matthew Bannister of the Press for arranging that, and for his helpful comments on the first draft of the book. I must also thank successive generations of students on my courses in business and politics at the University of Manchester on whom I have inflicted earlier versions of the arguments of these pages.

As will be plain, I have received much good advice from people who really know what they are talking about. I have sometimes been too stubborn, or incompetent, to take that advice; thus, all that follows is my responsibility alone.

The book is dedicated to Winifred, who has always shown a healthy indifference to politics and to business.

1 Studying Business and Politics

Comparing business politics

The business firm is one of the most important institutions in modern industrial society. The giant enterprise in particular is a major – perhaps *the* major – allocator of society's economic resources. It is also a great centre of power. The hierarchies of the firm subject numerous citizens to control – most obviously, over those who work in the enterprise, but also over suppliers and, in certain circumstances, over customers. The wider social impact of business activity – for instance in its effect on the physical environment – can shape the lives of all citizens, for better or worse. Hannah makes the point in writing about Britain:

The harshnesses of capitalism that remain may still bear down heavily on individuals, but they now do so less as a result of competitive market pressures on employment and wages, and more as a result of decisions which emanate from a managerial hierarchy which has supplemented the market as a means of co-ordinating economic activity. (1983: 2)

This power explains why the firm is a major concern of the state on both sides of the Atlantic. The fact that it is a major concern of the state helps explain another feature of the firm's political importance: business, either organized collectively or operating as a single firm, is a serious political actor in the governing systems of all advanced capitalist nations. As we shall see shortly, that has produced important debates about the power of business: about how far the effective operation of democratic government is compatible with, or alternatively is facilitated by, the role of business both as a hierarchy of authority and as a political lobbyist. Fully understanding the business firm, therefore, involves more than understanding it as an economic actor; it also involves understanding it as a political actor. That is what this book is designed to convey. Understanding the firm as a political actor is, however, not only important for understanding business, but is also vital for understanding the wider governing system. As we shall see, our judgement about the power wielded by business shapes our wider view of the viability of democratic politics.

These concerns help explain why this book introduces and compares business politics in two national systems. The United States is chosen for such obvious reasons that they need only be briefly summarized here. American business is the most powerful on earth, and beyond the United States is central to the operation of the global economy. As we will see in these pages, the American case also illuminates in a unique way the complex relationship between business power and democratic politics. The United Kingdom is also chosen partly for substantive reasons. It is not only the world's fourth or fifth (depending on measures) largest national economy, but is also one of the most 'globalized'. The City of London, which occupies a peculiarly important place in the British business community, is one of the three great world financial centres (alongside New York and Tokyo). The United Kingdom has for several years now also been the leading location for direct foreign investment in the European Union (EU) – and much of this investment is American in origin. The two business communities, we shall also see, are closely linked – and some of this linkage takes important organized political forms. But the significance of the United Kingdom goes beyond present importance. Famously, the United Kingdom was the first industrial society – the first society where many of the key institutions of modern business capitalism were developed. That pioneering experience has left important marks on the way business now works as a political actor – marks that crop up repeatedly in the following pages.

An important common feature binds the United States and the United Kingdom: they are both species of capitalist democracy. Yet, it is plain that there is no one single form of capitalism, but many models of capitalist economies. In the 'models of capitalism' literature, it is common, as was noted in the Preface, to treat the United States and the United Kingdom as leading examples of the same 'model': variously labelled as shareholder, stock exchange dominated, or liberal capitalism. Picturing the United Kingdom and the United States as belonging to a common model of capitalism obviously has important implications for the way we think economic activity is organized – as the different names of models suggest. But it also has important implications for how the relationship between business and politics is viewed: we might expect to find, if the United States and the United Kingdom are indeed part of a single family of capitalism, that (the relationship between business and the state is similar in both countries.) Part of the purpose of the following pages is to examine what are indeed the commonalities in the political role of business in this particular model of capitalism. But what will also emerge in the following pages are striking differences in political patterns between the two countries. These differences in turn have a great deal to do with the historical development of two sets of institutions: the institutions of business itself and the institutions of democratic politics. The answer we can give to a critical question – what is the relationship between business power and democratic politics? – depends a lot, we will discover, on which country we are talking about.

The two systems compared here, therefore, are important in their own right, and are also important analytically because they are so often held to stand for a particularly influential model of how to organize a capitalist economy. Of course, a full understanding of business and politics in advanced capitalism would demand something much more ambitious than is attempted in these pages. The market economy – where the business firm is a key institution – is now the dominant form across the globe, especially since the collapse of the command economies of the communist autocracies in the 1990s. The great economic crisis of 2007–9 will not change that, though it will change the relationship between states and markets. The relationship of business to politics outside the two giant North Atlantic economies is complex and diverse, and requires its own separate mapping. There also exists a world of global business networks that transcend nations, explored for example in Braithwaite and Drahos (2000). I have explained in the Preface how I deal with this bigger picture in the following chapters, but now turn to the established debates about business power and democratic politics.

Business power and democratic politics

Debates on business power go to the heart of our judgements about the viability of modern democratic politics. Most national economies in the world today are governed by some species of capitalism. That is, they allocate goods and services through market institutions designed to signal demand and supply, their most important productive resources are privately owned, these systems of private ownership are regulated in law, and they are typically embodied in the legal form of the business enterprise. At the same time, many of these capitalist nations also claim to practise democratic government. The attempt to combine democratic political practices with the existence of large and well-organized business communities dominated by giant firms is precisely what marks out the United States and the United Kingdom. A key question, therefore, is 'what does uniting democracy and capitalism do to business power and to democratic politics?' In a political system where nearly every adult may vote, but where business controls huge and unequally distributed resources, who actually governs? (Readers familiar with the literature on power in democratic systems will recognize this last sentence as a crib from the opening of a classic study of democratic politics Dahl 1961: 1.) Three particularly influential answers have been given to this question: pluralist, power elite, and structuralist.

Pluralism argues that there are many (a plurality of) ways of exercising power, many different resources that can be turned into power (e.g. money, skill, and votes), many separate domains where power can be exercised, and thus many different possible outcomes in any single instance of the attempted exercise of power (Dahl 1961 is still the classic account). Business, if it can organize and if it acquires political skills, has the potential to exercise overwhelming power, but that potential is not always realized. The reason for this has been most cogently described by Vogel (especially 1989 and 1996): Business has to operate in a competitive political environment, where there are many other organized interests, with whom it has to struggle for a say over policy decisions. What matters therefore is not just the resources it possesses, but how well it uses those resources in competition with rival interests. Two key influences determine success in this competition: how far business can operate as a united interest, something that observably varies greatly, and the political climate in which it functions. In this latter connection, Vogel has analysed the 'fluctuating fortunes' of business in America over the course of the twentieth century, fortunes that vary partly because there are long historical waves of popular hostility towards, or support for, important business institutions (Vogel 1989: 7–8).

The development of a fully worked out pluralist model was itself prompted by accounts of the distribution of power in American society which painted a very different picture of the power of business. According to Wright Mills' classic *The Power Elite*, the commanding heights of business were 'intricately and deeply involved' with governing elites – for instance with elites from the armed forces and the federal government. The result was to displace a 'democratic social structure' with a 'formal political democracy' that merely offered the rituals, not the substance, of popular control (Wright Mills 1956/ 2000: 274).

Although it was a critical account of the power of business, and although it was moved by a desire to democratize the capitalist economy, this *power elite* theory had links to older, more pessimistic pictures of how power works. This pessimism originated among a group of theorists who flourished in the early decades of the twentieth century in Europe. They developed a universal theory of 'elitism' as a critique of the claims of the new movements pressing for democratic control of political life. Power, according to these 'classical' elitists, would always be manipulated by a few, and thus the pretensions of democratic government were just that – pretensions (Parry 1969/2005). But in the American case, power elite theory also grew out of a more native intellectual strain: it rose to importance in the later decades of the nineteenth century and is usually called 'Populism'. It was a moral critique of the power of big business and of big government. That intellectual strain represented the response of a traditional, rural America to the first appearance of big business as a major institution in American life: to the growth of the first giant industrial corporations and to the emergence of financial markets, especially on Wall Street in New York, as major forces in the American economy, and indeed in American life (see Chapter 2 for more on this). Thus, the inspiration for power elite theory was the belief not that business as a whole was powerful (small business, according to Populism, was exploited and oppressed by the big business trusts) but that a privileged section of business was allied to other powerful groups, notably in government and the political parties, and was manipulating democratic politics.

Power elite theory is in this respect different in subtle, but important, ways from a third account, the theory of the *structural power* of business. It is labelled thus because it says that the very way business is organized in a market economy confers privileged power on enterprises. 'Structure' refers to the core institutional structures of the market economy: to the rules governing the ownership of property in enterprises; and to the rules governing the conduct of business life, such as who is entitled to take decisions about the allocation of resources, as in decisions about investment in new productive capacity or innovation in new technologies.

Theories of the structural power of business have come in many forms. Historically, the most politically influential was derived from Marxism. The original theories, much elaborated and changed over time, come from the work of Karl Marx (1818–83) who rooted them in a comprehensive theory of historical change. Marx argued that historical change was driven by changes in the 'means of production' – in the basic technologies and social practices by which societies organized economic life. Control of the most developed means of production was in the hands of the class that ruled in any society. In developed capitalist societies – the most innovative when Marx wrote and still the dominant form – this meant that the ruling class was composed of leading capitalists who controlled the most advanced sectors of business. The ruling class was a business class, whatever the formal political arrangements. Subsequently, numerous descriptions have been offered of how the public workings of democratic politics could be fitted to this account. One is that democracy is 'the best possible shell' for capitalism. In other words, it is the political system mostly likely to allow capitalists to realize their class interest, equipping them with a state able to think and act in the long-term interests of the capitalist class, often in defiance of the short term, sectional desires of particular groups of business people (King and Kendall 2004: 59–72). This tension between the interests of *particular* businesses or sectors and the wider *collective* interests of business is one we shall encounter often in the succeeding pages; and one strength of this Marxist account is that it tries to show how the separate interests of business firms and sectors can be organized into the collective interests of capital.

Marxism is, however, not the only source of a structural account of business power, and its influence has indeed waned in recent decades. The single most influential academic study of business power published in the last generation is Lindblom's *Politics and Markets* (1977; and see also Lindblom

2002: 236–50). Lindblom is especially concerned with one of the big themes of this book: the relationship between business power and democratic politics. He argues that only a highly attenuated form of popular control in any case exists in modern mass democracies. He dubs this polyarchy, signifying rule by competing elites. But even this circumscribed form of popular control is further hemmed in by the principles of a market economy, which give business a privileged position. The rules of property mean that business institutions own and control the most important economic resources in society. They therefore make the key decisions – about innovation, invest-ment, production, and marketing – that shape the economic fate of societies. Elected governments have little option but to accept that their fates are shaped by these independent business decisions. In this way, the rules of the market economy 'organize out' important decisions from any democratic political arena. There is no need for business to try covertly to manipulate government or to ally itself with other elites to form a single power elite. Without thinking, so to speak, it already occupies privileged ground. In Lindblom's own words:

> ... in any private enterprise system, a large category of major decisions is turned over to businessmen, both small and larger. They are taken off the agenda of government. Businessmen thus become a kind of public official and exercise what, on a broad view of their role, are public functions. The significant logical consequence of this for polyarchy is that a broad area of public decision-making is removed from polyarchal control. Polyarchal decision-making may of course ratify such an arrangement or amend it through governmental regulation of business decision making. In all real-world polyarchies, a substantial category of decisions is removed from polyarchal control. (1977: 172)

The pros and cons of these competing views of business power form a recurrent theme of the pages of this book, so are not rehearsed here. But we should notice one critical difference in assumptions that underlie the competing accounts. It has nothing to do with views about business, but rather concerns the way *power* is conceived and measured (Lukes 2005 is the classic explanation of this). The fundamental assumption of many *pluralist* accounts is that by accumulating studies of important decisions we can identify power holders. We identify a powerful group by discovering that it consistently dominates key decisions. The fundamental assumption of most *power elite* theories is that business power is less about exercising influence over single decisions (though this can happen) and more about location at the centre of networks which link business elites with other elites in society – like leading politicians, leading bureaucrats, or elites drawn from institutions like top universities and the armed forces. In Wright Mills' classic, power is the product of institutional position, and we identify power holders as those who 'are in command of the major hierarchies and organizations of modern society' (1956/2000: 4). This emphasis on the way power resides in particular enduring institutional arrangements, rather than being dependent on control over separate decisions, is obviously even more critical in the set of views that underpin *structural* theories. What unites theorists like Marx and Lindblom, despite their many other differences, is that business power is seen as a function of the way control over productive resources in a society is organized.

Many of the debates about the power of business, notably the debates stimulated by 'structural' accounts of business power, have implicitly made an important assumption: that power relations under capitalism are comparatively unvarying, at least for the same historical epochs. That assumption naturally follows from the argument that the fundamental rules of property ownership in a market economy ensure the privileged position of business. But that assumption is in turn implicitly challenged in what is sometimes called the 'models of capitalism' literature.

Models of capitalism and business power

tending to or able to change frequently or easily

Capitalism is an extraordinarily protean phenomenon, and this capacity for innovation and reinvention has from the beginning been at the heart of all the competing accounts of its character. In the classic literature, these accounts stretch from Marx's vision of the capitalist order as part of a process of world historical change (see last section) to Schumpeter's account of capitalism as a system dominated by 'creative destruction' – perpetual restlessness leading to endless cycles of innovation and the destruction of established firms and industries (Schumpeter 1943/1976: 81–6). It is not surprising, therefore, that the diversity of capitalism has given rise to a diversity of interpretations of the character of capitalism.

We can distinguish two different ways of tracking this diverse character, though they have recently begun to overlap: tracking across time and across space. Here we look at what each in turn suggests about the evolving character of business power.

Tracking capitalism across time created, at least until the closing decades of the twentieth century, a striking consensus among observers of otherwise very different intellectual and ideological persuasions: that capitalism's historical progress produced an increasing tendency towards more 'organized' forms. The character of that organization differed, true, according to intellectual and ideological persuasion. For the Austrian theorist, Hilferding, who was deeply influenced by Marx, it involved the development of systems of control with great banking complexes at their centre – a system of organized 'finance capitalism' (Hilferding 1910/1985). In the hands of cruder Marxist theorists, like the Russian revolutionary Lenin, it involved a theory that bound the development of capitalism to competition between states for global power – a competition to create empires, leading to Lenin's famous description of imperialism as 'the highest stage of capitalism' (1917/ 1975).

It is striking how far accounts outside this Marxist tradition also stressed the increasingly organized nature of the capitalist economy. Schumpeter, the scholar of capitalism who was most aware of the Marxist legacy and who saw capitalism as a restless historical force, pictured it as taking an increasingly organized form: monopoly replaced competition by small entrepreneurs, and the culture of the giant corporation came to resemble that of public bureaucracies (Schumpeter 1943/1976: 131–42). Just over a decade before the appearance of Schumpeter's great work, a study of ownership patterns by two American scholars laid the foundations for one of the most influential twentieth century accounts of the character of capitalist corporations. Berle and Means' *The Modern Corporation and Private Property* claimed to identity a landmark shift in the nature of enterprise ownership and argued that this in turn had huge implications for the way the corporation functioned economically and politically. The dispersal of share ownership, they argued, had fundamentally changed the dynamic of the modern capitalist economy by severing the direct connection between profit and the incentives that moved the managers of enterprises. The modern manager thus had more in common with a public-service bureaucrat than with an owner-capitalist. Indeed, there had been created 'a new form of absolutism' rendering null the idea that 'economic enterprise in America is a matter of individual initiative' (Berle and Means 1932: 124–5).

This view of capitalism as a social institution that over time was being reorganized into hierarchies controlled by professional managers, who in turn regulated competition, probably reached its zenith in the 1960s and 1970s, with the appearance of two highly influential studies (Galbraith 1967/1972 and Chandler 1977). Galbraith's *The New Industrial State*, as the title implies, drew out some of the wider political implications of changes in structure. In his account, the most important business institution – the giant corporation – was pictured as a key source of planning, in effect a governing institution of society (Galbraith 1967/1972: 72–85). Exactly a decade after the appearance of *The New Industrial State*, Chandler's *The Visible Hand* identified the giant corporation as the most important institution in American life – in other words, in the life of the most powerful nation and the most powerful economy on the face of the earth. The distinctive feature of Chandler's argument was conveyed in his riveting title. Against what Adam Smith had famously pictured as the invisible hand of the market in allocating resources, Chandler pointed to the giant corporation as a powerful organized hierarchy that had emerged as the most important allocator of resources in the United States. 'The modern business enterprise', he wrote, has taken 'the place of market mechanisms in coordinating the activities of the economy and allocating its resources' (Chandler 1977: 1).

These varying accounts of capitalist historical change have very different implications for the political roles of business – but they all have powerful implications for those roles. Just for illustration, consider two that are very different in inspiration, but which share some surprising common features: those that see capitalism mutating into a form of imperialism, where foreign policy serves the interests of the business class, especially that part organized into big corporations; and those that see the modern industrial state as a partnership between government and the giant corporation.

Chandler's work on the 'visible hand' provides a bridge between the two streams of the 'models of capitalism' literature identified earlier: those that stress differences across time and those that stress differences across space. The organizational innovations created by giant corporations in industries like railroads in the later decades of the nineteenth century endowed the American economy with institutions that produced high levels of productive efficiency. In his later work, Chandler became concerned with the degree to which these superior organizational forms were spread (or not spread) internationally. For instance, he ascribed some of the comparatively poor performance of the British economy in the twentieth century to the failure to adopt these superior institutional structures and practices (Chandler 1990). Lazonick fused Chandler's insight about the significance of national variations in business systems with a historical argument: that the American system of corporate organization was itself the product of a particular epoch and that it has been superseded as the most competitively effective national form by models, like the Japanese, better capable of long-term planning and coordination (Lazonick 1991: 57).

The insight that national models of capitalism might vary greatly was first introduced to contemporary debates in Shonfield's *Modern Capitalism* (1965). He put the varying role of a classic political institution – the state – at the centre of differentiation, and claimed to trace a close link between institutional differentiation and economic performance. Because he wrote during the 'thirty glorious years' of capitalist economic growth in the mid-twentieth century, he commended various models of 'continental' European capitalism. In particular, since this was the height of French economic success, he gave a central place to the state in steering business institutions and managing capitalist performance (especially Shonfield 1965: 151–75).

Prompted by Shonfield's classic, a huge literature subsequently has hinged on two propositions: that there are distinct national – or possibly regional – ways of organizing a capitalist economy and that the 'success' of models may be contingent on their national or historical setting. In other words, there is no 'linear' path along which we should expect all capitalist economies to develop. Since every nation has its own unique characteristics, in principle, there are as many national models of capitalism as there are nations on earth. In practice, a smaller number of distinct regional forms are usually identified. For our purposes, what is important is that these models convey very different pictures of the relationship between business and the state. Though the details of institutional differentiation have changed in each successive wave of the 'models' debates, the basic principles of differentiation have remained similar in the very different works of, for instance, Albert (1993), Coates (2000), and Hall and Soskice (2001). Different ensembles of states, firms, and unions recur in the various contrasting models: the American Hare versus the Rhine Tortoise (Albert), Liberal Capitalism versus Trust-Based Capitalism (Coates), and Coordinated Market Economies versus Liberal Market Economies (Hall and Soskice).

Apart from the very different implications which these models have for the political roles of business, there is one other particularly important implication of high relevance to this text. The various 'modellers' of capitalism consistently identify the United States and the United Kingdom with a distinctive variety. (For a rare exception that focuses on the special domain of corporate governance, see Roe 1994, 2003.) It is commonly labelled a liberal model, principally because it is believed to rely unusually heavily on the operation of free market forces – on economic liberalism, in other words. In this model, the power of the state is used to curb the influence of one important group that competes with business, labour organized into trade unions. Ownership, control, and the government of corporations are thought to be shaped unusually directly by market operations, especially by decisions of investors in highly developed securities markets organized on stock exchanges that trade the equity of leading corporations. Thus, this model is associated with what later in this chapter we will examine as a particular form of *corporate governance*.

Debates about models of capitalism took an important turn from the early 1990s. Until then, the success of first the German, and then of the Japanese economy, had led to the widespread view that a corporatist model of capitalism (with which Germany was closely identified) or a state-dominated model (closely identified with Japan) was at least a viable alternative to, if not actually preferable to, the Anglo-American model. In essence, in a corporatist model, business is a partner in economic management with the state and with organized labour; in a state-dominated model, business, with other social interests, is directed according to the strategic aims of the state (see, for instance, Lazonick 1991). The depressed character of Germany and Japan, coupled with a boom (on some indicators) in the United States and the United Kingdom for more than fifteen years after the early 1990s, led to a common argument, especially among some Anglo-Saxon policy elites, that the Anglo-American model was 'the model of the future'. The great financial crisis of 2007–9 cast doubt on that claim, to put it mildly – something we describe in Box 8.3 (p. 168).

The argument for the superiority of a liberal Anglo-American model was reinforced by a common claim that this model was also more attuned to the greatest structural development in the world economy in the last thirty years: the appearance of new waves of globalization, in which the highly developed financial markets of the Anglo-American world and the giant corporations of the American economy have both been central. There is widespread agreement that we have indeed been witnessing an era of globalization since the early 1970s. There is, though, some dispute about its historical novelty (Hirst and Thompson 1999). There is also dispute about the consequences of these developments for business power. At one extreme are those who argue that we now live in a world without borders: globalization is creating an economic order where nation states are powerless and where giant multinational corporations and their allies in other globally organized institutions are increasingly free to determine the economic fate of populations (reviewed, Scholte 2005: 13–48). On the other hand, theorists like Garrett (1998*a* and 1998*b*) argue that globalization is actually opening up new opportunities for national economic elites to control more effectively their economic fortunes, and to circumscribe the decision-making freedom of enterprises. (We examine these arguments more closely in Chapter 4.)

It will be apparent from this discussion that the two national systems occupying most attention in this book are peculiarly important in the debate about the way the global economy is developing. It will be equally plain that the 'liberal' Anglo-American model, if it indeed is a distinctive form of capitalism, entails a distinctive relationship between business and politics, and particularly between business and the state. Understanding these relations and deciding whether they do indeed constitute a common transatlantic model are therefore important for a reason even wider than understanding the connections between business and politics in these two nations; it affects how we view the wider capitalist global economy.

Policy issues and the power of business

Debates about the power of business matter because they are critical to our understanding of the character of democratic politics and to our understanding of the character of capitalist economies. But their importance goes beyond these analytical questions. The power of business is also tied up with a wide range of immediate policy issues that face the societies whose business systems are examined in this book. The power problem is therefore not just a problem for theorists of democracy and capitalism, but also citizens and policy makers face it every day. This section sketches five important areas where academic debates of the sort that have so far dominated this chapter actually overlap with these immediate policy issues.

THE ISSUE OF CORPORATE GOVERNANCE

The attempt to regulate business activity is almost as old as recorded economic activity itself (Braithwaite and Drahos 2000: 3–8). But the issue of 'corporate governance' is largely the result of the creation in the nineteenth century of the enterprise as a separate legal personality (Bowman 1996: 8–16; Pearson 2002). Corporate governance refers to two related matters: to the internal government of the firm and to the connection between internal governing arrangements and the state. Business life has to be conducted according to some rules, and if these rules are not adhered to then commercial transactions become virtually impossible. Such rules include specifications concerning honesty and fraud in the conduct of economic life, the enforcement of contracts, and the rules governing the conditions under which firms may trade (for instance, covering the conditions under which trading has to cease if firms cannot meet their debts, the heart of laws of bankruptcy, and insolvency). Corporate governance therefore involves a kind of 'contract' with the state: the enterprise gains privileges in return for observing obligations.

It is the terms of the 'contract' which are at the heart of modern issues to do with corporate governance: how explicit and detailed should be its terms and how onerous, or not, should be the obligations it imposes? In part, the substantive issues concern the practical conduct of business life: for instance, what kind of public reporting of the financial affairs of the firm is appropriate and how much state surveillance should there be of that reporting? How far, alternatively, could the rules be the product of non-legal self-regulation – for instance, administered by such institutions as stock exchanges as a condition of exchange listing? In part, the issues concern the structures of government within firms. It is not difficult to see that questions of structure soon widen beyond matters of institutional detail: they raise issues to do with both the internal power structures of the firm and the power balance between the firm and the state. On the former, the issues include the range of possible participants in corporate governance: should they, for example, include employees or be confined to legal owners? On the latter, they cover the extent to which the state should specify exact rules about corporate governing structures and embody them in law, or only lay down broad principles. Time and again in the following pages we shall see that there are big differences between the United States and the United Kingdom in the kinds of answers given to these questions.

THE ISSUE OF REGULATION

The issue of regulation overlaps with that of corporate governance, since it has much to do with the way firms conduct their internal affairs and with how they behave towards the society around them. Regulation, like corporate governance, is as old as the capitalistic business enterprise – indeed possibly older (see Ogus 1992). In the United States, its first modern manifestation dates from the revolutionary change identified by Chandler: the rise of the giant corporation. The power of these new corporate giants prompted claims that they could manipulate market competition; as we shall see in Chapter 2, from that claim originated American 'anti-trust' regulation. In the United Kingdom, regulation developed on a significant scale in the nineteenth century to try to cope with many of the consequences of industrialism – for example, pollution and damage to the health and safety of workers. We will see in Chapter 2 that these original developments were over the course of the twentieth century succeeded by waves of regulation that have affected both the internal practices of firms and the way they connect to their social environment. The consequence is that the daily life of business is penetrated by regulations, mostly embodied in law, and by public regulatory agencies responsible for their application.

Three sets of policy issues have been raised by the spread of regulation. The first is cost, as range and complexity have grown: firms have to invest significant resources in regulatory compliance. The second issue, which can itself seriously affect cost, is the style of regulation. A constant theme of the following pages will be the different roles played by the law and by regulatory enforcers in different periods and in different countries. Should regulation be essentially a matter of policing and prosecution, rather as we expect the criminal law to be enforced, or should it be a cooperative affair between the regulators and regulated? The third issue is in turn connected to regulatory style: it concerns the quintessentially political issue of the proper relationship between the regulator and regulated. The two must inevitably have a great deal to do with each other. Regulators develop knowledge and expertise that is valuable to regulated industries. 'Capture' of the regulators by regulated is a real danger: 'capture' occurs when the two are so cooperatively inclined that they inhabit a collusive world where regulation is conducted in the interests of the two parties, rather than in the wider public interest for which it has, formally, been designed. A common analysis of the 2007–9 crisis (discussed in more detail in Chapter 8) is that this kind of collusive relationship between market actors and regulators was a cause of the great financial crash.

THE ISSUE OF SCANDAL

Scandal is as old as the business enterprise, or at least as old as the attempt to create some systems of corporate governance and to regulate enterprise behaviour. For individuals, scandals have an obvious significance: whether those individuals are convicted in the courts as the perpetrators of particular scandals, are financially ruined as the result of fraudulent scandals, or have their health ruined by scandalous failures of safety regulation. But for the business system, scandals have a wider significance. If we view them historically, we quickly see that they do not happen randomly, but tend to come in clusters. The most recent were the set of financial scandals centred on American corporations like Worldcom and Enron, which had pioneered innovative business practices – practices that seem to have been connected to the scandals themselves (Brickey 2003). An obvious issue, therefore, is why scandals occur in this kind of pattern? (see Thompson 2000). There are broadly two explanations. One suggests that there are epochal changes in business behaviour which encourage scandalous practices: thus, a common explanation of the financial scandals at the turn of the millennium was that financial deregulation and increased competition loosened the grip of established institutions of regulation, and drove down standards of ethical behaviour in business communities. A second explanation traces scandals more to changing expectations about business behaviour: it is not so much that firms start behaving in newly scandalous ways, but that old patterns of behaviour, for a variety of reasons, are exposed as unacceptable (see Clarke 1981). In either case, the wider systemic consequences of scandals can be momentous. They can – as happened in the aftermath of the Enron and Worldcom scandals – cause large parts of the regulatory system to be overhauled. More fundamentally, they can affect the legitimacy of business institutions. 'Legitimacy' here means the moral authority of the business system – its capacity to convince the public at large that in the pursuit of profit, it nevertheless generally acts in morally acceptable ways and therefore can be trusted to act in the public interest. Any long-term loss of this kind of legitimacy can have damaging consequences for enterprises: immediately, it can lead to increased public control; more fundamentally, it can weaken business politically by strengthening the case of those who argue that the private enterprise system is driven by greed and selfishness. We shall find that these are themes in our two final chapters.

THE ISSUE OF REWARD

Arguments about greed and selfishness are connected to the issue of corporate and executive reward. Democratic capitalist systems of the kind examined in this book are marked by great economic inequality; one important source of that inequality is the business system. Business enterprises deliberately, and of necessity, create their own internal hierarchies of reward. Through a mix of competition in markets and the exploitation of other sources of advantage such as monopoly power, they also more widely distribute (unequal) profits between enterprises. The legitimacy of business enterprise thus depends not just on the management of scandals, but also on the ability to defend the moral acceptability of these wider inequalities. Justifying inequalities is plainly not only the task of the business enterprise or the wider representatives of business; but the enterprise, as both a beneficiary and a generator of inequality, is at the heart of the policy issues raised by inequality. Three illustrations make the point. First, the tax treatment of corporate profits goes to the heart of how much inequality the state under democratic capitalism can or should permit. Second, the tax treatment of the incomes of the very wealthy also puts the enterprise centre stage, since the super wealthy include – though do not only consist of – the business elite. Finally, the issues of both corporate reward and the rewards to leading executives bear on key problems of corporate governance. In the last two decades, the evidence demonstrates that the gap between the rewards of the elites at the head of business and employees lower down enterprise hierarchies has widened greatly on both sides of the Atlantic (Erturk et al. 2005: 54–6). This sense that the rewards to the super-rich in financial markets were indefensible was a key obstacle to the creation of rescue packages for banks in the great financial crisis of 2007–9. In the form of arguments about bonuses (the most important source of spectacular reward for the corporate elite), they have pursued financial services firms in the aftermath of the state bailouts that were organized on both sides of the Atlantic in the autumn of 2008.

THE ISSUE OF POLITICAL ENGAGEMENT

Everything we have seen so far in this chapter demonstrates that the business enterprise is an intensely political institution. Legally, it is a state creation. Practically, its internal government and daily operations are deeply shaped by public regulation. It is a major interest in society. Under democratic capitalism, much of the fate of elected governments, including electoral fate, depends on the success with which enterprises are conducted; and the resources businesses generate and distribute are critical to highly contentious political questions, such as how far state power should be used to moderate unequal distributions of wealth and income. Politics therefore cannot be separated from the conduct of business. The critical issues are about the terms on which business engages with politics and politics engages with business. As the succeeding pages will show, political engagement raises tricky questions of strategy and tactics for individual enterprises, for whole industries, and for the business community (insofar as it is a community). But it also raises wider issues for democratic politics. There are two main ways business can engage: by partisan commitment and by lobbying. The former involves a close alignment between business interests and political parties. That in turn, we shall see, takes different forms on either side of the Atlantic: for much of the twentieth century, the Conservative Party in Britain was identified as the party of business, while in the United States, both parties, Democratic and Republican, have historically operated as 'business friendly' parties. As we shall see in Chapter 6, this state of affairs has raised many policy issues. In the last thirty years, the most sensitive have concerned the escalating cost of party competition – and the extent to which this escalating cost makes candidates for electoral office unduly dependent on business (financial) support.

'Lobbying' is an inadequate shorthand term for a wide range of non-partisan strategies by which businesses, either individually or collectively, seek to shape policy. The issues raised take us right back to near the start of this chapter: to those debates concerned with the question of whether business is a privileged interest under democratic capitalism. 'Lobbying' is a competitive activity involving the mobilization of many different potential resources: votes, expertise, and money, to name but three. Business, especially large business, is often particularly well endowed with these resources – money and expertise being two obvious examples. We shall see that there are competing views of what kinds of practical policy issues this state of affairs creates, and these different views in some degree mirror the debates between pluralists and others that we encountered earlier in the chapter: on some views, business is one competitor among many in the process of lobbying; an alternative view is that the resources of business make it such a privileged lobbyist that its uniquely powerful resources need to be exposed, regulated, or even confiscated in the interests of defending democratic politics.

Capitalism, democracy, and the power of business

The fact that the countries that dominate this book are capitalist democracies shapes the most important themes of the coming pages. The marriage of capitalism and democracy is a common partnership in the world today, and has become commoner in the last three of decades: for instance, all the old 'command' economies of the former Soviet bloc, together with China, have tried to convert to market systems; and a smaller number have also seriously tried to accompany this with a conversion to democratic politics.

This marriage of capitalism and democracy is fruitful, probably beneficial to both, but often tense. The source of tension can be summed up in one word: legitimacy. The greatest modern scholar of the subject, Max Weber, argued that legitimacy – the readiness to accept the moral right of a hierarchy to exercise authority – lies at the heart of any successful governing system (1919/1970: 78–9). The legitimacy foundations of democratic political institutions are complex, but they are at heart connected to the practices of democratic citizenship: to a model of citizenship that is based on a presumption of equality. Whatever the realities of power in the actual making of policy, the claim of democratic government to obedience – its claim to legitimacy – rests on the notion that it occupies office as a result of a selection process (competitive election under some version of universal suffrage) where all citizens have presumptively equal weight in the process.

By contrast, authority in business does not rest on claims derived from the rules of democratic citizenship. To some degree, it rests on expertise: the management of the modern corporation is commonly in the hands of specialized professionals. It even more commonly rests on some performance criteria, notably measures of enterprise success like profit generation in a competitive market. But however the authority of business is legitimized, legitimacy it must have. The business enterprise, especially the big business enterprise, is a major centre of power in the societies of the advanced capitalist world. Chandler's 'visible hand' allocates highly valued resources – money, jobs, prestige. And those allocations have become much more unequal across the Anglo-American world in recent decades.

The hierarchies of power in business and the economic inequalities generated by business therefore have to be legitimized. Democratic capitalisms round the world offer no single solution to this problem. Indeed, much of what distinguishes the different 'models of capitalism' amounts to different models of legitimation. For instance, the 'corporatist' model identified with Germany pictures business as having public-service obligations; it is constrained by the need to operate in partnership with other important social interests like the state and organized labour. We shall see that part of what distinguishes American and British capitalism is that it has offered very different accounts of what could legitimize the business corporation, and all the power and inequalities it represents. But we shall also see that despite the common assimilation of the two countries to a single model, actually they have often taken different legitimation roads, differences dictated by variations in both their histories and their institutions.

It should now be obvious that understanding patterns of business and politics has to start with a careful account of the historical roots of business communities, and their relations with systems of politics and the wider civil society. That is the purpose of the next chapter.

2 The History of Business and Politics

Paths to the present

It is common to speak of the 'historical background' to the present, but in the case of business and politics, the phrase greatly understates the importance of the past. A country's historical experiences are critical to its modern day institutions. Examining the historical development of systems of business, politics highlights their *path dependent* nature. 'Path dependency' does not mean that the past determines the present, but it does mean that it constrains the present – lays out some paths that are more likely than others to be followed, and provides forks in the road of change that rule out some choices later in time.

This general observation about the path-dependent nature of historical development happens to be particularly relevant to our understanding of business politics in the two countries examined here. As we saw in Chapter 1, it is common to consider the United States and the United Kingdom as belonging to the same species of Anglo-American capitalism. But we will find in the following pages that historical experience has produced important divergences. These have helped shape profoundly different patterns of business engagement with politics on either side of the Atlantic. The differences turn on two features that are examined in the chapter: the timing of the development of business institutions and democratic institutions; and the cultures of democratic institutions themselves. Democracy, we shall see, has been shaped by business on both sides of the Atlantic; but business has also been shaped by its encounters with democracy.

This stress on historical timing and the way it creates path dependency shapes what follows. In each of the next two sections, I sketch the historical development of business and politics in our two countries. These are selective narratives designed to draw out wider analytic themes, to do with the way the histories of business institutions and democratic institutions have resulted in very different environments for business politics. Of the many differences in historical sequencing, the single most important to emerge in the following pages can be summarized thus: the institutions of business capitalism preceded the development of democratic politics in the United Kingdom, while in the United States, they grew up alongside democracy.

Box 2.1 Politics and market building: the case of the EU

An important theme both of this chapter and of the chapters that follow is that the markets which business firms inhabit are not natural forms. They are historically created institutions where politics is a central force in creation. That point is often not immediately obvious in the case of the two main country cases in this book simply because the process of market creation is the result of a long history of evolution; and because it is the product of gradual change, it can look like the outcome of a natural, inevitable process. The great insight offered by the history of market creation in the EU comes from the fact that it has been a much more historically compressed experience: it can be said to have begun only with the inauguration of the European Coal and Steel Community (ECSC) by the Treaty of Paris in 1951. Moreover, the process of market creation was the result of conscious design and ambition by a few key individuals who had a clear picture of what they wanted to create – and, albeit incompletely, have seen their ambition realized. The ECSC, which joined six countries, was the 'template' for what became the European Economic Community (colloquially the 'Common Market') inaugurated by the Treaty of Rome in 1957. The two key members of the ECSC were France and Germany, and it was substantially the creation of two men: Jean Monnet (1888–1979) a French technocrat and Robert Schuman (1886–1963). Schuman was French Foreign Minister at the foundation of the ECSC but had actually been born a subject of the German Empire. His lifeline was thus shaped by the upheavals of war in twentieth century Europe and their impact on national boundaries; and his ambitions for the ECSC were in turn shaped by these political experiences. In Monnet's mind, the ECSC was designed to do two things: to integrate what were then the core sectors of a modern economy – coal and steel – of France and Germany so that they could never again be used as the basis of war economies in the two separate states; and to 'spill over' integration from coal and steel into other sectors, thus creating a momentum for wider economic union. Thus, the ambitions from the start were as much political as economic. Likewise, the negotiations that created the Common Market were shaped by politics: some states, for instance the United Kingdom, took the political decision not to participate; and the nature of economic government in the new market was the result of hard bargaining between its six members, and especially between the big two: France and Germany. Although the ambitions of the EU after fifty years remain expressed in the language of the creation of a free market across all members – the same ambitions that were expressed in 1957 – each successive important stage in the creation of the market has demanded political choices. They include the choices to admit new members: for instance, the landmark admission of the United Kingdom (with Demark and Ireland) in 1973 was preceded by a long period of diplomatic bargaining. Even more fundamentally political was the admission of the ten new members in 2004, most from the Soviet Empire that had collapsed at the start of the 1990s. Accession in these cases involved bargaining not only about market practices and economic interests, but also about the construction of democratic political institutions. Likewise, each phase in the 'deepening' of the market has been a political act. The creation of a powerful system for regulating competition within member states, which largely began in the 1980s, was closely connected to the political ambitions of the European Commission, the main executive arm of the Union. (The role of the Union as a competition regulator is discussed more fully in Chapter 7). Even more fundamentally, the creation of a single currency, the Euro, its final introduction in 2002, and its present adoption by fifteen member states, has involved a long chain of political choices: for instance, to discard national currencies like the mark and the franc, and to reshape the power and operations of key nation state institutions, like finance ministries and central banks. When it comes to market making in Europe, in short, everything is political. These observations are well documented in the specialist academic literature on the EU, and can be most instructively followed in Milward's classic (2000) on the origins of the whole Union project and in more conventional textbook accounts like Bache and George (2006).

An obvious question to ask, faced with a chapter on historical development, is the following: what periods are we talking about? When does 'history' end and some more contemporary pattern begin? As we shall see, the answer is contingent on individual national patterns: the 'path' becomes 'dependent' at different moments on the different sides of the Atlantic.

The United Kingdom: business, oligarchies, and democracy

The single most important feature of the history of business politics in Britain can be simply stated: the development of business institutions preceded the development of democratic politics.

In part, this sequencing is due to something wider: the overwhelmingly important historical feature of British economic development is that the country was the global pioneer of the transition to industrialism. Economic historians debate the exact timing of the 'Industrial Revolution' in Britain, but there is no dissent that the century between 1750 and 1850 was crucial. In 1750, agriculture still dominated productive economic activity; manufacturing industry and extractive industries, like coalmining, operated on a small scale and were marginal economic contributors. A century later, though agriculture was still a major employer, manufacturing was the most innovative and dynamic part of the economy. Reliable figures about long-term economic changes only begin to appear from the start of the nineteenth century, but as an indicator of momentous change, we can note that the percentage of the population of England and Wales defined as 'rural' in censuses fell from 74 per cent in 1811 to 46 per cent in 1871 (Schofield 1994: 89). This momentous change created new industries, and in the process created new business interests and new business institutions. But these new business interests entered an institutional landscape that was already populated by existing interests and organizations. They had to coexist with these established interests, who in some cases were also their rivals and competitors.

Of these rivals, the most important lay in agriculture, the dominant economic sector before the rise of industrialism. Since the most significant form of wealth had been land, an aristocracy that had extensive wealth in land dominated politics before the Industrial Revolution. Much of the history of economic representation in the first century of the Industrial Revolution and much of the wider history of the political system was about the relations between old interests and the new business interests created out of industrialism – relations that were a complex mixture of rivalry and of alliance (Guttsman 1963: 34–108).

But alongside this diverse agrarian interest was a much more cohesively organized business community which, developing in the late seventeenth century, formed an important historical template for future forms of business representation and regulation. This was the commercial and financial community located in the geographical City of London – the original 'square mile'. While this part of the City was an ancient centre of commerce, there occurred three important developments at the close of the seventeenth and at the beginning of the eighteenth centuries that transformed its economic and political roles. First, there was institutional innovation, notably in the foundation of the Bank of England, which was designed to address the debt raising problems of the state (Clapham 1944: 53–103). Though a privately owned body, the Bank soon emerged as the state's 'banker' as well as the manager of public debt. Second, there developed new markets and the institutions that organized those markets, notably in insurance. An important institution dating from this period was the Corporation of Lloyds, the centre of commercial insurance services in London. Its origins lay in the coffee house of Edward Lloyd, which from 1691 was located so as to be close to the latest intelligence about shipping movements out of London (Kynaston 1995: 12). The link between shipping and insurance is the key. Insurance and reinsurance were important because they provided vital commercial services to maritime trading enterprises in the early phases of imperial colonization and the opening up of a global economy, a fact reflected in the early history of many great insurance companies (see, for instance, Supple 1970: 12–21). A third important development was the creation of uniquely close connections between the 'City' business community and the state elite. The links between commerce and imperialism, and the role of the Bank of England in the management of public debt helped bind the commercial elite and the state elite. In maritime insurance, the state elite and the commercial elite were linked because institutions like Lloyds were critical in underwriting many of the maritime enterprises that were central to the imperialist ambitions of the state and to important commercial enterprises like the slave trade. The City of London was at the centre of what Cain and Hopkins call the 'military-fiscal state' – an instrument for uniting business interests and military adventures in pursuit of empire and profit (1993: 71–84). Indeed, even to speak of, separately, a 'state elite' and a 'commercial elite' is to misunderstand the connections between the two. From the beginning these two elites were fused, drawn from a common pool, involving individuals who moved easily between the world of 'politics' and the world of 'commerce'.

The historical sequencing summarized here conditioned both the later economic and the political histories of British business. When the take-off to industrialism occurred, creating as it did new business interests and new business institutions, the City was already the location of a well-developed web of interests. It had a unique connection, symbiotic in character, to the central institutions of the state, notably to those concerned with imperialist adventures. The markets in the City were particularly attuned to one of the central purposes of that state – which was to colonize parts of the globe. These features gave the City a markedly 'global' orientation.

Rising alongside this well-established 'City' business interest, the new interests of industrialism acquired a number of distinctive features. They highlight a peculiarity of British industry compared with the experience of successor industrial economies: the take-off into industrialism largely happened without the participation of the commercial elite (Ingham 1984: 62–78). This bequeathed a key structural fault line in the British economy which fundamentally affected the character of business politics: an unusually clear separation between 'finance', meaning the institutions of the City of London, and 'industry', meaning the new enterprises created by the Industrial Revolution.

But early industrialism also bequeathed another feature that fundamentally affected the way manufacturing interests were represented politically. The early enterprises were marked by a powerful culture of individual entrepreneurship. The pioneering enterprises were owner controlled and, not surprisingly, there was a tremendous stress on the independence and autonomy of the firm. It was a kind of little kingdom to itself, a 'private association, which should have the minimum of government regulation and interference' (Gamble and Kelly 2001: 111; see also Parkinson 1994: 30). This was reflected in the legal history of enterprises. In the pre-industrial era, there had been a tradition of companies that were licensed, and to some degree controlled, by the state, but these were mostly connected to adventures in early imperialism. The culture of the enterprise under industrialism was very different. Even when the state began regulating the firm from the middle of the nineteenth century, two assumptions predominated: that owners, rather than other 'stakeholders', were kingpins and that such regulation as was conducted should be light touch (Carson 1970a, 1970b, and 1979).

Two early features of British economic development therefore critically shaped the political role of business: the establishment of a commercial/financial sector in the City of London, which had a privileged relationship with the state elite; and the emergence of a manufacturing sector with a powerful preference for the autonomy of the individual firm. The importance of these was reinforced by another feature of historical sequencing. The rise of the City as a privileged, powerful sector and the rise of the autonomous firm preceded two key features of the modern state: the development of significant administrative capacities and the development of democratic institutions. The resources available to the central state in Britain – measured by people or money – were tiny: for instance, the Joint Stock Companies Act of 1844, the critical legislation designed to control company fraud, 'led to the creation of a staff of two, a registrar and his assistant, to try to keep track of many hundreds of companies' (Porter 1995: 99). At the same time, the political elite was dominated by an alliance of 'old' and 'new' business interests. The old interests were symbolized by aristocrats, who continued to be prominent in government throughout the whole of the nineteenth century, and by members of the commercial/financial elite which increasingly 'fused' with that aristocracy, for instance through intermarriage. New interests were represented by those connected to manufacturing, who became increasingly prominent politically over the course of the nineteenth century (see Lisle-Williams 1984). In short, government was dominated by a number of connected oligarchies – aristocratic, commercial, and industrial. Democracy, in the sense of competition for the support of an electorate where all or most adults were entitled to vote, was only a demand, and not a widely supported demand: after the passage of the 1832 Reform Act only 7 per cent of adults still had the vote; even after successive reforms in 1867 and 1884 only 28 per cent had the vote in that latter year. Until 1918, property qualifications still regulated access of many to the vote, and even after 1918 property continued to play a residual regulatory role.

Business oligarchies therefore dominated politics and society before the rise of democratic politics or indeed before the rise of a state with any great administrative capacity to intervene in economic and social affairs. The effect of this was to confer on business a special position as far as the regulation of economic life was concerned. Over large parts of business life, notably in the financial and commercial markets of the City of London, the presumption was established that 'self-regulation' was the appropriate form of government. This meant that business institutions themselves – for instance, stock exchanges and Lloyds – set their own rules. Under pressure of the problems created by industrialism, the state did indeed begin in the first half of the nineteenth century to practise legal regulation of domains like safety at work, air pollution, and regulation of the purity of food sold to the public. But this system of regulation was guided by a philosophy of 'cooperative regulation' – a philosophy that stressed the importance of carrying business along in the regulatory process and not imposing measures in the teeth of business opposition. The resources that the state commanded, which in any case in the nineteenth century were sparse, were particularly limited in the case of institutions concerned with the regulation of business life; hence the puny resources noted earlier for the enforcement of company law.

Business therefore established itself 'early' in the government of economic life: before the appearance of either democratic institutions or the development of a state with significant administrative resources. Small wonder that policy was made and implemented in a business friendly fashion.

These are the conditions that governed the relations between business and politics at the beginning of the era of modern British politics. The most convincing date for this beginning is 1918. The First World War (1914–18) transformed the role of the central state in British society, greatly expanding its social and economic control functions, and the scale of its operations. While there was some retreat in the scale of government and of government control, after 1918, it never returned to the kind of state with which business had been used before the impact of war to deal – small, with a restricted view of its functions and with few resources. Business from 1918 was therefore faced with a much more formidable administrative machine than hitherto.

It was also faced in 1918 with a transformed political environment. The social upheavals of war (not least the entry into the industrial labour market for the first time of very large numbers of women) had caused substantial cultural changes. The kind of hierarchical society where business was used to intervening in politics was greatly weakened. One sign of this was the acceleration in the pressure for the enfranchisement of women, a pressure that resulted in the grant of the vote to all women over the age of 30 (if they were ratepayers or the wives of ratepayers) in the 1918 Representation of the People Act. The effect of other reforms – such as the extension of the vote to virtually all men over the age of 21 – meant that the 1918 General Election was the first to be fought under what can be called conditions of formal democracy: that is, with an electorate close to universal adult suffrage. (In 1928, women were finally granted voting rights on equal terms with men.)

These cultural and procedural changes were accompanied by great party political upheavals. Business entered the First World War with a party system dominated by two business friendly parties: Conservative and Liberal; they were distinguished mainly by the fact that they were to some degree allied to different sections of business. Divisions over the conduct of the war split the Liberal Party, and destroyed it in short order (and for ever) as a significant force in British politics. The Labour Representation Committee, which up to 1914 had been little more than a parliamentary faction operating as a lobby for the trade unions, now became part of a new mass Labour Party. Labour's emergence in this form was consolidated by its new constitution in 1918. In the general election held at the close of that year, following the end of the Great War, Labour emerged as the main opponent of the Conservative Party. It commanded the votes of a majority of manual workers and was close to a trade union movement that had itself grown greatly in strength and numbers during the War. Thus, business was now faced with a major potential rival in the party sphere, as well as with a newly functioning democracy. What is more, the destruction of the Liberal Party and the emergence of Labour were accompanied by a brief but frightening revolutionary movement when the whole business system seemed threatened by revolutionary socialism. The Russian Revolution in 1917, coupled with the collapse of both the German and the Austro-Hungarian monarchies in 1918, led to a wave of revolutionary unrest across Europe. Though this was quickly stemmed in Britain, the experience made plain to business, and any other defender of the established order, that as far as politics was concerned it would be anything but 'business as usual' after the War. (For two very different 'takes' on this process, see Cowling 1971; and McKibbin 1974.)

These new circumstances explain several developments in the organization of business representation during and around the end of the First World War. They are important because they helped shape business politics for much of the rest of the twentieth century. Three were particularly significant.

First, mostly under the pressure of the demands created by the vast war time economy, manufacturing industry for the first time succeeded in creating an enduring national 'peak' association to speak on its behalf: the Federation of British Industries (FBI) was founded in 1916 (Blank 1973: 13–15).

Second, again in part due to the pressures of war, the most formidable institutions of British business, the financial and commercial interests located in the City of London, reorganized the way they regulated their affairs and defended their interests in politics. The most important change transformed the role of the Bank of England. Before 1914, the Bank had been a fairly informally organized and specialized institution. It was run by a Court of Directors that provided a Governor who served for a fixed term of two years. It was important in organizing some financial operations, and had acquired also a function in preserving the stability of City markets: for instance, in the case of threatened collapses, especially in banking, it was acknowledged to be responsible for organizing rescue operations. But it had very little to do with 'politics' in the sense of dealing with central government, still less with the public world of party political debate. The impact of war and its aftermath changed all this. The Bank became a key actor in central government because it was vital in fulfilling a key function – raising the vastly expanded amounts in debt needed to provide the finances of the wartime state. This drew it into central government politics. The appointment of Montagu Norman as Governor in 1920 signalled a great turning point in the way it functioned. The short fixed term tenure was abandoned: Norman served as Governor until 1944. Under his governorship, the organization of City interests was radically reformed. The Bank established itself as the 'lead' intermediary between City institutions and the centre of government, notably in dealings with the Treasury. It thus acted as a kind of voice in government for the collective interests of the financial system. The Bank at the same time became increasingly active in the government of the City itself, regulating markets and competitive practices. Thus, its previous narrow remit in 'governing' financial markets was significantly extended. Partly, in order to carry out these functions, the Bank itself became increasingly 'professional' in its internal organization, and less an institution simply run by members of the City elite who formed the Court of Directors. Because of all these changes, the Bank also established itself in the eyes of central government as the governor of the City and as the 'gateway' between the system of government and City.

In this way, by excluding central government, it also managed to establish some protection for the City from the politics of the new democracy, preserving the historic system of self-regulation that left City markets to run their own affairs (Clay, 1957: 272–317; Moran, 1986: 22–7; Kynaston 2000: 42–4).

The third sign of change was in the party system. The destruction of the Liberal Party now left the Conservatives as the acknowledged party of business. Their success in electoral competition in the new democracy was critical for business interests. While the new Labour Party soon abandoned its brief flirtation with revolutionary socialism, it was nevertheless an institution organically connected to the main opponent of business in the industrial sphere, the trade union movement. And indeed, the Conservatives were highly effective, being easily the most electorally successful party in the United Kingdom over the next fifty years: in the half century after 1918 Conservative or Conservative-dominated coalition, governments were in office for thirty-seven of those years.

Thus, the experience of war and its political and social aftermath reshaped business politics in a way that affected operations for much of the rest of the twentieth century. Business equipped itself with powerful instruments for managing the new democracy. But these new instruments were also problematic, and their problematic character recurred across the succeeding decades. The attempt to position the FBI as the dominant peak association for business was from the start bedevilled by problems. The original ambition of the 'industrial statesmen' who were important to founding the FBI, like Dudley Docker, was to create a comprehensive voice for business as a whole (Davenport-Hines 1984: 84–7; Grieves 1989: 169). They appreciated that the *collective* representation of business interests would not happen automatically, but had to be created with an eye to something wider than the concerns of individual firms or sectors. But these ambitions were stymied, for reasons that recurred throughout the twentieth century: attempts to speak for business as a whole were obstructed by the existence of sectional business interests. The FBI entered an institutional landscape where there was already well-organized *employer* organization, concerned with collective bargaining with trade unions, and from the beginning these employer organizations were determined to protect their bargaining 'turf' (Wigham 1973: 103–4; Middlemas 1979: 116–18). The history of firm autonomy, which we have traced to the early experience of industrialism, also greatly limited the authority that any peak association – or indeed any kind of business association – could exert over members. The very diversity of business also proved an enduring problem. The most important sign of this was the problem of integrating small firms into a comprehensive peak association – a problem signalled by the existence of a separate National Union of Manufacturers catering for smaller businesses (Blank 1973: 20).

Box 2.2 The changing history of the developmental state and big business: the case of South Korea

---

The cases in this book focus, obviously, on Anglo-American capitalism. But in the longer historical perspective, the capitalist systems that have enjoyed the most spectacular economic success are those of East Asia: in the generation after military defeat in 1945, Japan re-emerged as an economic superpower; even more spectacularly, a group conventionally labelled 'Tiger' economies – of which the most important were South Korea and Singapore – leapt from third world to first world economic status in a few short decades from the 1950s. The most influential accounts of this transformation argue that it was marked by a particularly close connection between state agencies and big business: there was a 'developmental state' that strategically guided big business. Though debate exists about this thesis (see Johnson 1982; Samuels 1987; and Babb 2001), two points do seem well established: that there indeed existed in these systems a special kind of partnership between strong state agencies and business, especially big, organized business, and that from the 1990s this partnership entered a prolonged period of difficulty. South Korea illustrates the two great forces at work reshaping this state–business relationship, and they merit highlighting because they recur also elsewhere in the pages of this book. The two forces are democracy and globalization. The South Korean economic miracle originated in the 1950s under the first republic headed by President Syngman Rhee. His was an autocracy backed by the military that suppressed labour militancy and left big business in the ascendant. Fifty years later the country has been transformed into a (highly turbulent) competitive democracy (Pirie 2005, 2007) in which big business has to compete with other economic interests. The way globalization has created pressures for liberalization of markets and more transparency in the relationship between big business and public agencies can be traced to the intervention of global financial institutions: the great 1997 East Asian financial crisis was the catalyst transforming the regulation of markets in a more open and liberalized direction, and weakening the close partnership between big business and the state.

On some accounts, the conjunction of the crisis of the developmental state and the pressures of financial globalization have so changed things that we can no longer speak of a developmental state, but of a new *regulatory state*. For Jayasuriya (2001, 2005), the heart of the matter lies in the evolution of one key regulatory institution, the central bank: throughout the 1990s, central banks emerged as increasingly independent regulatory agencies with distinct mandates, normally attached to the goal of maintaining price stability. That emergence reflected the increasing hegemony of interests organized in the global financial markets, and was promoted by supranational agencies of global financial regulation. Alongside this, a number of more contingent forces helped foster institutional innovations that made it more difficult for the state to direct big business in strategically determined directions. For instance, pressures from global economic actors and from global supervisory institutions challenged the characteristically discretionary and collusive modes of doing business that were at the heart of the connection between big business and the state in South Korea. This in turn produced demands for more transparent and formally specified rules, and the creation of agencies to formulate and police those rules. Big business remains enormously important in the South Korean state of the twenty-first century, but the shape of the relationship is different from that which created the Korean economic miracle: it has to contend with a globalized economy in which very close partnerships between state and corporation have to be reconciled with demands for transparency and liberalization, and it has to contend with a system of domestic politics in which rivals to big business like trade unions cannot be suppressed in the straightforwardly authoritarian manner of the past.

The very success of the City of London in getting its political act together under the Bank of England also, ironically, created problems – for it reinforced at a political level the economic divide between finance and industry. That could be seen even as late as 1965, when the Confederation of British Industry was founded: the Confederation in its early years actually excluded financial services firms from full membership (Grant and Marsh 1977: 32).

The rise of the Conservative Party as *the* business friendly party, while it created opportunities for business, also created problems. The Party was a problematic tool of business interests. It was problematic for reasons that will be described in more detail in Chapter 6, but in summary, internally, the Party was biased towards particular sectors of business, with manufacturing being one of the weaker voices and externally, it was often forced to compromise between the interests of business and other social groups in the pursuit of electoral success.

The most important political legacies of the history of British business can thus be summarized as follows. Business inherited a history of division and fragmentation, notably one in which the autonomy of the individual firm was paramount and the City was a separate political grouping. It inherited a history of tension with the democratic state that had emerged after 1918. And it inherited as its main political 'manager' a Conservative Party that was often an unreliable steward of its interests.

The United States: business, Populism, and democracy

'The United States was born in the country and has moved to the city' (Hofstadter 1955/1972: 23). Hofstadter's remark catches much that is important about the historical character of business as a system of power in the United States. In the early history of the United States, not only was agriculture a dominant economic interest, but also powerful myths symbolically emphasized the importance of the farming life as the most valuable, and quintessentially American, mode of living. With this emphasis on the importance of rural America went a number of other features: a celebration of the small farmer as the archetypal business figure; a suspicion of big institutions, a suspicion of city life and the institutions associated with the city; and a corresponding suspicion of government, especially distant 'big' government. From the beginning, the United States was a commercial society: 'No nation has been more market-oriented in its origins and subsequent history than the United States of America' (McCraw 1997: 303). But a particular vision of the market was celebrated, and this vision marginalized, or even demonized, the worlds of large corporations and big government (Lipset 1964: 57 ff., 1996: 19 ff.). This explains, for instance, one of the great early divisions in American society: over the creation of a national 'federal' bank, which was rejected in the name of a 'democratic' model of America for fear of excessive central power (Hammond 1957: 405–50).

This starting point helps explain much about the formative historical era in the development of business and politics in American society: that covering the second half of the nineteenth century. A number of key developments took place. In this period, a predominantly agrarian society was transformed. This meant in part that an urban society and an industrial economy based on extraction and manufacturing developed: in 1850, 85 per cent of the American population was defined by census as living in rural areas; by 1900, the figure had fallen to 69 per cent; a century later, it was under a quarter (US Census Bureau 2008). But it also meant that the hitherto self-contained economy of rural America was 'commercialized': farming was integrated into wider markets, to feed both the rapidly growing cities and even to export to international markets. The Civil War (1861–5) reshaped the nature of political power, successfully asserting the authority of a newly powerful federal government. Public power fashioned a New York-dominated financial system, and in the process, 'a new class of finance capitalists was created' (Bensel 1990: 363–4).

Perhaps even more important, the economic consequences of the War accelerated economic and social changes that were already happening. For the first time, there developed a significant plutocratic class in the United States, immortalized in the idea of the 'robber barons' who emerged in the second half of the nineteenth century to dominate parts of the newly developing economy: for instance, Carnegie in steel, Rockefeller in oil, and Vanderbilt in rail (Josephson 1962). The wealth of this class was fabulous by American historical standards, and the economic and political power that it was able to exercise was correspondingly great: 'During the 1840s there were not twenty millionaires in the entire country; by 1910 there were probably more than twenty millionaires in the United States Senate' (Hofstadter 1955/1972: 136).

The plutocracy was partly responsible for major innovations in corporate organization, creating enterprises new to American society and indeed to the rest of the capitalist world. They consisted of giant corporations which captured and regulated markets in whole sectors and which developed their own distinctive forms of internal organization. They were a world away from that of the small farmer or storeowner who was the mythical centre of the traditional American economy. These corporations were soon to pioneer new forms of internal divisional organization that gave professional managers, rather than entrepreneurs, a central role (Chandler 1977: 6–12). The plutocrats were also associated with the rise of new centres of financial power, publicly often demonized as the 'Money Trust' allegedly organized on 'Wall Street', the great financial district of New York City. Indeed, whether demonization was justified or not, the period did see the rise of great financiers like J. Pierrepoint Morgan who used the financial markets to put together conglomerates in the new industries like rail and steel (Carosso 1973).

These great changes had political origins, and they had political consequences. The rise of the new giant corporations was not the result of some process of natural economic evolution; it reflected the exploitation of the political environment by creative entrepreneurs (Roy 1997: 10–20). The political consequences of the changes marked both American politics generally and the politics of the business community for over a century. The period under review here was one of extraordinary social and economic change – and of corresponding stress, notably for the 'old' economy and society of rural America, as it felt the impact of the new economic power and the new economic challenges. The most important political manifestations of this were the (linked) forces of Populism and Progressivism. 'Populism' was a great movement of agrarian radicalism that reached its height in the 1890s and then exhausted itself. It arose out of the stresses and problems imposed on small business rural America by the momentous changes of the second half of the century, and was a reaction against the figures and institutions that seemed to be behind, and to benefit from, those changes: the new plutocracy represented in the public mind by the 'robber barons'; the giant corporations that seemed to be able to control, rather than be controlled by, markets; the new centres of finance; and their perceived ability to control the terms on which small entrepreneurs, especially when facing hard times, could get credit. 'Progressivism' was a coalition with different social bases from Populism, with which it nevertheless shared some common features. It drew support from an emerging urban professional middle class concerned, in particular, with the weaknesses of systems of government which seemed to rely on patronage and corruption, often fuelled by the wealth of the new plutocrats (McConnell 1966: 30–50; Foley 2007: 266–76).

By the end of the nineteenth century, the impact of social and economic transformation, the stresses and strains to which rural American had been subjected, the legacy of the old myths of small town rural America, and the immense social problems of the rapidly growing cities all crystallized into new challenges to the power of big business in the United States. The challenge focused in particular on the alleged power of the 'Money Trust': the notion that the economy was being manipulated by a small number of institutions and individuals – the latter identified often with the 'robber barons' – so as to allow the exercise of excessive and harmful political and economic power. The belief in the power of the 'Money Trust' and the need to combat it was central to two important episodes in the history of business politics.

The first was the passage of the Sherman Act in 1890. This law was prompted by the debates over the alleged power of the corporate giants. It is agreed by most observers that the Act was aimed at the capacity of the new corporations to manipulate market competition, but critical interpretations have subsequently stressed the limited impact of the law, and its symbolic rather than substantive function. Critics of its effectiveness point to the extent to which the original proposals were shorn of sanctions during passage through Congress, and the extent to which later court interpretations created a jurisprudence which minimized the impact of the Act on corporate combinations (Bowman 1996: 63–9). The Act nevertheless has claims to be the founding measure for something that will loom large in these pages: a federal regulatory state aimed at controlling corporate power. And it also has significance because verdicts on it anticipate the long debate, which will also recur in these pages, about how far that state really does limit corporate power in America. The significance of Sherman is magnified because it did not appear in isolation. To this period also belongs the creation of the Interstate Commerce Commission (1887–1995) from which we can date one of the characteristic forms of business regulation for the next century – rate and service regulation, which extended over time into industries created by new technologies, like airlines and telephones (Stone 1991). Likewise, the passage of the Pure Food and Drug Act 1906 inaugurated a key, and enduring, history of federal regulation of both the food and pharmaceutical industries, leading to the establishment of a major regulatory agency, the Food and Drug Administration (Hilts 2003).

The second episode was a great outburst of hostility to corporate power shortly before the start of the Great War in Europe in 1914. In 1912, there took place a highly publicized set of Congressional hearings (commonly labelled the Pujo hearings, after the chair of the investigating committee), which 'exposed' the operations of the Money Trust, arraigned leading financiers like J. Pierrepoint Morgan, and in 1913, produced a report which claimed to document Trust manipulation of American economic life (see Carosso 1973). In the same year, there also occurred the first of a long line of (twentieth and twenty-first centuries) 'scandals' documenting the use by business of money and favours to influence the behaviour of leading figures in Congress (McConnell 1966: 11–29).

These are touchstone episodes because they resonate through the political history of American business. Movements critical of the exercise of American business power have deep historical roots. There exists a tradition of highly adversarial criticism of business institutions, in spite of the weakness of the root and branch opposition to capitalism offered by socialist movements in Europe and the relative weakness of trade unionism, the main rival of business for power inside the workplace. As we shall see later, this often shows itself as a highly adversarial system of business regulation – remarkably different from the legacy of cooperative business regulation that we sketched in the British case.

What is nevertheless undeniable is that none of the hostility to big corporate power widespread in the United States in the generation before 1914 did anything to halt the advance of the large corporation or the power of business. Nor did it hinder big industrial corporations in their brutal suppression of trade unions. Chandler documents what he calls the 'maturing' of the giant corporation during and after the First World War (1977: 455–83). The 1920s has been called an age of 'rascality': an era of outrageous business abuse, notably in the financial markets. It also saw, in the Presidency of Warren Harding (1921–3), the Administration with possibly the most corrupt links to business in US history (Sobel 1965: 235; McCartney 2008). Hostility to business, especially to big business controlled from Wall Street, thus went with massive, and often abusive, exercise of corporate power.

It was with this contradictory inheritance that the United States entered its greatest ever economic crisis – and the greatest ever crisis of the business order: that signalled by the great 'crash' on financial markets in 1929, rapidly succeeded by the Great Depression. That was an era of financial catastrophe, revelations of fraud, the collapse of production, and mass unemployment. Out of this came the 'New Deal', shorthand for a series of social and economic reforms introduced under the Presidency of Franklin Roosevelt in the 1930s. The 'New Deal' is a powerful symbol for a new relationship between government, business, and society – but the meaning of that symbol, we shall see, continues to be contested.

The New Deal was about much more than the relationship between American business and the political system, but it was indeed formative for that relationship. Roosevelt's reforms, quite simply, saved American capitalism. Faced with a collapsing financial system, a collapsing production system, and a collapse in the legitimacy of the business institutions, they stabilized the market order. Whether they succeeded in stabilization because they produced real economic changes or because of the political leadership symbolized by Roosevelt is a matter of continual debate (Foley 2007: 279). But, whether by real economic achievements or by the symbolic magic of Roosevelt's leadership, the reforms first rescued and then stabilized the market order in the United States.

The New Deal saved American capitalism in part because it radically changed the state structure that business had to deal with. Many of its radical structural reforms endure to this day. The best summary of these reforms is that they built new institutions of a *regulatory state*, and thus of a distinctively American way of ordering the relations between government and business. In doing so, reformers were of course able to construct on the foundations that had been laid down as long ago as the closing decades of the nineteenth century. The heart of this new regulatory state was a series of federal regulatory agencies that became emblems of the New Deal. The most important were concentrated on financial markets: for instance, the Securities and Exchange Commissions regulated stock markets, and the Federal Deposit Insurance Corporation safeguarded small deposits in banks and, as a corollary, regulated the prudential conduct of those banks. At the same time, the reforms also consisted of measures designed to put under closer control the amount of competition that was allowable in the financial markets: the Glass–Steagall Act (more formally the Banking Act of 1935) not only established a system of deposit insurance, but also enforced a separation between investment and retail banking. The New Deal's diagnosis of the cause of the Great Crash thus echoed historical themes that we identified earlier: it traced the problem to the excessive exercise of power by financial institutions and to their imprudence, rapacity, and fraudulence.

In turning this diagnosis into remedy, the New Deal established a highly distinctive *mode* of regulation that has ever since deeply shaped the relations between business, the state, and the wider political system. The most important feature of this mode is the dominance of the law and of legal argument. Established by statute, in a legal culture where law was already central to the regulation of social relationships, the regulatory process soon became heavily shaped by the courts and by juridical reasoning. Lawyers emerged as the key figures in negotiating the relationship between the new regulatory state and American business, both in the regulated enterprises and in the regulatory institutions. The law schools of the universities became important providers of skilled professionals for this new regulatory state (McCraw 1984: 243–4). We will in later pages see one consequence of this mode: the importation into the regulation of business of a distinctive feature of the wider American legal culture – its reliance on adversarial argument between opposing parties as a means of determining outcomes.

The creation of new regulatory bodies and new, legally informed ways of thinking about business policy can be thought of as involving the imposition of constraints on business institutions – a common perception among critics of the New Deal from within the business community. But this was not the whole story. Another feature of the regulatory state that the New Deal created reminds us that business institutions in America, whatever popular hostility they aroused, still entered the New Deal with formidable power resources. The most important resource was ideological: attachment to the market order still dominated the minds of Americans. The aim of the New Deal, as we have seen, was to stabilize, not replace, the business order, and so from the beginning, the institutions of regulation it created worked under important limits, some of them self-imposed. The institutional structure and the actual practices of the new regulatory bodies ensured that there was a great deal of cooperative regulation with business, with market actors encouraged to run their own affairs. Indeed, this turn to a more organized, regulated capitalism had already begun in some sections of big business even in the 1920s (Hawley 1978). The single most important regulatory institution established by the New Deal, the Securities and Exchange Commission, provides a good example of the actual style of the new regulatory state. The Commission was designed to regulate the institution – the stock exchange – that had been the heart of the scandalous collapses in 1929. But from the start the leadership of the Commission was drawn from the very markets where scandal had originated: its first chairman, Joseph Kennedy, founded the fortune of the Kennedy political dynasty by financial speculation in the 1920s. More important still, the Commission worked through a kind of 'franchising' system: it delegated responsibility for regulation to the stock exchanges themselves, mostly restricting itself to authorizing and supervising these self-regulatory bodies (Seligman 2003: 103–23).

The New Deal helped redefine the relationship between business and the state in America, and helped also to lay the foundations for a quarter century of great business power in the United States. The 1940s and the 1950s now seem like a golden age of the power of the corporation, especially the giant corporation. It was the age of 'Fordism' (see Box 2.3, p. 36): an age when big industrial corporations had finally worked out a cooperative relationship with privileged sections of the unionized working class. Out of the New Deal came an alliance between many of the big corporations at the heart of the manufacturing economy – such as the auto industry – and powerful sections of the American trade union movement. 'Business unionism' put a premium on securing favourable deals for workers in particular industries and firms, and locked some powerful unions into a political alliance with some large corporate employers. The cooperative relationship between business and state on which the New Deal was predicated was also greatly strengthened by the economy of world war between 1941 and 1945, and by the economy of the 'cold war' that soon succeeded the end of formal hostilities. This was an era of what has been called 'Pentagon capitalism' (Melman 1970). The American state emerged as a giant customer for large corporations in the defence and the allied industries. The contractual relationships in these business deals did not resemble those of a conventional market; they involved close and enduring partnerships between the upper reaches of the state and significant parts of corporate America. Many parts of the United States – such as the giant Californian economy – also rested heavily on defence contract work. And reaching out from the defence core there were numerous other sectors where similar collaborative relationships developed – for instance, in the rapidly growing health technology industries, which often used technologies allied to those in the defence sector (Brown 1979; Trajtenberg 1990; Foote 1992).

The collaborative economic relationships between key parts of business and the state were also reflected in political practice. The top of the American federal government for much of the 1950s (for instance, President Eisenhower's Administrations 1953–60) was heavily populated by the leaders of corporate America (see McQuaid 1982: 170–7, 1994: 106). In Congress, the importance to the economies of the constituencies of individual congressmen of lucrative federal contracts, notably in defence, set up a struggle for the spoils of spending. This encouraged the development of close relationships between leading Congressional figures, leading figures in the executive, notably in defence administration, and leading corporate interests. This was the era of 'iron triangles', in which a triangle of interests covering key policy areas like defence in Congress, the Executive, and business often combined to bargain in a closed world where other actors and interests were excluded (Cater 1965: 26–48). It is not a coincidence that this golden age of business power in the 1950s also produced some of the major studies of power in American society that argued for the existence of a power elite uniting the top of corporate America with leaders of political institutions: among the most important were Wright Mills' study (1956/2000) of the power elite nationally and Hunter's pioneering study (1953) of its workings in one city, Atlanta.

The 1950s were also a golden age for business legitimacy, especially for big business. We need to express this with caution since it is obviously partly a judgement about popular perceptions of business, and evidence about perceptions from the past is often unsatisfactory. Nevertheless, the weight of the evidence that we have is convincing. The performance of the business system after the creation of the original wartime economy was by historic standards highly satisfactory: it delivered full employment and, by the 1950s, hitherto unimaginable consumer prosperity for the mass of Americans. Globally, this was an era not only of American political might, but also of American economic dominance. In important sectors, especially in manufacturing, corporations had established a stable business relationship with big trade unions. The era of the New Deal had already helped reconcile Americans to big business: Galambos' study of media treatment of business argues that even by the end of the 1930s it had helped 'ease Americans into acceptance of big business' (1975: 247). Studies of the media treatment of business indicate a generally deferential approach – something that was to change radically by the 1990s (Berry 1999: 123–30). The opinion poll data that we have indicate historically high levels of approval of, and trust in, corporate America: at least, historically high, we shall see in later pages, by the standards of today (Vogel 1989: 7–8).

The election of the Democratic candidate, John F. Kennedy, to the Presidency, as the successor to the Republican Eisenhower in 1960, might be taken to signify a prolongation of the golden age of business power. Kennedy was after all the son of the same Joseph Kennedy whom we encountered earlier: the speculator who made a vast fortune before the Great Crash and then

---

Box 2.3 An industrial statesman and politics: Henry Ford and 'Fordism'

Henry Ford (1863–1947) is principally known as the founder of the Ford automobile empire. Politically, he is known as the sponsor of extreme right wing views, notably of a virulent anti-Semitism. But Ford's production methods also meant that his name was attached to an influential theory of the workings of the American and West European economies in the half-century after the close of the First World War (1918). Ford pioneered the application of a highly advanced division of labour to automobile production, typified by assembly line working. It enabled huge advances in productivity, the mass marketing of cheap consumer goods, such as Ford's famous Model-T car, and the consequent creation of an economy with a virtuous circle of production and consumption: productivity advances allowed marketing of cheap consumer goods; this created mass demand; meeting the resulting mass demand boosted employment in the most productive industries already paying high wages; and the workers in those industries in turn became customers for mass-produced consumer goods. Ford's own empire spread to the United Kingdom and other parts of Europe; more important, the model of production and consumption that lay behind his industrial success also spread (Holden 2005). Hence the inauguration of an age of Fordist consumption and production. (One of the earliest coinages of the word is by Gramsci, in 1971: 279–318) The new industries like automobile production that Ford pioneered were critical to the stabilization of capitalist democracy on both sides of the Atlantic in the wake of the Great Depression of the early 1930s. In the 'long boom' that stretched in the Anglo-American economy from the late 1940s to the early 1970s, Fordist production, allied to mass consumption, was the engine of the boom. Politically, it involved two components. First, it was connected to a particular theory of state management of the economy influenced by the great British economist Keynes (1883–1946). Keynesianism gave the state a central role in managing demand in the economy, and thus stabilizing the mechanisms of mass consumption that were critical to the workings of the Fordist model. Second, it involved a partnership between the great corporations, like the Ford Motor Corporation, who were central to Fordist production, and the political and industrial representatives of part of the labour force – that part which was fortunate enough to be employed in the industries that had benefited from the huge productivity advances of the Fordist division of labour. Fordism thus was closely linked to a system of consensus politics binding big business to the best-organized sections of the work force. It was thus truly an Anglo-American phenomenon, but it was more, for the Fordist model also lay at the root of post-war economic success in other giant European economies, like Germany. Its history also shows the complex forces linking industrial statesmen like Ford and the practice of capitalist democracy. Ford undoubtedly pioneered key elements of what became labelled Fordism, notably those that enabled huge productivity advances and the creation of an economy of mass consumption. But Fordism was also a political alliance between progressive forces, in business, in the organized labour movement, and among pro-business politicians. It thus represented views that were worlds away from Ford's own brand of reactionary right wing politics, with its attacks on labour unions and Jews. Accounting for the end of the Fordist era in the early 1970s is complicated, because it involves accounting for the fundamental changes in the character of advanced capitalism that brought the 'long boom' to an end. But that Fordism did exhaust itself cannot be denied. As a symbol of its exhaustion, the last generation has also seen the continuing decline of the automobile industry in the mid-West, including the decline of Ford as an automobile producer: in short, the decline of the original heartland of Fordism.

played an important part in the business regulatory system of the New Deal. Kennedy's victory was won on a campaign part funded from the family wealth – itself a sign that business finance was now important to the increasingly expensive task of winning electoral office in America. But in fact this moment was a watershed in business politics, and is an appropriate point for our historical sketch to end. Business was soon to enter a world very different from the golden age. It would still be one where corporate power was exercised impressively, but the way power could be exercised, and the conditions under which it could be wielded, were to change profoundly. The character of the wider political culture altered greatly in the next decades, the late 1960s being a particularly critical period of change. Likewise, the lobbying world in which business had to operate began to be transformed, and the world of regulatory politics created in the New Deal was reshaped. In summary, business could still exercise great power, but it had to exercise it in a more competitive and combative political environment – one that characterizes the modern relationships between American business and politics that we shall see recurring throughout the rest of these pages.

Varieties of capitalism and varieties of democracy

The 'varieties of capitalism' literature has assimilated British and American capitalism to a single model. But our sketch here suggests that this is overstated: varieties of capitalism theories have a lot of illuminating things to say about capitalism, but rather less to say about the political setting of capitalist business systems, in particular about democracy. British and American business has a lot in common, but also exhibits marked differences. Some of the difference has to do with the contrasting character of core capitalist institutions, like corporations; some has to do with the relations between business and the wider political system; both have to do with contrasting historical experiences.

The single most important feature of the British system is that most significant British institutions and practices predated the rise of formal democratic politics, or were, latterly, an attempt to manage democracy so as to minimize its impact on business power. There were two critical episodes in the development of the politics of the business system. The first was the original development of the City of London as a key centre of (globally important) financial activity and as a significant concentration of power well connected to London-based political elites. The second was the Industrial Revolution, which created the first industrial society, the first great centres of industrial capitalist power, and the first attempts to solve the problem of how politically to manage an industrial society.

The results of all these are summarized in the preceding pages. The great centres of economic power colonized the state. They established over large parts of the economy – notably the financial sector – the presumption that business should be allowed to conduct its affairs without the intervention of government. These notions were systematized in ideologies of self-regulation. Where the state was drawn in to control aspects of the new industrial economy – such as the health and safety of workers – the new industrial elites in the nineteenth century managed to defend a minimalist framework of regulation. This was expressed in an ideology of 'cooperative regulation': in other words, in the notion that even where state agencies had power of legal compulsion, it should be used sparingly, and enforcement agencies should give priority to working in cooperation with regulated businesses. The critical years in laying down a template for modern relations between business and politics were those during and immediately after the First World War: business began successfully to organize itself as a national lobby, it forged an alliance with the Conservative Party as 'the' business party, and it reinforced ideologies of self-regulation and cooperative regulation as a protection against any inter-ventionist ambitions by the newly democratic state.

The key political problem for business in Britain for much of the twentieth century, therefore, was how to maintain patterns of power and privilege that had been established before the rise of democratic politics. The problem for American business was different. It lived in a more business friendly envir-onment than was inhabited by British business. There was no significant legacy of an aristocratic culture hostile to commerce or manufacturing. Business was a high status activity and business elites were important parts of the political elite. But business institutions had to live with two conditions that were weak or absent in Britain. The first was formal democratic politics – not complete, but much more extensive than existed in the United Kingdom throughout the nineteenth century. The second was a set of cultural expect-ations that were hostile to big business. The American state was anything but laissez-faire in its treatment of business. Shaped by Populism and Progressiv-ism, it intervened much earlier than did the British state in the regulation of key areas of economic life, such as competitive practices. In the aftermath of the great world economic crisis at the end of the 1920s, it moved much more extensively than did the British state to control large parts of business – building a powerful set of institutions that we now summarize as the American regulatory state.

Historically, the American business community not only enjoyed greater status than did its British counterpart, but it also had to operate in an environment where its privileges were more likely to be contested. As we shall see in later chapters, this has had important consequences that distinguish the two national systems: in the organization of business lobbying, in the relationships between business and partisan politics, and in the wider relations between business and society. In the next chapter, we turn to the first of these: the way business organizes itself for lobbying purposes.

3 Organizing Business

Business collective action and the politics of the firm

The organization of any interest for political purposes is a problematic affair, but it is especially problematic for business interests. We know why from the first two chapters of this book. There is a tension between the desire of business to maximize its political impact by organizing collectively and the pressure felt by individual enterprises to compete with business rivals. The tension has been made more acute by the historically fragmented organization of business interests on both sides of the Atlantic.

This chapter is about how business organizes now in the face of these problems. Organizing collectively is not the only source of business power, but it is an important one. The descriptions in this chapter highlight some big themes. The importance of national setting reappears. Here, however, I emphasize the importance of differences, not just in historical experience, but also in the wider national institutional setting – albeit that this setting is itself historically shaped. How business organizes, or fails to organize, is in part the product of the wider policy-making system within which it has to operate. It also follows that when the wider system changes, the way business organizes politically also has to change – an observation that will recur in these pages.

Studying how business now organizes also emphasizes another feature that has cropped up in our first two chapters: the sheer difficulty of creating and maintaining institutions that promote collective interests. We shall also see that a common organizational experience of recent years has made this problem more acute. The individual firm, we know, is an institution that is politically shaped: even the basic legal form of the company is a political creation. But the significance of the individual enterprise, especially the large enterprise, as a carrier of business interests has grown in recent years. The firm has become an intensely political institution, and this raises many questions about how to organize the business community behind a common purpose. As we shall see by the end of the chapter, the effect of the great financial crisis of 2007–9 was to magnify the extent to which giant firms, especially those in the financial sector, have this intensely political character.

Box 3.1 The evolution of business lobbying in the EU

We now have more than two decades experience of the evolution of lobbying in the EU since the passage of the original legislation to complete the single market (1986) – and this legislation is agreed to have stimulated a lobbying boom in Brussels. In its effect on business lobbying, it probably had a more profound impact even than the original creation of the 'Common Market' by the Treaty of Rome in 1957. Coen's work (1997, 1998, 1999, 2002, 2007a, 2007b) allows us to chart the development of a changing, and distinctive, lobbying system. The picture encompasses more than lobbying by business, but business is the most numerous, the best organized, and the best resourced of the lobbying interests, especially in Brussels. Present estimates suggest that about 20,000 lobbyists operate in the city alone. There are over 1,400 formally organized interest groups, and over 260 law firms and public affairs firms. (Some of the most important of the former are branches of American multi-national law firms who have long operated in Washington as combined 'fixers' and specialist advisors on regulatory issues.) The biggest change over time in the case of the EU is, simply, growth in scale: there was an 'explosion' (Coen's word 2007b) in numbers in the 1990s, and this was connected to two developments: the shift of much responsibility for regulatory decision making from national governments to the European level and the rise of Qualified Majority Voting as a decision mechanism within the Council of Ministers, which put a premium on putting together alliances supporting particular positions at the European level, for under Qualified Majority Voting it is no longer enough to line up a single national vote to veto a proposal. A second change over time is the widening range of institutions and arenas that are targeted by business lobbyists. When Coen surveyed the lobbying community in the mid-1990s, he found that attention to the European Commission predominated. But when he replicated his survey a decade later, he found that, while the Commission was still the most important object of lobbying attention, there was a much wider spread of activity including, for instance, the European Parliament. The change reflects the more complex distribution of policy-making responsibilities in the Union's institutions and the development of a more sophisticated array of lobbying techniques by business interests. This greater sophistication may be connected to a third striking development: a shift on the part of business lobbyists from collective to individual action. This is reflected in the composition of the lobbying community itself: Coen estimates (ibid.) that about 40 per cent of lobbyists can now be classified as individual actors (single firms, think tanks, and law and public relations firms) as distinct from collective actors like trade associations. What is doubly striking about this development is the way it resembles a shift which we noted (see pp. 47–8) at the level of our two national cases: there we saw that firms, especially big firms, were either using their own in-house lobbying expertise, or hiring in professional lobbyists, to advance their interests. Individual lobbying is a sign of growing sophistication – a capacity to identify individual corporate interests and to pursue them in a single-minded fashion, rather than relying on exerting influence through some industry- or sectoral-level trade association. But the behaviour of firms in Brussels also reflects their behaviour in London and Washington in one other way: individual action, though rising in importance, does not rule out collective action. There is a premium, especially in dealings with the Commission, in being seen to be a 'team player'. Support for the collective action exemplified by the workings of trade associations therefore complements the focused approach reflected by individual actor lobbying. The individual firm, whether in Brussels, London, or Washington, has a delicate balance to strike between acting as a team player and pursuing its own special interests.

The United Kingdom: fragmentation and firm autonomy

We saw in the first two chapters that there were powerful pressures obstructing the organization of business interests in Britain: the autonomy of the firm, the legacy of organizational rivalries between different representative associations, and the existence of differences of interest between diverse sections of business. The more recent history of interest organization helps show the shaping influence of the political environment of business and the way this combines with changes in the character of business itself. It is possible to divide that recent history in a reasonably clear way: one pattern predominated until about thirty years ago; in the intervening decades, a new pattern has been fashioned. I first sketch that older pattern and then show how it has changed.

By the mid-1970s, the organization of British business lobbying had reached a historic peak of cohesion. The Confederation of British Industry (CBI), founded in 1965, over the next ten years enjoyed a dominant role as the voice of British business. Indeed, so successful did it seem as a template that the report of the Devlin Commission in 1972 on Business Representation advocated the creation of a single Confederation of British Business modelled on the CBI (Devlin 1972). In that decade, the Confederation was virtually a 'governing institution', to use Middlemas's phrase (1979: 371–6). It participated in the shaping and the implementation of a wide range of public policy. But this was only the most visible sign of the collective organization of business interests and their incorporation into the state machine. The same pattern could be seen in numerous instances at the sectoral level. Employers were organized to bargain collectively with unions – the function of employers' associations like the Engineering Employers' Federation. They were also organized as producers in trade associations. In both guises, they were often closely connected to arms of the state: the system was epitomized by the creation of 'Economic Development Committees' within the National Economic Development Council (created 1962). These 'little Neddies' were designed to create, at sectoral level, institutions that united business representative bodies, trade unions, and the state in economic planning (Blackaby 1979: 21–2; Ringe and Rollings 2000).

This pattern of business representation reflected in part the wider organization of interest representation in the British political system, and this in turn was shaped by the character of state organization and political representation. These shaping forces were a mix of institutional and policy features.

The most important institutional development was the rise of the interventionist state in Britain over the course of the twentieth century. As we saw in Chapter 2, the surge in state intervention during the First World War prompted the creation of the first enduring 'peak' associations claiming to speak for business as a whole. A new high tide of peacetime state activism rolled in during the fifteen years after 1960, when the state responded to national economic decline by trying to manage the economy in an increasingly interventionist way. We have already encountered a major institutional sign of this: the creation of the National Economic Development Council in 1962, and the creation of the network of sectoral 'little Neddies' below it. These drew business, both at the level of peak associations and trade associations, into bargaining with the state and trade unions in the pursuit of a more planned economy. The high point of this occurred during the second half of Edward Heath's Conservative Premiership (1970–4) when an attempt was made to manage even prices and incomes by law, through a tripartite partnership between business, labour, and the state. In this, the CBI was assigned a central role. In short, in this era, the collective organization of business was greatly encouraged by an interventionist state looking for a unified voice of business nationally and for business voices in individual sectors and industries.

The rise of state intervention coincided with a long-term change in the structure of the policy-making system and in the wider system of interest representation. Business representation was inevitably affected by these developments. Over the course of the twentieth century, the state not only became highly interventionist, but also became increasingly centralized on a small, homogeneous system concentrated in London. In the language of political science, policy making was made in *policy communities* – socially well-integrated small groups where decisions could be sorted out informally and confidentially. In the sphere of business, the extreme model of this was the organization of the City of London. In the City, business lobbying was channelled through the Bank of England; there was little formal organization of any kind, and the 'representation of interests' was bound up seamlessly with the wider organization of markets under the eye of the Bank of England. 'Lobbying' in the sense of crudely making a case to government for some particular policy was something City interests rarely had to do (Moran 1986: 12–28).

This tendency towards the informal coordination of business interests by a metropolitan elite was strengthened by one long-term structural development within the business system itself. Over the first three quarters of the twentieth century, ownership and control in business became increasingly concentrated in a small number of big firms (Supple 1992: xi–xxix) who typically dominated their industries, and equally typically were closely integrated into the metropolitan policy community of London: for instance, the share of the 100 largest manufacturing companies in output rose from about 15 per cent in 1910 to about 40 per cent by the end of the 1970s (Hannah 1983: 91–2). This metropolitan centralization was strengthened by the development of a dense system of 'interlocks' between large concerns: networked connections, made through cross share ownership and cross directorships, helped create a well-integrated business elite which was in turn well connected to governing elites in Whitehall and in Westminster (Scott 1997: 119, 2003). The Governor of the Bank of England remarked in evidence to a public inquiry in 1957 that 'if I want to talk to the representatives of British Banks, or indeed of the whole financial community we can usually get together in one room in about half-an-hour' (Radcliffe 1960: 52). But up to the mid-1970s almost the same could be said of the most important figures in British business – that they were few in number, knew each other well, and mixed in a small, informal world. This, then, is the system of business representation that was consolidated over the first three quarters of the twentieth century. It is also the system that has since been dismantled.

The changes can be summarized under two – superficially contradictory – headings: there has been a shift away from the collective representation of business interests and there has also been a shift to more formal organization in the representation of business interests. I summarize this as the simultaneous shift to more lobbying by individual firms and to more professionally organized lobbying by business.

The decline in the importance of the collective voice of the business lobby is clearly seen in the fate of its most important peak association, the CBI. Although the Confederation remains probably the best-known 'peak' organization, it has suffered a number of blows over the years. The circumstances of the Confederation's creation meant that it had a strong bias towards manufacturing. The FBI, the most important 'parent' of the Confederation, actually excluded retailers and the finance sector, and the CBI partly replicated this bias towards manufacturing: at its foundation, it only allowed firms from the retail and the financial services sector to join as 'associate' members (Grant and Marsh 1977: 32). While this restriction has long been removed, the Confederation remains dominated by manufacturing – and this is precisely the area of British business that has been in relative long-term decline. The Confederation claims to speak for 240,000 businesses, but this figure is arrived at by grossing in the membership of trade associations and federations that are its affiliates; it has only about 2,000 individual companies in membership. In the new millennium, it was actually a smaller organization, measured by numbers employed, than in the 1970s. In terms of sheer financial muscle, the CBI is vastly outweighed by the British Chambers of Commerce, but the latter is a geographically decentralized institution and it has a bias towards small business (see Chapter 5). The richest representative of manufacturing is probably the Engineering Employer' Federation (which owes its wealth to a valuable property portfolio). But the Federation too has powerful regional components and a weak national voice (Grant 2000; Gribben 2005).

The main collective voice of business has therefore been weakened by the way long-term structural changes in the economy have diminished the significance of the sector that dominated the CBI. But the Confederation also suffered because of changes in the styles of policy making under which it had prospered in the 1960s and 1970s. The critical event was the election of Mrs Thatcher as Prime Minister in 1979: under her, government turned away from the notion that economic management involved a partnership with 'peak' associations like the Confederation and the Trades Union Congress. Instead, it asserted the independence of the state in managing the economy. The National Economic Development Council was not abolished until 1992, but after 1979 it, and the system of 'little Neddies', was an empty shell. Moreover, the first two years of the Thatcher Premiership saw a recession which greatly damaged the manufacturing sector from which the Confederation disproportionately drew its members, and witnessed a spectacular falling out between the Confederation and government (Grant and Sargent 1987: 123–5). The Confederation remains an important lobbyist but it has never regained its quasi-governing status. The falling out with the Thatcher Government also created space for rival voices which claimed to speak for the interests of British business in a way more sympathetic to the Thatcherite Revolution. In particular, from the 1980s, the Institute of Directors, an organization which specializes in individual membership for leading business figures (rather than the institutional membership of the Confederation), established itself as a distinctive voice, often successfully allying itself with the more radical economic policies of the Conservative governments of that time. Thus, there has been a decline in the degree to which business in Britain speaks with a unified voice over matters of long-term strategy in relation to the defence of the business system.

The problems of the CBI reflect difficulties at what are sometimes called the 'macro' level – the organization of the business system as a whole. But there have been organizational problems too at the 'meso' level – in the ability of business in particular industries or sectors to organize for a common purpose. We have already seen that the 'little Neddy' networks first atrophied, and were then abolished. Employers' associations have also been the unintended casualties of public policy. One of the historic strengths of business had been organization as employers for collective bargaining purposes in institutions like the Engineering Employers' Federation. But under the impact of economic recession and the weakening of trade union power as a result of the Thatcher Government's legal reforms, national systems of collective bargaining declined. Individual enterprises preferred to deal directly with a weaker and more divided trade union movement. Paradoxically, this also weakened employer solidarity. Over the 1980s and 1990s, membership of employers' associations fell: in the 1980s alone, the 'density' (proportion of eligible firms in membership of employers' associations) fell by a half, and in the 1990s, many associations just went out of existence (Milward et al. 1992: 45–6; Greenwood and Traxler 2007). Nor did trade associations – the alternative form of collective organization at the sectoral level – do much to plug this gap: studies in the 1990s and at the turn of the millennium showed that the majority of associations were poorly resourced and poorly organized (May et al. 1998; MacDonald 2001).

What all this change amounts to is a decline in the capacity of the business system to engage in collective action for the defence of its interests. That decline has important implications for the future political health of business as a whole – something examined in Chapter 7 – but it need not entail a decline in the political clout of individual firms: recall the distinction made in Chapter 1 between defence of the collective interests of the business system and those of individual enterprises. The evidence is that, if anything, the ability of individual enterprises, especially large enterprises, to defend their interests has greatly improved over the last couple of decades. The decline of the system-wide organization has been accompanied by the rise of firm level political action. This is the second change identified earlier. Firms, especially big firms, have become increasingly professionally competent at managing the lobbying function and have increasingly put resources into that function.

Grant (1984) first identified this trend in the mid-1980s. It involved the development of specialized government relations units within firms, especially within the biggest firms. This represented the professionalization of a lobbying function that, insofar as it had hitherto been done at firm level, had involved informal lobbying by senior executives. 'Lobbying' in the old system meant cultivating personal contacts between senior executives and senior policy makers, often based on affinities of class, education, or prior career. It hardly felt like lobbying in the sense of accosting policy makers to put a case to them; it was just a natural product of social connections. But firms now began actively to cultivate public agencies, to try to manage their relations with government, and to try actively to anticipate, and influence, developments in public policy.

These fairly modest initial institutional developments have over the intervening decades developed into much more ambitious strategies for representing the firm. This broadening in ambition and range arises from a realization, often after bitter experience, that the political capacities of the individual firm are not just a matter of having a government relations department. The ability of a firm to defend its interests is a function of wider public perceptions of the enterprise – something borne home to firms like Shell and BP, for example, who have been involved in public relations fiascos involving safety, environmental issues, and their accounting practices (see Sklair 2001: 198–254; and Nilsson 2009). Damage limitation in these circumstances demands something more ambitious than a government relations department; it requires the capacity to manage the reputation of the firms. Even damage limitation to repair reputation is not enough. Large firms like Shell or Marks and Spencer are increasingly conceived as 'brands' which need active fostering, and the management of the reputation of the brand is inseparable from managing the political capacities of the firm. As a result, the fairly modest original development of a government relations function has now spilled into broader domains of corporate public relations and brand management.

Operations of this sophistication are daunting even for the largest and best resourced of firms, and the rising interest in integrating government relations, corporate public relations, and brand management helps explain another feature of the changed world of business representation: the explosive growth in recent years in the numbers of firms offering services in these areas. There are, certainly, some difficulties in documenting exactly the scale of the industry or the pace of growth because there is – unlike the United States – no centrally available register of lobbyists. One estimate is that the industry has doubled in size (to about 3,000 full-time lobbyists) since the early 1990s (House of Commons Public Administration Select Committee 2008: 132). But this must only be the tip of the iceberg, because 'lobbying' is not a specialized trade. It overlaps with public relations: the Chartered Institute of Public Relations estimates that there are over 48,000 employed in PR in the United Kingdom (cited in House of Commons Public Administration Select Committee 2008: 132). It also overlaps with the provision of legal services by big commercial law firms, who offer everything from the most specialized services in negotiating regulatory problems to high-level 'fixes' based on elite contacts. This very imprecision about what constitutes 'lobbying' is in itself revealing, for it alerts us to an important point. What firms do is no longer just 'lobbying' in the specialized sense of accosting policy makers and trying to persuade them to adopt a particular policy. (The origin of the term lies in the practice of accosting legislators in the central lobby of Parliament.) It is about managing the whole political and cultural environment of the firm: cultivating political contacts with an eye to their long-term use; monitoring the stream of public policy, and public policy proposals, so as to sense dangers to, or opportunities for, the interests of the enterprise; and, especially if the enterprise operates in retail markets, managing the enterprise as a brand (see also Davis 2000, 2002, 2007; and Miller and Dinan 2000).

This is a daunting list of tasks, and it is not hard to see why enterprises have outsourced so many, and thus contributed to the growth of what we for shorthand call the lobbying industry. Organizing a specialized lobbying function for a single enterprise is an expensive business beyond the resources of all but the largest firms. Even for the very biggest firms, many of the services are most economically bought 'off the shelf' as required, in the same way that firms contract for services like corporate advertising. For smaller firms, hiring a lobbyist is plainly a more efficient way of trying to exert some influence over the policy process than relying on the enterprise's own limited expertise.

It should be plain that the turn to firm-level lobbying and the increasing professionalization of the lobbying function are connected. On the one hand, institutions for the collective defence of business – like the CBI and many individual sectoral associations – are weaker than in the past. On the other hand, the political environment demands more active and formal intervention than in the past; the kind of club like informality typified by the old City of London just does not work any longer. It does not work in part because the social cohesion of the business elite has declined, but it also does not work because the social cohesion of governing elites is not what it was.

The best summary way to appreciate this latter change is to recall our characterization of the policy-making system that dominated for much of the twentieth century in the British system of government: it was highly centralized in London and it was dominated by socially well-integrated communities in distinct domains which closely connected elites at the top of government and elites at the top of the organized interests, especially business interests.

That world has been disrupted in three ways by developments of recent decades. The first has already been referred to: there is now a large body of case study evidence showing that the world of small, well-integrated, informally organized policy communities is giving way to larger, more dispersed and more difficult to navigate constellations of networks that demand more formal modes of control (the authoritative account is Rhodes 1997). A second development is the rise of important centres of policy making in the devolved political systems created by the Labour Government's reforms after 1997. Considerable uncertainty surrounds the extent to which business finds it easier or harder to work in the new policy networks created by devolution to Edinburgh and Cardiff; but what is certain is that new networks have indeed been created, and that business has to master these if it is to influence the considerable range of policy decision now subject to devolved authority. (For a summary of impacts, see Jeffery and Wincott 2006; Mitchell 2006; Morgan 2006; and Wincott 2006.)

A third development is illustrated in Box 3.1 (p. 41) and can therefore be more summarily described here. The United Kingdom has been a member of the EU – and of its policy-making systems – now for over thirty years. There was a surge in the range of business regulation that entered EU domains of competence after the passage of the Single Market Act in 1986 (Armstrong and Bulmer 1998), and a concomitant surge in the level and intensity of business lobbying in the main Union institutions, notably in the Commission in Brussels. Though the lobbying system in the institutions of the Union is fluid because the Union is still developing, a number of features stand out. The rising importance of the Union has created new systems of policy making where modes of lobbying unfamiliar in the British setting are important. Firms simply cannot rely on the personal contacts forged in the Westminster system. There has been rapid development around the Commission in Brussels of a professionally organized lobbying industry. Some of the pioneering firms in this industry are American. They include multinational American corporate law firms with long Washington experience of providing advice and advocacy services to business, especially in lobbying over regulation in the American

Box 3.2 How the French business elite organizes itself politically

'They order this matter better in France'. The famous opening line of Laurence Sterne's *A Sentimental Journey through France and Italy* (1768) provides our theme here: the French business elite may not order representation *better*, but it certainly orders it *differently*, for instance, when compared with the patterns of operation for the United Kingdom described in the body of this chapter. The example emphasizes the importance of national setting to the workings of the politics of business. Shonfield (1965) first popularized the notion that there was a distinctively French relationship between the state and business. Maclean, Harvey, and Press (2006) and Harvey and Maclean (2008) give us an up to date picture of this distinctiveness, drawing out the differences with the United Kingdom. The French business elite is more socially homogeneous and selective, is more closely linked together, and owes its career more to the state, than is the case in the United Kingdom. While products of the leading public schools and two elite universities – Oxford and Cambridge – are disproportionately represented at the top of British business, the predominance of elite educational institutions is much more notable in France: a very small number of schools provide entrants to the *Grandes écoles*, the small group of elite higher education institutions that are separated from the wider university system. The numbers of *Grandes écoles* graduates are also much smaller than the numbers graduating even from the elite UK universities. This compactness is then underpinned by a dense system of interlocking directorships at the top of the leading French enterprises, and this is further reinforced by the greater persistence of family dynasties at the top of French business. All these factors create a much higher level of social integration and informal closeness, in the French than in the British, business elite. But the crucial difference for the practical politics of business representation is provided by contrasts in patterns of recruitment to elite positions in business. Although movements by civil servants into business are becoming commoner in Britain, there are still two quite distinct career hierarchies for ascending to the state, and the business, elite. The two tend only to be joined in late career, when the cohorts have reached the top of business and government. In France, by contrast, the pattern has been for the products of the *Grandes écoles* to move initially into positions in elite institutions of the state, where they strengthen the networks they have already formed through the experience of common education. Then in mid-career, they commonly engage in the practice of *le pantouflage*: shifting to positions in private enterprises that carry them into the upper reaches of the business elite. At this stage of career, it is common to move to and fro between state and business posts. Thus, the French business elite is not only itself socially powerfully integrated, but is also seamlessly integrated with the governing elite by ties of educational origin, common career, and participation in common social networks. These features underpin Shonfield's original argument that the French state was much more coherently strategic in its policies towards business than was the state in Britain. It leads Maclean, Harvey, and Press to argue (2006: 173–4) that the French state is still much more willing than is the state in Britain to sponsor and to defend technologically advanced sectors of business, sectors that often demand long-term commitments of resources which markets may not be willing to provide. Thus, institutions not directly connected to, or shaped by, business, like those in the education system, can have a crucial impact on the form and effectiveness of business as an organized system of political power.

system. While patterns vary from sector to sector, the weight of the evidence is that Brussels lobbying has strengthened what we have here been calling 'individualization'. Individual firms have found Brussels a happy hunting ground, partly because they have the resources to invest and partly because for long periods the Commission has looked to the biggest firms for advice and cooperation in the policy process (Coen 1998, 2007; Woll 2006).

To some degree, the turn to 'do it yourself' lobbying by the enterprise and the turn to more professionally and formally organized lobbying are pulling the British system of business representation in different directions. On the one hand, individual enterprises are striking out on their own in the defence of their particular interests. But the professional lobbyist, paradoxically, operates in a rather different way. An obvious tactical problem for any single enterprise is that simply defending its own interests can, in an environment where the language of the public interest is constantly used, appear selfish and illegitimate. The lobbyist's role lies partly in spotting the potential to create alliances uniting the promotion of raw economic interests to more culturally acceptable ends. In part, the lobbyist is looking to encourage firms with common interests, if only short term in nature, to operate cooperatively; and in part is looking to transform public perception of the crude self-interest of a business into a cause that appeals more widely. Thus, the lobbyist's skill lies in recognizing when the interests of business coincide with those of groups like charities or advocacy groups and in creating campaigns that support narrow self-interest with the legitimacy of less self-interested institutions. McGrath beautifully illustrates the process. Firms faced with a government proposal to impose a levy on blank audiotapes were put together by a lobbyist with the Royal National Institute for the Blind (RNIB), which opposed the proposal because the blind were heavy users of audiotapes. Business provided the resources; the RNIB provided the unanswerable emotional arguments. For the RNIB, it was a 'white sticks and dogs job' (McGrath 2005: 306): flooding the Central Lobby of the House of Commons with crowds of blind and partially sighted protestors against the proposal.

This is the kind of cold calculation that modern business needs to advance its interests in the UK policy process, and, we shall now see, it needs it even more in the case of the United States.

The United States: organizing business under decentralized government

We saw in Chapter 2 that the shape of business power and representation was heavily influenced by the distinct historical paths taken by national business systems. But it is more than a matter of historical setting. The description of Britain in the last section highlighted another feature of national setting: the way the organization of contemporary business representation is shaped by the wider character of the governing system and by the changing character of the national system of economic government. A similar pattern of influence prevails in the United States. For nearly a century, the United States has been a dominant global power, and thus a key problem for American business has been how to shape foreign economic policy in the interests of business. We shall see a striking pattern here: many of the leading national institutional voices emerged at the moment when this consciousness of American global prominence developed. Issues of foreign economic policy have thus closely shaped the national organization of business in the United States. But it has also been shaped by domestic political factors. A divided, dispersed, multi-level system of government has faced business with problems of tactical and strategic cohesion much more acute than in the British case – where, as we saw, for much of the twentieth century there existed a close integration between political and business elites at the metropolitan centre in London. Until recently, a description of organization at the centre covered most of the important ground in the United Kingdom, but in the United States, organization in Washington is only one part of the picture. Organizing business interests in Washington is a very different matter from organizing business interests in, say, Austin (the capital of Texas). This decentralization is mirrored in a party system that reflects the multi-level character of the political system and the diversity of American society.

These features immediately give us a clue to the organizational shape of the American business lobby. American business as a corporate body has been good at organizing, but poor at organizing in a unified way. We can see three different institutional solutions to these problems of cohesion.

First, there are institutions organically connected to the business elite, but freed from the constraints of individual membership firms or associations, and therefore in principle able to take a strategic view that transcends the parochial interests of firms or sectors. Two of the most important are the Conference Board and the Council on Foreign Relations. The Board – which now has a multinational institutional reach – is a body for individual members of the business elite. It in effect serves as a think tank for business, and dates from 1916 – the eve of America's entry into the First World War and the eve of the moment when the United States began to flex its muscles as a global power. The Council on Foreign Relations, an organization also composed of individual members – not all drawn from the business elite – dates from almost the same critical moment: the eve of the Versailles Peace Conference in 1919 when the United States, emerging as the dominant power from the First World War, was preparing to try to shape the post-war settlement in line with

President Woodrow Wilson's vision of America's providential global mission (see Parmar 2004).

Both the strengths and weaknesses of these strategically minded institutions are inherent in their membership structure: precisely because they are freed from the constraints of the demands of individual firms they can think in ways that transcend the interests of particular sectors and enterprises; but this kind of strategic vision is often of little use to sectors and, still less, to individual firms. Hence the existence of – in the language of political science – 'peak associations', the second institutional solution to the problem of cohesion. Everything we said in Chapter 1 emphasizes the need for national business systems to create institutions capable of expressing and promoting some common interests, and the institutionally fragmented character of both the system of government and the system of business in the United States makes that task especially important. Just to sketch even the main national bodies claiming to speak for business as peak associations is to get a sense of how important the task is and how hard it is to perform successfully. The oldest association, dating from 1895, is the National Association of Manufacturers. The Association advertises itself as a broad-based business membership body, but its historical origins lie in Cincinnati in the mid-west manufacturing heartland, and its priorities are well flagged in its name and its self-image: 'the leading advocate of a pro-manufacturing agenda ... Manufacturing is the engine that drives American prosperity' (National Association of Manufacturers 2007). It is, in other words, best considered as a kind of pan-sector representative association for manufacturing as a whole. A similar characterization best describes the National Federation of Independent Business, which as the name implies has its roots in small- and medium-sized enterprises – the special concerns of which are examined in Chapter 5.

The closest the United States has to a unifying peak organization for business as a whole is the US Chamber of Commerce, a body – like the British CBI – with associational and individual members. It conforms to the pattern we identified earlier: like other important voices of business, it originated – in 1912 – at the moment of realization of American global might (Jacobs 1999: 17–18). In the words of Smith's authoritative study, it 'comes closer than any other association in representing the overall business viewpoint' (2000: 40). This broad base of membership is also a predictable source of difficulty: the Chamber has a history of caution in expressing views on any contentious issues precisely because of the need to conciliate its very diverse membership (ibid.: 42–7).

It is this very caution that the Business Roundtable, founded in 1972 from the merger of three separate groups, is partly designed to circumvent. It is an organization for the very largest corporations in the American (and therefore in many cases in the world) economy. Membership is relatively small – presently about 160, concentrated in the Fortune 500, and encompassing almost all the Fortune top 100 (Jacobs 1999: 15–17; Business Roundtable 2008). It tries to solve problems of consensus and strategic cohesion by insisting on the direct participation of corporate leaders: it is, in its own words, 'an association of chief executive officers of leading US companies' (Business Roundtable 2008). It is hardly a surprise, therefore, to find that it is at any one moment a 'Who's Who' of the American business elite. The Roundtable itself is the child of an even older attempt at creating a coherent strategic voice for the corporate elite: it grew out of the Business Council, an organization created in the 1930s to liaise with the top of the federal government as 'the executive committee of the nation's corporate elite' (McQuaid 1982: 32). But the Roundtable marks an important tactical development, one we shall see again later. The Business Council functioned in an informal way, relying heavily on private connections with the very peak of the political elite, going right up the President. The Roundtable, while also exploiting these connections, functions in a much more open and formally organized way. Through an array of task forces, it produces a stream of documents arguing the business case. It also engages in very public advocacy, for instance, in appearances before Congressional committees (Business Roundtable 2008). The political skills it demands of its CEO members are thus very different from – and more demanding than – those required in the old Business Council 'schmoozing' mode.

In the United Kingdom, to describe the main national peak associations is, we found, to describe the main forms of collective representation by large and medium size business. Once we descend to the local or even regional level, we are mostly in a world of small business representation, simply because of the twin British features of centralization of the business system itself and of the system of government. But this is just not so in the United States: the third institutional solution to the problem of cohesion is to organize below the federal level. There are powerful business alliances 'beyond the beltway' – that is, beyond the world inside the beltway (freeway) that rings Washington, DC, a common image for the world of politics in the national capital. But attempting to characterize business organization, still less business power, in this hugely diverse world beyond Washington, immediately takes us to fundamental arguments about the significance of business power. A large number of studies of state politics and of politics in important cities, spanning more than half a century, document the significance of this kind of organized representation, but there is substantial disagreement about what conclusions can be drawn about the power of business at state level and more local level from these studies. The pictures vary from domination by a business elite to one where business is one of a range of interests struggling for control over a range of issues (a sampling ranges from Hunter 1953 to Polsby 1980). Similar competing pictures emerge in a later generation of studies of the role of business in urban coalitions, many of them organized in large cities in the face of the challenges of globalization. In some accounts, the coalitions are substantially controlled by big business; in others, business is one interest competing in policy cockpits populated by many different groups (Stone 1989; Rast 2001; Paul 2005). The persistence of these different pictures owes something to irresolvable methodological differences (a particularly marked feature of the debates about the power of business in community studies) and in part to the sheer diversity of political cultures and systems at state, city, and even more local level in the United States.

The competitive world of 'peak' associations coexists with an equally competitive, and hugely diverse, world of more specialized interest representation. Virtually, every conceivable interest is organized at industry and sectoral levels. In the United States, this pattern of organization has two particularly distinctive features that impact on the way business organizes for the purposes of interest representation.

First, much more than in the United Kingdom, it has been marked by a highly 'professionalized' approach to lobbying. The largest firms now routinely have their own 'in-house' lobbyists, particularly organized in Washington; we discuss this in more detail in the following chapter. A key function of representative associations is the provision, likewise, of in-house lobbying services. A study by Heinz et al. found that most representative work done by these associations was indeed done by their own 'in-house' professionals (1993: 63–6). There is also a long-established practice, mostly organized in the biggest law firms, of the provision of advice and contacts, a service which mixes 'fixing' via contacts with specialized legal advice in a highly juridified regulatory setting. There also exists a large industry of registered professional lobbyists, 'hired guns' available to anyone prepared to pay. Surveys of the lobbying industry – for instance of the registered lobbyists in Washington – show business to be its overwhelmingly important customer (Baumgartner and Leech 1998: 93–8). And, as we document below, this industry has grown hugely in recent decades.

Second, the organization of interests is entangled with the most important form of public intervention in, and public control over, business life in the United States: that described in the preceding chapter as the rise of a regulatory state in American economic life. There is an almost ubiquitous pattern here: private business associations are deeply involved in the regulatory process, and their organization is often shaped by that involvement. There exists what Wolfe calls the 'franchise state' (1977: 108–75). This is a system where key areas of social and economic life are conducted through a partnership between state bodies and private interests. Business is 'organized', but it is not always explicitly organized as a lobby. It is organized because it has been assigned a privileged position in the making and delivery of public policy. The most developed form of this occurs in those areas of economic life where there exist systems of publicly overseen institutions of self-regulation. For instance, most financial markets are organized in this way. The result is that the regulatory bodies governing these markets – for instance, on the New York Stock Exchange – are major institutional actors in shaping the character of business interests in their markets and in negotiating about the management of those interests with public bodies.

But this pattern of licensed self-regulation is only the most extreme example of the way the existence of the regulatory state conditions the organization of business representation. The most important feature of economic regulation is that at its heart is a dense network of exchanges between regulated industries and regulatory bodies – ranging from the consensual to the highly adversarial, but always dense. The organizational life of an industry, and of individual firms, is shaped by the daily reality of regulation. Nor is this confined to relationships between regulated and regulatory agencies. Regulation politicizes economic life in the United States, in the sense that it creates high stakes in regulatory outcomes, and thus creates incentives for numerous groups to enter regulatory struggles. At stake are the interests not only of the most obviously engaged parties – the formally empowered agencies and the regulated firms – but also a wide range of societal claimants: formally organized lobby groups in domains like environmental policy, groups like unions representing workers, and countless activist groups ranging from those representing aggrieved citizens to those representing investors. Much of this spills over into organized litigation and counter-litigation. The effect is deeply to shape institutional patterns, both within firms and across industries and sectors. (In Chapter 7, we look more closely at some of the consequences for business of this intensely political and juridical pattern to regulation.)

A summary of the institutional pattern described above could run as follows. The organization of business interest representation in the United States displays great diversity; tremendous organizational density; and overlapping, multi-sectoral, and multi-level structures. 'Organization' means much more than the organization of what would conventionally be recognized as business lobbies, important though these are. This is a 'snapshot' of the organization of business representation, but we also need what we provided in the case of the United Kingdom: a sense of how the system of business representation is developing over time. Important changes in the organization of the American business representation system can be summarized under four headings.

THE ORGANIZED POPULATION IS CHANGING

We saw above that some of the most important early groups – like the Conference Board – were designed to voice a strategic vision of the interests of business independent of the sectional demands of particular firms or sectors. Yet, it is obvious that what constitute the best strategic choices, in alliance with American state, are not always immediately clear: they have to be argued out, and will always have a contingent, uncertain character. These arguments take place in an open, liberal culture where there is great variety of resources, views, and links with different interests. This helps explain an important long-term development: the multiplication of 'think tank' like groups devoted precisely to this task of formulating a strategic vision. There is competition between these groups to gain prominence as the authoritative voice of strategic business interests. The Business Roundtable itself has some of the elements of such a strategic body. Likewise, the Public Affairs Council was founded in 1954 because the then President, Eisenhower, 'felt that the business community needed to be more strategic in how it dealt with government' (Pinkham 2005: 267). In Chapter 7, we will see more details still of the expansion of this 'think-tank' business. But despite the constant appeals to the rhetoric of strategy, this is actually a rather unstrategic world. It is crowded and competitive, with different institutions claiming to act as the strategic guide of business, often offering very different visions of the interests of the business system or visions so encompassing that it is unclear what strategic priorities animate them at all. Among the better-known founded in recent decades are the Heritage Foundation (1973) and the Cato Institute (1977). We will also discover in the next chapter that there has also been a tendency for this world to itself become globalized, with the creation of bodies like the World Economic Forum (1971), the Trilateral Commission (1973), and the World Business Council for Sustainable Development (1995).

THE SCALE OF RESOURCES DEVOTED TO BUSINESS LOBBYING IS GROWING

This picture of growing institutional competition to act as the strategic voice of business is paralleled by growing competition for voice in the more 'sectional' domains of business representation. Thus, a second major development is the growth in the scale of business lobbying, the resources invested in it, and the complexity of the lobbying process, over the last three decades. A simple index is the growth in the numbers of lobbyists. From the 1960s to the 1980s, numbers grew from an estimated 3,000 to 10,000. By the turn of the millennium that had grown to over 16,000; by 2005, under the business friendly Bush administration, the numbers had more than doubled to over 35,000 (Heinz et al. 1993: 10; Bimbaum 2005).

And that is only the picture in Washington: one estimate is that around 40,000 more are registered at state level (Rush 2007). Business is by far the most important client of these professionals, as a number of surveys of the lobbying system show (Schlozman and Tierney 1986; Baumgartner and Leech 1998; Gray et al. 2004). 'Within firm' lobbying capacity has not only grown in scale, but has also been increasingly institutionalized in the creation of specialized departments designed to manage the (variously labelled) government relations or public affairs function (Martin 2000: 36). Within firms, there has also occurred a development similar to one we noted in the case of the United Kingdom (indeed it would be more accurate to say that it was first developed in the United States): the 'government relations' function has itself typically been generalized within firms into a more comprehensive function involving the management of the external reputation of the firm, and has been increasingly recognized as an important specialized function within corporations.

THE TACTICS OF REPRESENTATION ARE CHANGING

The growing investment in expertise is itself connected to a third development: a change in the way business lobbying is done. A generation ago, lobbying in Washington was a matter of knowing the right people: it relied heavily on informal 'fixing' (McGrath 2005: 89, 222). Hence the importance of well-placed individuals in locations like prestigious law firms who had valuable contact books, often based on their experience in public service. These kinds of informal contacts have not disappeared, but they have been overlain with a much more institutionally complex system of business representation. In part, this is a matter of more formality and professionalism in the presentation of client cases, but it is more than that: it is a matter of being more active and anticipatory in monitoring and shaping policy developments, in building a reputation with policy makers, and in forming alliances with other interests, often interests beyond business. Professional lobbyists are especially important here, because part of their skill lies in putting together different groups with shared, contingent interests in particular cases – interests that they might not spontaneously recognize. We have already noticed this in the case of the United Kingdom, but it is so well developed in the United States that it has acquired a label: 'Bootlegger–Baptist' coalitions, which unite 'moral' with sectional business interests (Yandle 1983; Eisner 2007:11). The lobbyist's skill lies in spotting potential commonalities of interest between narrowly sectional business interests and groups that can claim the moral high ground, thus conferring legitimacy on business interests that would otherwise struggle to represent themselves as anything other than narrowly selfish.

Box 3.3 The Transatlantic Business Dialogue at work: the EU–US summit of June 2008

The Transatlantic Business Dialogue (TABD) is a group of 35+ large European and US corporations. The Dialogue (the name fails to convey fully the extent to which it is an organization which produces a stream of reports and argument) was not the creation of business, but of states: it began in 1995 as an initiative of the European Commission and the US Department of Commerce. It promotes the creation of an integrated marketplace free of barriers to trade across the Atlantic. It follows the 'round table' format pioneered in the United States: that is, it is an invitation only body, and members are represented by CEOs or equivalent. It is an ever-present at meetings of the annual EU–US government summits. Consequently, its leaders were present at the June 2008 summit in Ljubljana, Slovenia. (The summit was held there because Slovenia held the Presidency of the EU at the time.) The Executive Board of the TABD meets twice yearly, at the annual EU–US summit and at the annual meeting of the World Economic Forum. (On the latter, see Box 8.2, p. 158.) The EU–US summit is partly an occasion for the kind of platitudinizing about strategy combined with networking that is the central to the lives of chief executives of large corporations. But the experience of the 2008 summit shows that the Dialogue is also plugged into the operational debates about the hard detail of policy. It presented to the Summit leaders its report 'Driving Forward Transatlantic Economic Integration'. Though the headline summaries of this report consist of platitudes ('Enhancing cooperation on energy supply and climate change') the detailed report is a substantial document which tackles the hard problems of liberalization, for instance in respect of Intellectual Property Rights. More important, its content and tone mirror the simultaneously published report to the government leaders by the Transatlantic Economic Council (TEC). This is a body set up in 2007 consisting of representatives of the European Commission and the US government. Nor is it surprising that the TEC document resembled that produced by the business leaders, because the Council has been tasked by Summit leaders to convene a Group of Advisers which includes the co-chairs of the TABD, and the Advisers are in turn tasked to consult their major stakeholders. (From 2008 to 2010, the two co-chairs are Jürgen Thumann, a former President of the Federation of German Industries, and James Quigley, CEO of the US accounting giant Deloitte Touche Tohmatsu.) The TABD's participation in the annual EU–US summit is thus now institutionalized. Not only are the meetings of its Executive Board programmed to coincide with the Summit, but also the Board routinely presents its view of policy priorities to leaders at the summit, and, as we have just seen, the two co-chairs are an important part of the advisory group that turns into hard policy detail the platitudes of the summit communiqués. The adoption by the 2008 Summit of a series of 'Lighthouse (high priority) Projects', for instance, reflected directly the briefings from the TABD which the Transatlantic Council transmitted to summit leaders, in respect of such things as action to protect intellectual property rights against copyright piracy. The TABD also plays an important part, especially through its institutionalized place on the Group of Advisers to the TEC, in the vital stage of following up the Summit leaders' general pronouncements: at the start of September 2008, the European co-chair of the TABD travelled to Brussels to launch a period of consultation on the Transatlantic Economic Dialogue's programme, and on 25 September 2008, he hosted stakeholder meetings in Washington and in Brussels to present the results of the consultation and to consider next steps ahead of the third (2009) TEC meeting. Hence, the institutionalized presence of the TABD at the heart of Trans Atlantic trade diplomacy answers a question posed often in this book: how far does participation in elite networking actually translate into hard bargaining over the detail of policy? The answer here is 'on many important occasions it does'. The details of the TABD role can be traced through the Dialogue's excellent web site (at www.tabd.com).

THE REGULATION OF BUSINESS LOBBYING IS GROWING

One reason for the shift to more professionalized and formally organized lobbying is a fourth institutional development: increasing regulation of the lobbying system. This goes to the heart of business lobbying, because it is scandals created by the business lobbying which have prompted regulation. In Chapter 6, we will see that there is now virtually a generation of regulatory reform seeking to control the financial relations between interests, mostly business interests and parties. There is also virtually a century of scandal-driven change in regulating the relationship between lobbyists, Congressmen, and policy makers, dating back at least to the Mulhall scandals of 1913 (McConnell 1966: 11–18). The most recent comprehensive reform at federal level was the Lobbying Disclosure Act of 1995, but the viability of this was placed in question within a decade by a further series of scandals. The most important involved bribery by a leading lobbyist, Jack Abramoff. It led to the resignation of the Republican Majority Leader in the House of Representatives in 2006 and the jailing of a Republican Congressman for accepting bribes. The period saw a sharp acceleration in the pace of regulatory reform, especially of the giant lobbying industries that operate at state level. Twenty-four states enacted new disclosure rules between 2003 and 2006 alone (Center for Public Integrity 2008). The most recent federal legislation is the Lobbying Disclosure Act of 2007, a measure that attempted to impose complex new rules governing the disclosure of relationships between legislators and lobbyists (Mitchell 2008). The one thing we can say with certainty is that it will be only the latest in continuing instalments of regulation.

Business lobbying and the crisis of the business system

In Chapter 2, we saw how distinctive were the historical circumstances shaping business politics in the United Kingdom and the United States, and how these distinctive historical origins had set the two systems of business politics on different paths. The account of the institutional structure of business representation presented in this chapter has re-emphasized this story of distinctiveness: notably, distinctiveness imposed by the contrast between a centralized and a decentralized systems of politics. These differences remain important. But we have seen that there is also some striking convergence. This is partly because the political environment within which business in Britain has to organize has become less centralized: increasingly, it works within a system of multi-level government embracing both the economic government of the EU and the world of devolved national government. But there are other commonalities that are more particular to business representation itself: the long-term problems involved in organizing business for collective action; the growing sophistication and resources of lobbying by individual firms; the growing professionalization and specialization of the lobbying function; and the growing integration between business lobbying and interlinked service industries in public relations, legal representation, and lobbying itself.

The great economic crisis of 2007–9 gave a decisive push to these developments, and in particular to patterns of cross-national convergence. Every leading capitalist democracy – not just the two that are our subjects here – experienced a profound crisis of its financial institutions. The intensity of the crisis was peculiarly severe in the United States and the United Kingdom. In both cases, it drew political leaders and leaders of financial institutions into frenzied bargaining in an attempt to avoid a full-scale collapse of financial systems. A remarkable feature of that episode, however, was how irrelevant were the institutions of collective representation on the side of business. Political leaders and business leaders were obliged to confront each other directly. The force of crisis allowed no time or space for pondering collective interests, long-term strategy, or the creation of alliances. Out of that experience came seismic changes in economic structure and in the character of the links between business and government. Governments once again assumed the role of steering their economies, especially their financial systems. The critical relationships forged were those between political elites and enterprises, especially enterprises in the banking system. A new age of enforced partnership between big business and big government was inaugurated. Never before had the importance of the giant firm been so great. The change reinforces the significance of the next chapter, which examines more closely the political role of the giant enterprise, especially the giant multinational enterprise.

4 Politics and the Giant Multinational Corporation

Why giant firms matter politically

The preceding chapter sketched the most important institutions that try to represent business interests, and Chapter 5 will describe the (often unique) politics of small business. But another kind of enterprise – the giant corporation – made several appearances in the preceding chapter, and these appearances already suggest that we need to look at the corporate giant in more detail. We do this for three reasons.

The first is, simply, the economic weight of these enterprises. What constitutes a 'giant' firm is hardly obvious. But granted the uncertainties of measurement, both our everyday experience and the more systematic evidence of statistics show us economies where a small number of very big firms are peculiarly important. Just take, to begin with, some everyday instances: our shopping centres are dominated by a small number of retail giants; we fuel our cars, and indeed buy those cars, from one of a small number of giant firms; and much of our leisure involves consuming products or services – for instance, in music, book, or film – that are produced by corporate giants. And to take the example closest to hand: you are reading a book written on hardware, and with software, produced by a couple of giants, Toshiba and Microsoft. (The political evolution of Microsoft, we shall see below, is indeed highly revealing.) When we turn from everyday experience to the more systematic evidence of the statistics, the arithmetic overrides any subtleties of definition: for instance, the most recent UK statistics show that the officially defined large firm sector accounts for only 0.1 per cent of enterprises by number, but 41 per cent of employment and 49 per cent of turnover (BERR 2008c).

But the second reason for looking at the corporate giant is that it is not only a special kind of institution economically, but is also, we shall see in the pages that follow, special politically. It has some special strengths, and also some special weaknesses. It is often a highly politicized institution, both in the sense that its internal operations are deeply shaped by its political environment and

Box 4.1 The European Round Table of Industrialists: a voice of the European business elite

The 'round table' format for business representation was invented in the United States: for details, see pp. 52–3. It was intended to solve two recurring problems of business representation: that of coordinating collective action amongst large numbers of firms and that of ensuring that firms commit key personnel to business representation. The 'round table' format tries to solve problems of commitment and collective action by involving a comparatively small number of firms, by recruiting them by invitation only, and by requiring that they be represented at the most senior (such as chief executive)) level. This was exactly the format adopted in 1983 when a group of seventeen leading industrialists met on the initiative of Pehr Gyllenhammar, at the time chief executive of Volvo, to found the European Round Table (ERT) in Paris. A photograph (reproduced on the ERT web site) of the inaugural meeting is also a portrait of the European industrial elite at that time: it includes chief executives of (then) leading enterprises such as Shell, Siemens, Fiat, and Volvo. But that first portrait also contains two figures not then active in business, whose presence is critical to understanding the point of the ERT: they are Etienne Davignon and Francois-Xavier Ortoli. Both were members of the European Commission, the key executive body of the EU: Davignon was Commissioner for Industry and the Single Market and Ortoli was Commissioner for Economic and Monetary Affairs. The prompt for the meeting was a question addressed to Gyllenhammar by Davignon: 'whom do I call when I want to speak to European Industry?' From the beginning, in other words, the ERT was sponsored as a business representative body by the leadership of the Commission. In the intervening quarter century, the ERT has maintained both its original organizing principles and a presence as a key insider in debates about economic reform in the EU. It has expanded to contain within its ranks the very elite of European business ('industry' now being a misnomer insofar as it suggests a concentration on manufacturing): it has forty-five members, chief executives, or board chairs of leading European multinationals. On the model of the US round table, these members are expected to chair or serve on one of the 'Working Groups', that in turn draw members from firms represented in the ERT. At the time of writing, there were seven of these, covering topics like International Accounting Standards, Foreign Economic Relations, and Competition Policy. Moreover, the ERT is plainly perfectly placed to practice high-level networking. 'Every six months', it claims, 'the ERT strives to meet the Head of the Government that holds the EU Presidency to discuss priorities' (http://www.ert.be). There can be little doubt, given the calibre of those who head the Round Table, that this 'striving' is successful. Van Apeldorn (2000) has documented the key role played by the Round Table in the creation of a single market and a single European currency. But the ERT has two plain weaknesses. While its membership is kept deliberately confined, it nevertheless is a heterogeneous organization, with members from eighteen countries and many different sectors. (Membership is not even confined to the EU: the chief executive of the Eczacıbaşi Group from Turkey is a member.) It also has a tiny permanent staff (a secretary general and only six office staff) and we know that effective lobbying, especially in the European Union, depends critically on the possession of expertise and a capacity to monitor the complex development of policy. In short, it is not clear how far the ERT is able to go beyond the generalities about high strategy that are meat and drink to chief executives of multinationals (for more on the ERT, see http://www.ert.be/home.aspx).

in the sense that it is a key participant in both the high politics, and routine politics, of economic life.

The third reason for the special focus of this chapter is flagged in the reference to 'multinational' in the title. Not all corporate giants would be categorized as multinational in their operations, and conversely there are instances of enterprises that would not by conventional measures be classified as giant in scale but which nevertheless are multinational in their reach (e.g. Pilling 2006). But in the Anglo-American world, giant firms nevertheless do commonly operate on a multinational scale, and multinational enterprises are usually easily classifiable as giants by most accepted measures. It is not hard to see that multinational reach introduces quite fresh political experiences. It forces firms into encounters with more than one state jurisdiction, and as a result has important consequences for the way they must operate politically. Another dimension still has been introduced by the changing shape of the world economy. It is well established (for a review, see Scholte 2005: 13 ff.) that the period since the early 1970s has seen an acceleration of the pace of globalization. The multinational corporation is at the heart of this process. That explains why, in addition to our account of two national systems, this chapter contains a separate section on the politics of the multinational corporation in the global economy.

The giant firm and politics in the United Kingdom: the transformation of a private political world

The giant firm has some key advantages as a political actor, and some key disadvantages. The case of the United Kingdom illustrates these two features. Some of the advantages are so obvious that we can deal with them summarily. Economic weight makes the giant firm a key player in the shaping of economic life and in the delivery of economic policy. While the economy-wide weight of giant firms is great, in some particular industries and sectors it is not only striking, but also growing. A vivid example which consumers experience every day is provided by the grocery trade. In 2000, the three largest supermarket chains (Tesco, Asda, and Sainsbury) accounted for 45.3 per cent of UK-wide grocery sales; within the short period to 2007 that large figure had grown further, to 55.5 per cent (Competition Commission 2008). In addition, in the United Kingdom since the mid-1980s, a particularly important category of giant firm has been created by the privatization programme which began in earnest in that decade. A handful of industries, chiefly concerned with the provision of what had historically been considered public utilities – energy, transport, water in particular – were consolidated in the private sector but subjected to distinctive regimes of public control via specialized agencies. The creation of this special regulated category of, principally, giant enterprises has as a consequence created a distinctive set of relationships between these enterprises and public institutions. The regulated enterprises were from the beginning highly political entities, since their competitive advantage and, in cases like rail where they operated under a publicly granted franchise, their very presence in markets, depended in part on how they managed their relations with public regulators. Unsurprisingly, therefore, these privatized enterprises have developed specialized units to monitor their regulatory environment and have developed institutional means of negotiating with public agencies, notably with their specialized regulators (Coen and Willman 1998). The size of this closely regulated sector was quite unexpectedly expanded in the autumn of 2008 by the consequences of the global financial crisis – expanded not by privatization but by an extension of public control. The state was obliged, in order to prevent the collapse of the biggest banks, to take substantial ownership stakes. In effect, the giant British banks were turned into regulated public utilities, and key decisions – about executive pay and lending policies – suddenly became political in character.

The significance of the development of these politically highly organized regulated enterprises lies not only in the size of the sector, however, but also in the fact that their rise reflects a wider development in the political character of the giant firm. We noted this in the previous chapter, drawing on the work of Grant (1984): he first charted an important institutional innovation, the creation of the specialized government relations department in the largest firms.

The initial developments spurring this change happened from about the mid-1970s, and reflected changes in the political environment of the giant firm. For just about the first three quarters of the twentieth century, as we saw in Chapter 2, the policy-making system in the United Kingdom provided a congenial home to corporate giants, and the structure of these giants evolved to fit that system. The policy-making system was centralized on a small Whitehall-based network; giant firms thus centralized their board-level operations in the metropolis, and their leaders became incorporated into the policy-making elite. As a result, big firms often did not 'lobby', in the sense of formally organizing to put their points of view in Whitehall; their chief executives just had everyday access to the policy-making elite in a private political world. The distinguished American observer of UK politics, Samuel Beer, has a revealing story illustrating this symbiosis. Attending the annual dinner of the Chamber of Shipping – the main trade association for the shipping industry – in 1958, he discovered that the Minister's after dinner speech on government–industry relations had been jointly drafted by his civil servant with main responsibility for shipping and the civil servant's opposite number in the trade association (Beer 2006: 699–700). In the 1960s, the two giant firms in the overlapping sectors of chemicals and fibres, ICI and Courtaulds, were led by quintessential policy insiders: Sir Paul Chambers (chairman of ICI, 1960–8) had come from a glittering civil service career; and Sir Frank – later Lord – Kearton (chairman of Courtaulds 1964–75) was a favourite big businessman of the Wilson Governments between 1964 and 1970, chairing the institutional centrepiece of its industrial policy, the Industrial Reorganization Corporation from 1966 to 1968. And as chairman Kearton pursued a pro-big business policy, encouraging mergers in the search for giant 'national champions' that could compete for the United Kingdom against foreign multinationals (Paine 1982; Bowden 2000).

Even by the 1970s, these tightly knit, metropolitan policy communities were losing their cohesion. Indeed from 1979, there was in power a government under Mrs Thatcher that thought this policy-making world involved an unacceptable 'corporatist' bargain with big business. It became necessary for the giant enterprise to organize more formally in order to lobby and to influence policy.

In the intervening years since Grant first identified the phenomenon, the initially narrowly conceived 'government relations' function in the corporate giant has become both broader and more complex. Many specialized functions inside large firms have become increasingly sensitive politically: market regulation, health and safety, equal opportunity policy, financial compliance – all involve tracking, and to some degree trying to influence the shape of public policy. In short, giant firms now have to manage their influence on public policy as part of a strategy designed to shape both the regulatory environment and the reputation of the enterprise. We shall return to this phenomenon below in considering the management of firm reputation.

This growth in the complexity of the task of managing the giant firm as a political actor has also been influenced by two other developments over the last three decades, which can be summarized as globalization and Europeanization. We know from the preceding chapter that both these have had important consequences for the wider organization of business lobbies, but there are also some important, and obvious, ways in which they have affected the workings of the individual giant enterprise as a political actor. We explore the issue of globalization in more detail later, but for UK giant firms its political effects may be summarized in the following terms. The UK economy is almost uniquely hospitable to the giant firm organized along multinational lines. It is, for instance, the most popular location of direct foreign investment into the European Union (UNCTAD 2006: xxii). The roll call of foreign multinational giants with significant operations in the United Kingdom is also a roll call of the global multinational elite. In the City of London, the United Kingdom has a set of market arenas that are central to the trading activities of giant firms, and not just those domiciled in the United Kingdom.

And the UK economy is itself peculiarly 'globalized' – exposed to the consequences of the great burst of globalization of recent decades. This has transformed large numbers of hitherto UK firms into parts of globally organized multinationals.

In short, globalization has greatly changed the institutional reach of the giant firm in the United Kingdom, and has made considerably more complex the range of interests it contains. A similar point can be made about Europeanization, particularly in its impact on the range of arenas where the giant firm is a political actor. The renewal of the project to create a single integrated market was closely connected to the ambitions of multinationals, including UK multinationals (Van Apeldorn 2000). The European Commission has been particularly anxious to draw giant firms into both the stage of consulting over and later implementing policy (Coen 1998, 2007). Indeed, as we see from Box 4.1 (p. 62), the Commission was important in the founding of the ERT of Industrialists. The result has been to magnify the range and complexity of the political activities of the giant firm: it now has to operate in a whole set of policy-making arenas outside those of the United Kingdom and in the process to form alliances with interests and institutions beyond the United Kingdom. That helps explain why some of the most important members of the ERT of Industrialists are British corporate giants or giants with a major presence in the United Kingdom: they include Unilever, Astra Zeneca, British Airways, BP, and Rio Tinto.

We thus have a picture of the giant firm in the United Kingdom as a political actor that has gone through a distinctive evolution: the range of interests it contains has become more complex, the range of political arenas in which it has to operate has widened, and the institutional complexity of its internal political organization has grown significantly. These changes have been due in part to internal institutional changes (the development of new functional capacities inside firms), to changes in the UK political environment (the decline of a centralized, socially integrated, metropolitan focused policy-making system), and to external political and economic changes (summarized in the twins of globalization and Europeanization).

The pattern of change here might be summarized as the growth of formality in the way the firm organizes itself politically, and the increasing integration of what began as a fairly specialized lobbying function into a wider process that attempts to manage the reputation of the firm. Giant firms are often also *brands* (consider the Marks and Spencer brand) and the reputation of the brand has to be managed. Thus, the political effectiveness of giant enterprises now depends on something more diffuse and hard to control than professionally organized lobbying. Two emblematic episodes that occurred within a few short years of each other illustrate this. First, there was the PR disaster suffered by Shell in 1995 when, faced with a well-organized movement of opposition that was damaging its market position, it was forced to retreat on a plan to sink an oil rig (Brent Spar) in the North Sea (Nilsson 2009). Second, there was the destruction of the accounting firm Arthur Andersen in 2002 when its apparent complicity in the Enron scandal – a primarily American affair but with global consequences – in short order destroyed trust in a hitherto highly respected multinational accounting firm with a large presence in the United Kingdom. Giant firms are peculiarly vulnerable to reputational damage because of their visibility. Well beyond the world of operational lobbying, therefore, the last decade or so has seen the growth of a whole world of 'reputational management' aimed at the giant firm. In Power's phrases, there is a 'reputation constellation' that giant firms have to manage, and which has spread into, for instance, the development of 'corporate social responsibility' as a means of promoting reputation (2007: 130–4).

It is plain that the management of enterprise reputation is critical for the operation of the giant firm as a political actor, and it seems equally plain that the rise of the problem of reputation management in Britain is symptomatic of an important change in the strategic environment with which the giant enterprise has to deal. This involves a shift of methods, of arenas, and of environments. It means a shift from informal, elitist networking to professionally organized management of interests; from an overwhelming concentration on the outputs of the Whitehall policy system to a concern with trying to manage policy at a multiplicity of governmental levels; from a social and cultural environment when the giant enterprise was relatively unchallenged to one where reputations are contested.

The rising importance of enterprise reputation as something that the large firm has to manage in order to operate as a successful political actor is connected to key institutional features of the firm. Two merit special attention: the sheer complexity of the institutional processes and the interests that are now typically contained within a giant enterprise, and the vulnerability of the giant enterprise arising from its salience as a social institution.

The giant firm is an intensely political institution, not only in the sense that it plays a large part in the public policy process but also in the sense that it is an institutionally complex organization, typically with different divisions, and run by different specialists in different parts of the organization. It produces its responses to policy problems by its own internal political process that has to mediate between the views and demands of the different parts of the organization. The very subject of business strategy arose from the realization that the appropriate strategy for an enterprise in the market is not obvious; firms in similar circumstances make different choices, as a result of an internal process of decision making. The same is true of political strategy. The policy positions firms adopt, and the operational tactics they employ to advance those positions, are partly determined by the balance of influence between different divisions, and between different professional groups inside the firm. The giant firm cannot be viewed as a kind of black box that efficiently identifies some definitive firm interests and adjusts political tactics accordingly. The firm is internally divided and is also penetrated from without: in other words, a whole external regulatory world permeates the enterprise. The political consequence is that, just as giant firms often make mistaken choices in the field of conventional business strategy, so they have to overcome internal divisions to avoid comparable mistakes of political strategy.

A second source of political difficulty arises from the perception of the giant enterprise as indeed part of a wider system of big business. We know that in recent decades the perception of big business in Britain has become increasingly unfavourable, as measured by opinion polling data (the issue is discussed further in Chapter 7). This does not condemn the individual enterprise to a hostile public reception, but it does create a climate against which the corporate giant has to seek protection. The development of the initially narrow 'government relations' function into a whole industry of public relations, investor relations, brand management, and reputation management which we documented above is in part a response to this climate. The existence of such a climate helps explain why the public perception of the worth of an enterprise can be so volatile.

One solution to this problem is illustrated by the career of Richard Branson and his Virgin enterprises. It is well known that Branson's market strategy is built on the notion that the Virgin 'brand' has a value which is transferable across different markets and sectors; he has opportunistically entered markets as different as rail and air travel, pop music, and telecommunications. But he has allied this to a distinctive highly personal political strategy: he networks avidly among the political elite and cultivates a public persona as an idiosyncratic, ageing hippy figure, softening the perception of Virgin as a calculating institution and generating huge free public relations material in the process.

The success of this fusion of political networking and marketing is a source of debate (Bowers 2000; Branson 2007; Dearlove 2007). But in any case, it depends critically on Branson's own idiosyncratic personality and his record as an entrepreneur. More bureaucratically organized corporate giants find this new world of branding and political management trickier to manage. Take the case of the long-established oil giant Shell. Its reputation was badly damaged in the 1990s, as we noted earlier, from the furore over the attempted disposal by sinking in the North Sea of the derelict oilrig Brent Spar. (Shell took all the public hostility because it was contractually responsible for disposal, despite the fact that in its working life the rig had been jointly operated with another oil giant, BP.) The salvaging of Shell's reputation was still progressing when in 2003 it was damaged by yet another public relations disaster, this time arising from its oil business in Nigeria, which tied it to corruption and murder by the ruling regime. Then, in 2004, it was struck by an internally delivered blow – the revelation that its accounting practices had

---

Box 4.2 Big business and politics in Russia

The only certainty about the relationship of big business and politics in Russia is that they are intertwined to a degree greater even than in the world of the advanced capitalist democracies. Hanson and Teague (2005) identify the main area of uncertainty: Is big business the creature of the Russian state as it developed under the Presidency of Vladimir Putin (2004–8) or is the state the creature of big business? The history is quite recent. The reform, and then collapse, of the former Soviet Union in the late 1980s and early 1990s produced a massive wave of privatization of the assets of the former command economy, where all significant productive property had been publicly owned. The privatization mostly involved the appropriation of hugely valuable assets by key individuals, many of whom were tied to the former *nomenklatura*, the organized system of Communist functionaries in the Soviet Union. The fabulously rich 'oligarchs' who emerged out of that process owed much of their wealth, in particular, to appropriation of Russia's vast natural resources in fields like oil. An almost seamless web unites 'big politics' and 'big (energy) business': for instance, Dmitry Medvedev, Putin's successor as Russian President, is a former chair of the board of directors of Gazprom, the largest Russian energy corporation. The structure of the business system has some of the conventional marks of big business lobbying that we would recognize from the two national cases that provide the material for this book. The oligarchs control the main employers' association, the Russian Union of Industrialists and Entrepreneurs (RUIE). As Hanson and Teague show, the RUIE aspires to act as a conventional lobbying organization in the manner of a body like the British CBI, putting its case to the Duma (Parliament) and to the big economic ministries (2005: 758–60). Business is also a major participant in Russian elections: in the state Duma elections of 2007, for instance, one estimate was that up to 50 per cent of the candidates of the Putin-supporting 'United Russia' were from business (Mereu 2007). Over the period since 1990, numerous big foreign multinationals have also established a presence in Russia: they include McDonalds (whose most profitable franchise is in Moscow), IKEA, and the Ritz-Carlton Hotel chain. But Russia is also a difficult and often dangerous place to be a big business figure. Big oil, which has been a key to the success of the Russian economy, has proved to have an especially problematic relationship to the Russian state. One of the most successful of the 1990s oligarchs, Mikhail Khodorkovsky, who had translated early connections in the Konsomol (the young Communist movement) into a vast oil empire, Yukos, found that the value of his business was largely stripped away by tax prosecutions. He is presently serving a prison sentence (until at least 2011) on a mix of tax and criminal convictions – the legitimacy of which are widely contested, on the grounds that they arise in part from struggles for political control in the Putin era. Another tricky field has involved control of the mass media: the television tycoon Boris Berezovsky now lives in political asylum in the United Kingdom after being vanquished by Putin allies in a struggle for control of a major television station. The British-based oil multinational, BP, was involved in a hugely tortuous struggle with its Russian partners for control of oil resources that are estimated to account for as much as 25 per cent of BP profits; in September 2008, it was obliged to reconstitute the board of its joint venture, with the BP-nominated chair stepping down. The present relationship of big business to politics in Russia is sometimes compared to the era of the 'robber barons' in the United States (see Chapter 2). But there are important differences: even the rough and tumble of late nineteenth century American politics coincided with a robustly independent legal system, and the integration of big business and the state is much closer at the top of the Russian system than was ever achieved in the founding period of American capitalism.

consistently overstated the value of its oil reserves, and therefore the reserves of the company (Nilsson 2009). Shell may be considered unusually unlucky (or incompetent), but it illustrates how a mix of a diverse and complex range of operations, coupled with high visibility, can make the reputations of many giant enterprises highly vulnerable. We shall see some of these patterns repeated in the case of the United States.

The giant firm and American politics: great strengths and great weaknesses

The political condition of the giant enterprise in the United States resembles its condition in the United Kingdom, but in an exaggerated form. Virtually everything we can say about the political position of the corporate giant in the United Kingdom can be said about the corporation in the United States; but in virtually every instance corporate political strength and corporate political vulnerability are magnified in the American case.

The strengths are well documented, and need only brief rehearsal here. As we saw in Chapter 2, the work of business historians like Chandler (1977) has demonstrated that the giant corporation is not just a concentration of economic resources but is one of the key institutions in American life. In a society without a traditional aristocracy, business leaders – which almost entirely now means those who head giant corporations – enjoy a special kind of social ascendancy, and the giant corporation has enjoyed an especially prominent place as an institution in both the economy and in the culture. In the words of Marchand in his history of the creation of a cultural presence for the corporation: 'by the mid-1940s, the great corporations had attained a conventional, largely uncontested standing that most corporate leaders could recognize as an acceptable substitute for soul' (1998: 5). The big business elite has a kind of cultural ascendancy that it has been difficult for its UK counterpart to achieve (Lipset 1964: 84–5, 175).

Not only does the giant corporation have strengths that resemble, but exceed, those in Britain, it has also gone through a similar lobbying evolution to the one we identified in the case of the United Kingdom. And as in the United Kingdom, this evolution is largely a function of a combination of two factors: the changing nature of the political environment of the giant firm and its changing internal organization.

The alteration in the lobbying character of the giant firm is epitomized in a remark made about political tactics by Thomas Watson, one of the dominant CEOs in the history of the US computing giant IBM: 'IBM doesn't lobby' (Hart 2007: 6). The remark, even when it was made in the early 1970s, harked back to the 1950s and 1960s. It did not mean that that IBM had no relations with the system of government. On the contrary, government was a major customer and a wide range of public policy affected the fortunes of the firm. It rather summarized a particular, informal political relationship that lasted from the 1930s to the end of the 1960s, the period when the Watson family dominated the firm, and it was characteristic of the political relationships enjoyed by many corporate giants. It was summed up, again by Watson, as follows: 'the most graceful and effective way to [cultivate politicians] is in person, and . . . probably the worst way is to have a Washington office staffed with professional lobbyists' (quoted ibid.).

The 'giant firms don't lobby era' had four distinctive features. First, giants like IBM were comparatively simple political institutions. They 'did not lobby' because relations with government were to a substantial degree conducted informally by a small number of people who did not think of themselves as 'lobbyists'. Of these, the most important was the chief executive himself, a key part of whose job was to act as the voice of the firm – but a quiet voice, exploiting connections at the top of the Washington system to advance corporate interest.

Second, if the chief executive was a de facto lobbyist who yet did not think of himself as such, this was because the CEOs of many of the most important giants were naturally integrated into elite policy-making circles. This was particularly so after the Republicans came back into the White House in 1953, when the Administration drew substantially on the leaders of large enterprises to fill key posts within the new Administration. But it was also true of periods when Democrats controlled the White House. The Watsons, the founding family of IBM who provided its chief executives from the 1930s to the 1970s, were emblematic in the ease with which they mixed with, and served, Democratic and Republican Presidents. More widely, an institution like the Business Council, which we encountered in the last chapter through McQuaid's histories, ensured that the leadership of the biggest corporations was guaranteed informal access to the very top of any administration, Republican or Democrat (McQuaid 1982, 1994).

Third, by the 1950s, the giant corporation was operating in a benign political environment. It had stabilized its reputation after the failures of the 1920s and the Great Depression. It was associated with the long period of economic growth that began at the start of the decade and with the rise of the United States as the dominant global economic power. Though we have to be careful in interpreting polling data, it does seem that approval of the giant corporation as a benign American institution was high – possibly at a uniquely historical high. (This too is discussed more fully in Chapter 7.) A close instinctive identification between the interests of the giant corporation and the national interest reduced the need to do anything so explicit as 'lobbying'.

This benign environment was also reflected in the fourth feature of the 'corporate giants don't lobby' era: the absence of serious organized rivals to, and critics of, the giant firm. True, there were in the extractive and manufacturing industries of the industrial revolution, like mining, steel, and automobiles, well-organized unions with a powerful place in the institutions of collective bargaining. But these were really partners of the giant enterprises, divided by some interests but also united by the common aim of defending the economic health of 'their' industry against any damaging public policies. In the wider civil society, it was rare to find significant institutional critics of the large enterprise or indeed of the business system as a whole. Churches and universities, though they contained some individual critics, as institutions were either indifferent or supportive. The same could be said of the older environmental movements, like the Sierra Club. Movements that, as we shall see later, were to emerge in later decades as critics of the corporate giant – in churches, in ethical consumer groups, and among environmentalists – were either not yet born or still in their infancy.

The third and fourth of these features – the benign climate of opinion and the absence of a competitive lobbying environment – have greatly changed in the last generation but, since they form a major theme of Chapter 7, I do no more than mention them here. I concentrate instead on what has happened to the giant firm as a lobbying operation. In summary, it has become more overtly political, more professionally organized, and more institutionally complex. Now, corporate giants definitely do lobby.

A sign of this change is the growing 'politicization' of the role of the chief executive. This may seem an odd way to put things, since I stressed above the centrality of the CEO to representation in the 'old' system. But recall the point of the 'IBM doesn't lobby' era. A fairly seamless integration into the federal governing elite meant that when the heads of giant firms put their points it did not feel like 'lobbying' or 'politics'. But over the recent decades, presence in the lobbying system, especially in the Washington lobbying system, has become an important part of the 'job description' of the CEO of most giant enterprises. 'The biggest single change in management during my career', a leading CEO told a researcher in 1995, 'has been the increase in time that managers spend dealing with government' (quoted Hart 2004: 61). The chief executives of 'the largest corporations typically devote up to half their time in dealing with extracorporate concerns, and government is the most important of these concerns' (Lehne 2006: 81). We saw in the last chapter that the foundation in the 1970s of the Business Roundtable for the largest corporations, with its requirement that CEOs be directly involved in the organization, demanded open, active political involvement. Likewise, the skill set demanded of a chief executive has changed, to encompass ability to operate in the lobbying world: in face-to-face negotiations and in public forums such as appearances as witnesses before Congressional Committees.

Just how damaging the absence of the right presentational skills can be is shown by the public relations disaster suffered by the tobacco industry over the long campaign to link cigarette smoking and cancer. In a famous encounter with a Congressional committee at a public (and televised) hearing in 1994, the ineptness of a whole slew of tobacco industry CEOs had the industry and its leaders pilloried as liars in a pure piece of theatre orchestrated by a shrewd and media savvy Committee chair (Derthick 2005: 55–6, 111–15). A very striking demonstration of the politicization of the role of the chief executive can be seen from Hart's study (2002) of 'the political education of Bill Gates and other nerds': in other words, the political evolution of high-tech corporate giants who have risen with great speed in the last couple of decades. These were often founded by individuals with high levels of scientific education but little natural feel for, or taste for, politics. The founders have subsequently been forced to acquire lobbying skills, or to buy them in. Microsoft initially tried to get by without any organized lobbying operation, but by 2007, it employed sixty-three professional lobbyists in Washington alone (Callan 2007). Google, the most spectacular high-tech successor to Microsoft, is now experiencing a similar evolution: it has formed its own Political Action Committee, and has hired politically well-placed advisors on both sides of the Atlantic (Lehne 2006: 166; Wray 2006).

The change therefore partly consists in a change in the role of a single individual, the chief executive, but it also involves profound institutional change in the political practices of the giant firm. Some of the changes parallel those already identified in the case of the United Kingdom – though it would be more accurate to say that they were pioneered in the United States and then diffused elsewhere. These changes reflect a more enduring feature of the giant American corporation, one repeatedly emphasized by business historians and students of business organization: it is a complex and extended series of specialized divisions and hierarchies. Chandler's famous image of the corporation as the 'visible hand' in a wide range of societal allocations catches this. Internally, it is an elaborate allocative mechanism with an active political life of its own, as all such mechanisms must have. The long-established literature which documents the rise within the giant corporation of specialisms in its management teams – specialists in functions like personnel as well as in the technologies of production and distribution – reinforces this picture of the existence of an elaborate internal division of labour, stretching to the rise of the specialist 'public affairs' function in the largest corporations (Boddewyn 2007: 156).

Professionalism and the growth of internal organizational complexity are linked. The 'political' function has become increasingly specialized, both internally and externally. The 'government relations' function that we identified in the case of the United Kingdom was pioneered in the United States and the evolution of that function as described in our UK section has if anything been even more radical on the other side of the Atlantic. The vast professional lobbying industry in the United States mostly has business, especially the largest corporations, as its customers (for some representative statistics, see Heinz et al. 1993: 10, 83; and Derthick 2005: 103). The allied activities of brand management, of corporate public relations, and the wider management of corporate reputation are likewise highly developed. So although chief executives do, now, indeed have a political function as a key part of their role, by contrast with even a generation ago they are trying to perform this role alongside a large apparatus of professional representation, lobbying and the management of organizational reputation. Some of this is done 'in house' and some 'outsourced' to the overlapping industries of lobbying, public relations, brand reputation management, and plain old-fashioned legal advice.

The consequences for the internal political cohesion of the giant corporation have been well explored in Martin's study (2000) of the internal processes by which enterprises make decisions about what positions to adopt on critical public policy issues. The lesson of her study might be summed up in terms that we used earlier: just as the appropriate business strategy for any enterprise is not obvious, but has to be hammered out through a process of argument and decision, so the appropriate political strategy is not obvious. Often the scale of economic enterprises and the variety of markets that the corporate giant is active in mean that what constitutes the 'interest' that the enterprise should defend is not at all obvious – it depends on which set of groups inside the firm dominate the definition of corporate interest at any single point. Take the position of the corporate giant DuPont in one of the biggest issues facing US policy makers and business in the last two decades: how to respond to the proposal to create the North American Free Trade Agreement (NAFTA) between Canada, the United States, and Mexico. (NAFTA was finally inaugurated under President Clinton in 1994.) DuPont's overall corporate position supported a free trade agreement; its fibre division, by contrast, opposed, reflecting its location in a sector of the US economy which feared cheaper Mexican competitors (Sklair 2001: 103).

The idea that multidivisional corporate giants can be internally divided in their interests is a fairly obvious one. But a more subtle and important aspect of corporate division is introduced by Martin's analysis of firms as 'stuck in neutral'. This happens when the specialized professionals inside the institution, like personnel and legal specialists, act as bearers of the values of wider professional communities. In this way, the firm is penetrated by numerous societal influences, and becomes itself a kind of cockpit for wider societal struggles (Martin 2000: 3–19).

To summarize, the political activities of the giant corporation in the United States have been increasingly conditioned by the more explicitly political role for the chief executive; by a growing professionalization of political activity externally, through the huge lobbying industry; and by professionalization internally through the rise of specialists controlling functions like personnel and regulatory compliance.

Some of these developments – notably more formal organization and more professionalism – are also evident in the way the giant enterprise in the United States has evolved its modes of collective action. Since we discussed some aspects of these in the preceding chapter, we can deal with them summarily. From the 1930s to the 1970s, the most important institution of collective action for big business was the Business Council. McQuaid's histories (1982, 1994) show it to have been a product of the 'big business doesn't lobby' era. It had a low public profile, and very little by way of formal organization. It relied heavily on the coordinating activities of a small number of business leaders and on informal access to the very highest levels of the federal government, notably to Presidents of both parties. The foundation of the Business Round-table in 1972, the details of which are in the preceding chapter, marked a step change. The Roundtable demanded the engagement of executive officers at the highest political level, expressed in the requirement that member enter-prises normally be represented by their CEOs or by officers of equivalent seniority. It turned to more formal organization and to open lobbying, typified in the way CEOs now have to take responsibility for heading up Roundtable 'task forces'.

When the leaders of giant firms meet in a Roundtable setting, they are attempting collective action in a constituency of more or less equals. But there is another form of collective action which has also undergone a complex evolution in recent decades: in the relationship between the giant firm and the conventional, historically established mode of collective action for business – the representative association (trade or employer) organized at industry or sectoral level. The increasingly organized and activist political character of the giant firm might lead one to expect that it would abandon the often unsat-isfactory compromises involved in working through sectoral or industrial representative associations. This has not happened, because the representative association is of use to the giant firm and because the corporate giant can often control it. There is a significant cultural value attached to collective representation: representative bodies help soften the image of the corporation and make it seem more than a narrowly sectional voice. The activities of professional lobbies assist this further; one of their most important innov-ations in recent decades has been the fostering of advocacy coalitions which allow 'selfish' business interests to ally with cause groups which are viewed as more benign than business in the public eye. Indeed, this can stretch to the very creation of such groups, behind which the corporate giant can conceal itself. The United Seniors Association, for instance, is ostensibly a lobby group for senior citizens in health and social security; in reality, it is closely allied to big pharmaceutical firms (Congress Watch 2002). Giant firms have

---

Box 4.3 An American multinational enters UK supermarket politics: the case of Wal-Mart

---

In June 1999, the American retailing giant Wal-Mart bought the UK supermarket retailer Asda. The takeover pitched Wal-Mart into the competitive marketplace in the United Kingdom, and it also pitched it into the political marketplace, for success in retailing at this level is not only a function of market strategy, but is also a function of political strategy. Wal-Mart has been a by byword for ruthless price competition in the United States; we shall see in Chapter 5 that its success in this respect has depended in part on its ability to circumvent regulatory restrictions erected in Federal law on the use of the marketing and buying power of retailing giants, controls erected to defend the position of small retailers. Wal-Mart's overseas expansion, which began in 1991 with a Mexican acquisition, has been rapid. By 1998, it had entered Europe with a German acquisition (Burt and Sparks 2001; Rowell 2003). But it has faced serious political difficulties in replicating its American formula in foreign markets: in Germany, for example, regulatory restrictions on the creation of new stores meant that it had to enter the market by buying an existing chain, and it immediately faced the entrenched power of the German unions in retailing. In the United Kingdom, it prepared the way for the ASDA takeover by using a resource which would not have been available to a smaller organization: gaining access to the Prime Minister. In January 2008, two *Daily Telegraph* reporters used the Freedom of Information Act to secure the release of an official minute of a meeting between the Prime Minister (Tony Blair), some of his senior advisors, and Bob Walters, the chief executive of Wal-Mart International (Hope and Hall 2008). The note of the discussion conveys a good flavour of the way an American multinational prepares the way to cope with domestic regulatory obstacles in advance of entering the British market. Mr Walters stressed that 'the main obstacle to entering the UK market was zoning and planning controls – Wal-Mart had concluded that they could only come into the UK by acquisition of an existing company' – as it did six months later in the case of Asda. He contrasted the United Kingdom with the German market: the latter was already 'sophisticated', but in the United Kingdom, 'Walmart had seen low hanging fruit. There had been a lot of waste and scope for improvements in transportation.' Wal-Mart was thus offering a price war ('the opening of Wal-Mart's stores typically began price wars') in a British retailing system that it pictured as charging excessive prices; in the meeting, the suggestion that British prices were 30 per cent higher than abroad was floated. But it is one thing to gain access at the highest level, another to turn that access into policy concessions. The Prime Minister's minuted response does not go beyond anodyne remarks about providing a stable macroeconomic environment and welcoming competition on prices. (Just how marginal the firm was to the concerns of the Prime Minister and his official is suggested by the fact that the minute misspells Wal-Mart's name.) Wal-Mart's subsequent political history has been a familiar mix of struggles with local authorities to gain planning permissions for larger stores and opportunistic alliances with some retailers against others: In the autumn of 2008, for instance, it was joining Waitrose, Marks and Spencer, and the Association of Convenience Stores before the Competition Appeals Tribunal, to oppose a move by Tesco to have struck down a proposed new competition criterion that would take into account size of market share in considering planning applications by large retailers (Wood 2008). The new rule, proposed by the Competition Commission, was aimed at Tesco's dominant position – hence its appeal to the Tribunal.

also learnt to circumvent the limitations of collective action at the sectoral level. They can often manage associations, exercising control over the positions adopted by representative bodies, using their resources – of money and personnel – to dominate them, or even sponsoring their very existence (e.g. Hart 2004: 50). Although the giant American corporation is thus often mired in institutional complexity, it is also highly opportunistic. If it can, it will hedge its bets by pursuing numerous concurrent institutional tactics to advance corporate interest – and one of these is via collective action at industry or sectoral level.

The giant firm and global economic lobbying: the problem of strategic cohesion

Giant firms do not have to operate on a multinational scale, but most do, and that is especially true of the giant firm in the Anglo-American arena. An obvious point follows: in describing the giant firm as a political actor, we cannot do only what we have done so far in this chapter – describe its operations in discrete national political settings. The very existence of the giant multinational creates not just a multinational economic sphere, but also a multinational representational sphere. The point is especially important in the case of the two systems that are the subject of this book. The United States is particularly important to this multinational sphere because of the economic weight of US multinationals, while the American presence in representative organizations in that sphere is particularly marked. The United Kingdom is particularly hospitable to the multinational sphere, in part because it is a major centre of inward investment by multinationals and in part because the City of London is one of the nerve centres of the global economy.

This multinational representational sphere is the subject of hugely contentious debates concerning both the power of multinational corporate elites and the capacity of states to manage their economies in the face of global markets (for the authoritative overview, see Scholte 2005). In these debates, more prosaic matters are often neglected, and they are our focus here. In particular, how do firms actually try to operate as political actors in this sphere?

It is an important implication of the development we sketched earlier – the rise of the giant firm as an increasingly sophisticated, and well-organized, political actor – that it is likely to invest a lot of effort in promoting its own sectional interests in the multinational sphere. The biggest multinationals are as opportunistic globally as they are within national systems. They use their centrally developed representative resources directly to lobby 'foreign' governments. Their chief executives can expect to be as active lobbying national political authorities across the globe as lobbying political authorities in 'their' jurisdiction. Trade, production, and location decisions are all highly sensitive politically, and corporations must constantly recognize this fact. Their activities as economic institutions are intimately tied up with the politics of the international economic system. At the very top, their leading executive officers routinely include individuals whose careers have involved moving continuously between leading positions in the corporate and state worlds. They expect to both lobby public authorities across the globe and to use their special connections with their 'home' government to mobilize it in defence of their interests.

As an example of the kind of personality that prospers in this world consider the glittering career of Peter Sutherland. Born in 1946, Sutherland began his public career as a member of the Fine Gael party in the Republic of Ireland. He served as a member of Fine Gael governments, and then was nominated as a member of the European Commission under the Presidency of Jacques Delors. He was the founding director general of the World Trade Organization, and after narrowly missing out on succeeding Delors as president of the European Commission he moved into business. At the time of writing, he chairs both the oil multinational BP and the British subsidiary of the global investment banking firm Goldman Sachs. He is on the steering committee of the Bilderberg Group and is a vice-chairman of the Trilateral Commission (both are described below). He is also a vice-chair of the ERT of Industrialists, and is a financial advisor to the Vatican.

Corporate leaders like Sutherland specialize in networking at the very highest levels, operating interchangeably across national–international and public–private boundaries. But we know from our account of how the corporate giant operates domestically that this kind of networking is only part of the picture. It happens alongside something more systematic: processes of image management for the firm that often involve participation in collective action through trade associations. This kind of participation in collection action is replicated in the multinational sphere.

Many of the giant multinationals are long-established actors in national economic systems beyond their home state, and provide key personnel in national trade associations: for instance, the president of the Society of Motor Manufacturers and Traders (the leading association for the automobile industry in Britain) in 2008 was a senior vice-president of Toyota Europe. The global character of City markets is reflected in the long-established presence (established 1937) of the Association of Foreign Banks (Association of Foreign Banks 2007). But though multinationals commonly subscribe to national representative associations, it is hard to be certain how important this is to their representational activity. It is certainly one way – and a comparatively cheap way – of showing themselves to be 'good citizens' with a long-term stake in the economy in which they are operating. But the most systematic study of trade associations in Britain reports that foreign multinationals (not just American) often show little interest in national associational activities: their minds, and their balance sheets, are elsewhere (MacDonald 2001: 4).

What this limited participation in national associational life also suggests is that the global, rather than the national, sphere is critical for the representational activities of giant multinationals. Here there is a world of multinationally organized associations with a dizzyingly wide range of functions. To organize this complex world, we can schematically distinguish between three different kinds of representative institution.

The first are specialized representative associations that are designed to function in the multinational sphere. A striking example, documented by Coen and Grant, is the Transatlantic Business Dialogue. This was established in 1995 as a joint initiative of the European Commission and the US State Department, to 'coordinate business responses to international trade, standards and regulation questions' (Coen and Grant 2001: 37). It joins the chief executives of leading US and European Companies. It is a striking instance for several reasons. It shows the almost seamless unity that in the multinational sphere joins institutions in the 'public' and the 'private' realms. It reinforces one of the themes of our account of national operations: the way politically sensitive duties are now central to the job description of chief executives. It shows how important is the EU to the organization of the multinational sphere. It shows, in the involvement of the State Department, the way multinational representation is linked to the high politics of foreign (economic) policy. And of course it incidentally shows, in the inclusion of European firms, that the institutions of this sphere are not constrained by the national boundaries of the two cases that we use in this book. (A case study of its work is provided in Box 3.3, p. 58.)

Notice that, almost in passing, the account of the TransAtlantic Business Dialogue mentioned its role in considering regulatory policy. Regulation is a critical consideration in economic life because the terms of regulation – the organization of regulatory institutions, the substantive content of the rules – is key to competitive advantage (or disadvantage) in markets. It is central to competition in the multinational sphere and pervasive across all sectors of economic life. This naturally explains the importance of the second main institutional form that representation in the multinational sphere takes: participation in regulatory and standard setting bodies. In Braithwaite and Drahos's classic study *Global Business Regulation*, there is a revealing tabular summary of this world (2000: 476–7). It shows, to use a metaphor of which Braithwaite and Drahos are fond, a global web of organizations, individuals, and social groups. The regulation of 'Contract and Property Rights', for instance, encompasses major American national trade association (like the Motion Picture Association of America) and individual corporate giants like IBM. It is a web that joins individual corporate giants with national governments: the regulation of telecommunications includes the governments of both the United States and the United Kingdom and corporate actors like Time-Warner. Some regulatory spheres are made up of segments of national governments, individual agencies often operating in highly technical spheres: for instance, the International Organization of (national) Securities Commissions for the regulation of securities markets. The web is also marked by an elaborate division of labour even between corporate giants: they include not only producers of goods and services, but also commercial standard establishing bodies, such as credit and bond rating agencies like Moody's (see also Kerwer 2005; Sinclair 2005).

This multinational world of economic regulation is simultaneously highly political and highly technical. It is highly political because it helps determine the rawest of all political struggles: over economic interests between corporations and states. It deeply influences who gets what in the global economic struggle. But it is highly technical because the bread and butter of debate typically focuses on issues that are technologically complex (consider the regulation of telecommunications or of pharmaceuticals) or administratively complex (consider the regulation of financial institutions.)

One by-product of participation in the specialized worlds of regulation and standard setting is that it creates social networks where highly placed actors (like leaders of important public institutions and CEOs of multinational giants) can, mixing with similar elite figures, have the opportunity to discuss strategic issues of global economic management. But collective action by multinational corporate elites, if it is to shape the economic and political setting of the corporation, has to transcend the technical details of economic life, important though these are. Hence our third form of global representation, one where the corporate elite can more directly consider issues of broad strategic significance to do with the management of the global economy. An institution that we have already encountered – the TransAtlantic Business Dialogue – is obviously addressed in part to this task. But there are other more specialized mechanisms that also contribute: inter-corporate networks, and institutions explicitly created to provide forums where the corporate elite can hammer out common strategic positions on the largest questions of economic and political management. Chroniclers of inter-corporate networks (the joining of corporations into networks by ties of co-ownership and co-directorships) have often argued that the existence of dense networks within national economies is a powerful aid to the cohesion of the corporate elite and to its ability to generate a common strategic outlook and a capacity for common action (see for instance Useem 1984). Moreover, the work of Carroll and his colleagues demonstrates that these networks are particularly dense-linking corporations across the North Atlantic – precisely, of course, where American and UK enterprises are prominent (Carroll and Fennema 2002; Carroll and Carson 2003).

The obvious difficulty in ascribing strategic significance to inter-corporate networks lies in demonstrating that they actually lead to common discussion or common action. This is why particular importance lies in the other institutional mechanism identified above: in multinational organizations that exist precisely for the purpose of agreeing strategic priorities between multinational corporate elites. The most important, in chronological order of creation, are the following. The *International Chamber of Commerce* dates back to 1920, and was inaugurated partly to settle international economic differences between business arising out of the First World War (Kelly 2005). The *Bilderberg Conferences* are periodic and informal gatherings of transatlantic elites that date back to a first meeting in 1952. The *World Economic Forum* was set up in 1971 (Graz 2003). The *Trilateral Commission* was established as the leading capitalist nations entered economic crisis in 1973 (van der Pijl 1998: 124–6). The *World Business Council for Sustainable Development* was established in 1995 as global environmental issues began to press in on multinational corporations.

Of these, the World Economic Forum is probably the best known, chiefly through its annual meetings in the Swiss ski resort of Davos. These highly publicized occasions are by no means confined to the leaders of giant multinational corporations. They are designed to create a forum where these figures mix, both for business and pleasure, with other strategic elites, notably from government. In recent years, the range of institutions and individuals attending has also widened considerably, to include various celebrity activists, like ageing rock stars, and carefully selected figures from the world of non-governmental organizations (NGOs). The considerable work the Forum does in the period between these meetings is likewise addressed to large strategic questions facing the global economy (e.g. Graz 2003).

In these very characteristics of the WEF lies the difficulty in estimating the significance of strategic forums designed for the multinational corporate elite. Undoubtedly, they potentially address one of the key problems that has recurred in this volume – the problem of business solidarity – because they encourage the corporate elite to think beyond its own immediate, parochial corporate calculations, in a way that is difficult to do, for example, in the world of standard setting and regulatory negotiations. Undoubtedly, also, they highlight a key social feature of the multinational corporate elite: the way the boundaries between that elite and other elites, notably in government, are blurred, with very high levels of transfer and overlap between the two. The doubt arises from uncertainty about the practical impact of all this. The World Economic Forum annual meeting is, perhaps, an extreme example, because it is so high profile. But it is such an extraordinary jamboree, involving some people of real power and all kinds of opportunistic publicity seekers, that it is hard to see how it can act in an effectively strategic fashion, as distinct from providing a useful opportunity for the multinational corporate elite to network and prepare the ground for deals – exactly what a strategic institution should not be doing. (For more on the World Economic Forum, see Box 8.2, p. 158.)

The essentially political character of the giant corporation

In modern capitalist democracies such as the two core cases in this book, all business is political: that is, the state is constantly present in various guises in the life of business, and the wider political environment is critical to the fate of business interests. But for the giant corporations examined in this chapter, the salience of the political is especially high. I have expressed this in the accounts above by picturing the giant corporation as an institution with special political strengths, but also with special political weaknesses. The political strengths of the corporate giant have been well rehearsed in the specialist literature on business and politics and in the wider literature on the political economy of modern capitalism. They can be summarized as arising from the impressive resources available to the corporation when it overtly intervenes in politics; the central place of the corporate giant in the functioning of a modern capitalist economy, meaning that no state can manage economic life satisfactorily without its compliance; and the special advantages of mobility which come to the corporate giant when it is organized – as it usually is – on a multinational scale.

The special political weaknesses of the corporate giant are in some degree a mirror image of its strengths. The very scale and range of activities, interests, and divisions contained within corporate giants often leave them immobile in the face of the diverse and complex interests which they have to defend. The sheer visibility of the giant corporation means that it constantly has to battle with the problem of creating and maintaining its reputation, and the reputation of its brands. This interacts with a final source of weakness, mentioned only in passing here but a major theme of Chapter 7: the extent to which corporate giants now face critical institutions in civil society, both domestically in the United States and the United Kingdom, and in global civil society.

But before we turn to that issue, we need to deal with other facets of business and politics: in the next chapter, we look at the political fate of very different business enterprises, those small in scale.

5 Small Business and Politics

Small business, collective action, and political innovation

Most businesses are small businesses. This generalization is true even granted a well-known problem – that, simply, of defining 'small'. There plainly can be no hard and fast rule in supplying such a definition. The *measurement* of size can be by turnover, market share, and number of employees. The *criterion* of 'smallness' is naturally fuzzy: even if we agree to a scale of measurement – say number of employees – there is nothing obvious to tell us how to identify a particular size with 'smallness'. The result is that specialist studies of small business are obliged to use a range of conventional measures. Some of the commonest are administrative. For instance, the official UK definitions for some years have used numbers of employees as a benchmark: small is 0–49 employees; medium is 50–249; and large is 250 or more. The US Small Business Administration, by contrast, defines 'small business' as any enterprise with fewer than 500 employees.

One might quarrel with classifications which put a firm with 250 employees into the same category as one with several tens of thousands, or indeed one with a single employee in the same class as one with almost 500. One might also feel that these handy administrative measures often fail to capture the complexity of enterprises. Yet, while these problems are not trivial, especially for anyone wishing to study small business closely, they need not be serious obstacles for our purposes. For instance, if we return to our opening generalization – that most businesses are small businesses – the British data immediately verify that point: over 99 per cent of all firms in the official database are small by the official criterion (Department of Trade and Industry 2007).

This figure gives us some inkling of both the potential political problems and the potential political muscle of small firms. As we shall see, when we turn to Britain, small business was given low priority among policy makers for much of the twentieth century, and the drift of policy advantaged large corporations. In many respects, the American state behaved in a similar way. The economic (and political) weight of any individual large firm – let alone of any individual giant corporation – will vastly outweigh that of any single small firm in virtually any conceivable circumstances. The measures for Britain tell an entirely typical story: as we saw in the previous chapter, in the United Kingdom, the 0.1 per cent of enterprises defined as large account for 41 per cent of employment and 49 per cent of turnover (BERR 2008*c*). Yet, the total weight of small firms in the economy – especially if we use a measure such as numbers employed – still outweighs that of giant corporations, on both sides of the Atlantic. The economic weight of small firms is reinforced by cultural factors. Though in different ways, and for different historical reasons, we shall see that there are powerful strains in social values on both sides of the Atlantic that attribute a particular virtue to running a small firm.

Small business nevertheless faces formidable obstacles as a political operator. Three recur in this chapter. The first takes us back to a feature which has already been important in these pages: the sheer heterogeneity of business interests. It is unclear whether it is meaningful to speak of a small-business sector. It is even more doubtful that one can speak of distinct small-business *interests* – or, at least, get small businesses that operate in so many disparate markets to recognize and act on common interests. The second obstacle arises less from heterogeneity than from sheer numbers. These numbers in principle give small businesses considerable 'clout', for instance in electoral competition. But as we shall see, they also stand in the way of creating one of the conditions for political success: effective organization. The point lies behind some of the most important modern theorizing about the political weakness of small business (Olson 1965, 1982), but it can be expressed simply in an everyday sense: organizing the three or four largest supermarket chains behind a common position is problematic, but at least only a tiny number of institutions have to be persuaded; uniting small shopkeepers behind a common front involves the considerably more daunting task of coordinating several tens of thousands of separate enterprises. By one recent measure, there were 34,000 small retailers in London alone, and over 243,000 in the whole of Great Britain in 2004 (Greater London Authority 2006). This problem of creating common organization links to a third obstacle to effective political action. Interest representation demands resources – money, skilled people, and expertise. Large corporations usually have these, small firms hardly ever. The question of how the small-business sector can accumulate the resources needed for effective interest representation goes to the heart of the political problem it faces. But as we shall also see, these very problems have often been a source of political innovation in the sector.

Box 5.1 What does business do when it lobbies? The case of the UK Federation of Small Businesses in Brussels

---

Business lobbying does not happen automatically; it has to be organized. Behind generalizations about business influence lies a quite mundane world of everyday activity. The case of the work in Brussels of the UK Federation of Small Businesses (FSB), the largest UK voice of small business, illustrates what the daily reality of business lobbying means – and it also shows how alliance with, and influence in, grandly titled European organizations can give European legitimacy to otherwise sectional national concerns. Small businesses rely much more than do giant firms on collective action because, separately, they do not have the resources to monitor and intervene in the highly specialized issues that are the material of regulation making in the EU. In September 2008, for instance, the Federation was monitoring the following in the EU: the Agency Workers Directive, which regulates the employment of temps, principally to strengthen the UK government's 'opt out' from key parts of the Directive; the Working Time Directive, which regulates length of working hours; and a proposal from the Commission for a Small Business Act which would for the first time create, in the Federation's own words, 'a new European Private Company Statute to make it easier for businesses to trade across Europe, a reduction in VAT rates for locally provided services and the consideration of some exemptions for small businesses from regulation' (Federation of Small Businesses 2008a). Organizations like the Federation have a tricky double task of persuasion to carry out: they have to persuade policy makers to their point of view, and they also have to persuade their own members that it is worth continuing to pay subscriptions to the organization. The Federation's 'list of achievements' for 2008 is therefore particularly revealing because it shows what the Federation leadership considers worth stressing for a membership which has to be convinced to continue subscribing. The list highlights a series of films made in October 2007 illustrating, in the Federation's own words, 'what business people could do with the seven hours they spend filling out forms each week.' The film was launched in Brussels by the Enterprise Commissioner, Günter Verheugen, and copies were emailed to all MEPs and Commissioners; how many actually watched the film is not known. The FSB also highlighted its role in 'convincing the European Parliament and Council to modify proposals that would have required retailers to write their contracts in the laws of every EU member state in which they did business'. As a result, it claims, 'firms will retain the right to apply UK contract law to cross-border sales'. Through its membership of the European Small Business Alliance (ESBA), the FSB argued that it gained representation on the European Parliament Committee for Standardization (CEN), allowing it to oppose measures such as the standard concerning 'Enhanced Supply Chain Security', which it claims could have been damaging to FSB members (Federation of Small Businesses 2008b). The relationship with the ESBA is a striking instance of a theme noted often in the text: how representative associations can be created and colonized to add legitimacy to more sectional activities. The grandly named ESBA actually only has members from six EU member states (on its web site the ESBA adds Gibraltar to the list of national members to create seven). It has a Brussels office of only three staff. It is an FSB creation and it is heavily under FSB influence. It was founded in 1998 by Brian Prime, who was one of the original founders of the FSB in 1974. He served as President of the ESBA until 2006, and was succeeded by Tina Sommer – the present Director for International Affairs of the UK FSB. Three of the six members of the Executive Board of the ESBA are officers of the UK FSB (European Small Business Alliance 2008). In other words, the ESBA mostly serves to give extra 'European' legitimacy to the FSB's campaigns.

Small-business politics in the United Kingdom: decline and revival?

The problematics of small-business power are well illustrated by the British case. Until the opening of the First World War, small business occupied an important position at most of the key levels of the British policy-making system. Although mergers and amalgamations had already begun to reshape the British economy, large firms were still only starting to emerge as power-fully organized interests: no unified national voice existed for them before the First World War. If we look at the economic composition of political leader-ship, what is striking is the extent to which it contained a large body of representation from small-business interests. Local government in this period still remained particularly important. Many functions – health care, trans-port, energy, water, etc. – were controlled at the local level. Local government in turn was dominated by small business. The same is true of the many boards responsible for services – like Poor Relief – that were ancillary to the formally organized local-government system (on the domination of local government by a 'shopocracy' in particular, see Winstanley 1995).

Over the first three quarters of the twentieth century, four developments damaged the political interests and power of small business. First, the struc-tural balance in the economy shifted away from small to large enterprises: for instance, in 1909, the share of employment of 100 largest enterprises was 9 per cent; by 1970, it had risen to 41 per cent (Supple 1992: 1). A more everyday sign of the change could be seen in almost every high street, in the displace-ment of small retail enterprises by large chains. Second, the very arena where small business had been so dominant – local government – declined. Many key functions – health, transport, energy, water supply, etc. – were removed to higher levels, and even those that remained – such as school education – were subject to closer central control. Third, while business did indeed continue to dominate some local communities, the rise of the Labour Party after the First World War led to the control of whole swathes of local government by Labour authorities. Many local authorities became in effect one-party systems, and many of these in turn were dominated by Labour interests unsympathetic to business.

A fourth development in some ways paralleled the wider changes in economic structure: there was an alteration in the mind set of policy makers. For much of the twentieth century central government favoured 'bigness', especially in business organization. The high point was probably reached in the second half of the 1960s when the state Industrial Reorganisation Cor-poration actively promoted mergers to create large 'national champions' in many industries (Mercer 1994; Bowden 2000). The domination of the British economy by big firms was not the product of impersonal economic forces; it was the result of policy decisions, and policy pressures, that encouraged amalgamations and mergers, in the belief that large-scale organization brought economies of scale, and an improved ability to face foreign competition (Bolton 1971: 79–81).

Over much of the twentieth century, therefore, the long pull of political and economic change was damaging to small business. But even in the hardest of times there were some countervailing forces. While the party system had changed so as to create in organized labour a powerful rival at local level, small business did cement an enduring alliance with the Conservative Party, and given Conservative electoral success across the twentieth century, this was a source of some influence. (We shall have more to say about this when we examine political parties in Chapter 6.) Even in districts where small business was electorally weak, it also retained some residual political advantages. Until 1948, business proprietors had a second vote in parliamentary elections by virtue of their proprietorship. Perhaps more important, from early in the twentieth century, there was a flowering of middle-class associational life which encompassed, if it was not completely restricted to, small business: networks that grew (in many cases they were exported from the United States) included the Lions Clubs, the Round Table, and Rotary. As a single example: Round Table was first established in Britain in Norwich in 1927; by 1937, there were 125 Tables in the United Kingdom and by 1968 over 1,000. The standard studies of local politics testify to the importance of such voluntary associations in the life of small business (see Birch 1959: 166–7; Jones, G. 1969: 135–6; Saunders 1979: 313–14).

At the national level, however, the story for much of the century was one of almost perpetual decline. Although some national associations for the representation of small business were formed in the early part of the century (the National Union of Manufacturers, with a pronounced bias to small firms, appeared in 1916), small firms were marginal to policy making at national level (Bolton 1971; May and McHugh 2002: 76). In policy terms, as we have seen, there was a consensus on the advantages of large-scale business organization. And in political terms, the Conservative Party, while still heavily influenced at local level by small business, at national level either became disconnected from business or was influenced increasingly by large firms that were already well integrated into national economic policy making. Indeed, even in the interwar years, the connection between big business and the Conservative backbenches in the House of Commons was 'close and pronounced' (Guttsman 1963: 296). How far this long decline has reversed in Britain in recent decades is uncertain; there are contradictory signs.

There has undoubtedly been an important change in the policy climate, such that May and McHugh (2002) speak of the rise of a 'new policy consensus' favouring small business. Just how far the close detail of policy has indeed favoured small business is, as May and McHugh also show, open to dispute. But that there has been a sea change in assumptions, by contrast with the era of 'big is beautiful', is undoubtedly the case: 'it is clear that all governments since 1979 have been concerned about small business and have endeavoured to implement policies for its benefit' (May and McHugh 2002: 79). The beginning of the change probably dates from the publication of the report of the Bolton Inquiry on Small Firms (1971). But shifts of policy climate like this are vulnerable to the moods of fashion that tend to sweep over policy makers. The rise of the new consensus led, for instance, to the creation of a Small Business Service inside the former Department of Trade and Industry, but the pendulum of fashion has seemed more recently to swing away, under the Premiership of Gordon Brown after 2007. He created a 'Business Council' which was dominated by executives from giant enterprises; and in reshaping the Department of Trade and Industry into a new Department for Business Enterprise and Regulatory Reform, he also transformed the Small Business Service into a less important Enterprise Directorate (BERR 2008a, 2008b).

Nevertheless, despite these swings of high-level policy fashion, it does seem that the long structural decline of small business was at least arrested in the last couple of decades of the twentieth century. Unsurprisingly, there were sharp differences between sectors: in retailing, for example, the years actually saw an accelerating march by big firms, typified at everyday level by the decline of outlets like small retail newsagents, and the domination of the grocery sector by a tiny number of supermarket giants. But overall, the actual share of total economic activity (variously measured) seems at least to have halted its historical decline, though the rate of birth and death among small firms is so volatile that it is hard to make confident generalizations (BERR 2008a). There is even some evidence that, while small businesses have declined in some important sectors, parts of the economy most successful in creating new jobs, and in pioneering technical and institutional innovation, have been dominated by small firms. Thus, Bryson et al. (1997) document particularly rapid small-firm growth in what they call information intensive business services, such as IT, consultancy, and research (see also Supple 1992: 1).

This structural revival, or at least stabilization, has been partly matched by some revitalization of the institutions of small-business representation. In part, this reflects a wider change in the lobbying system in Britain. The relative decline of political parties as agents of representation (documented in Chapter 6) has been compensated by the mushrooming of a wide range of 'special-interest' groups. Some of these have spectacularly mobilized parts of the small-business sector: for instance, the fuel protests which briefly brought the economy to a halt in 2000 were based on an alliance of small-business people, notably in agriculture and road haulage (Doherty et al. 2003). Some of the recurrent objections to large-retail developments have also involved alliances between small retailers and others, such as supporters of so-called sustainable local economies (Corporate Watch 2008). This kind of opportunistic alliance represents a considerable act of political learning by small-business interests – allying their sectional concerns with more broadly based public-interest campaigns.

In addition to this engagement with single-issue politics, there has also occurred a wider institutional development: a marked revitalization of the specialist institutions of small-business representation. In the 1970s, there were a number of failed efforts to organize the very smallest businesses in bodies for the self-employed. The work of Jordan and Halpin (2003, 2004) documents how subsequently a particular small-business organization – the FSB – seems to have partially solved the collective-action problem originally identified by Olson (1965): it has built a well-resourced lobbying organization by using shrewdly targeted selective benefits to attract a considerable membership. Meanwhile, the Chambers of Commerce – which at local level were historically dominated by the small-business sector – enjoyed a considerable augmentation of their roles as managers of local economies, notably as a result of their incorporation into systems for skills training at the local level (Fallon and Brown 2000).

We should nevertheless be wary of ascribing too many policy consequences to these institutional changes. Jordan and Halpin document the growth in resources of the FSB, but their studies do not examine how far this increased mobilization has turned into an impact on policy. Attempts to identify small-business communities at the local level have suggested that, at the very least, small-business participation in institutions like the Chambers of Commerce or in local partnerships designed to link the public and private sector is now very patchy: Curran et al. (2000) and Bassett (1996) paint a picture where extensive parts of small business are disconnected from any representative or policy-making institutions. The sheer struggle for survival in a small enterprise leaves little extra headroom for participation in representative bodies. Likewise, case studies of the mobilization of business interests at local level – the level where historically small business was important – are discouraging for anyone who believes we have entered a new era of small-business influence. One marked feature of local and regional economies in the last quarter century has been the creation of coalitions of public and private agencies addressing issues of local economic development. The coalitions span specialized, non-elected development agencies, consortia of elected local authorities, representative bodies like the Chambers of Commerce, and private enterprises. A striking feature of the case studies of these coalitions is the way they show small business to be marginalized, and large firms to be dominant. This is a pattern identified, for instance, by Thornley et al. in their study of economic planning by the Greater London Authority that was established in the new system of Greater London government after 1997.

Likewise, Phelps et al. in their case study of Croydon – a major 'success story' in the development of a new service sector at local level – show domination by big business-service firms (see Thornley et al. 2005; Phelps et al. 2006; and see also Saunders 1979; Peck 1995; Peck and Tickell 1994). Greater London is a particularly striking case, for not only is it the most successful region in the British economy, but also the political reforms introduced by New Labour after 1997, such as the introduction of a directly elected mayor, might have been expected to open up the policy-making system to a diversity of groups, including small business.

The explanation for these difficulties in penetrating policy making partly has to do with the small-business sector itself, and partly to do with the changed policy-making environment in which it has been obliged to operate in recent decades. We know that some of the institutional connections that once advantaged small business, especially at local level, have either been dissolved or greatly weakened. For all the revival of the Chambers of Commerce movement, we saw above that some of the most economically dynamic sectors have become disconnected from the Chambers, and indeed from other small-business-representative organizations. The case of Croydon cited above (Phelps et al. 2006) also suggests the weakening of another bond that was historically important: the Conservative Party has ceased to be a significant channel of influence in Croydon, reflecting a wider national decline in the membership and activity of the party at local level – something we examine in more detail in the next chapter.

The weakening of party ties, and the decline in the importance of party as a medium of interest representation, is not something confined to Conservatism, as we shall also see in the next chapter. The decline of party reflects a wider change in the interest-representation system which has to some degree worked to the advantage of small business, but to some degree worked against it. One undoubted reason for the long period of national policy indifference to the interests of small business for much of the twentieth century is implicit in the account we gave in Chapter 3 of how the business-representation system operated for most of that century. The institutions of business lobbying marginalized the role of small business in part because they were embedded in a particular kind of political system in Britain. This system was centralized on a small political community in a very concentrated district of central London. Being a metropolitan insider was crucial to affecting policy, and this became more important still as non-metropolitan systems of government, most obviously local government, experienced a century-long decline. It is no accident that the most successful business-lobbying organization of this period, the FBI, founded in 1916, prospered as precisely that kind of 'insider' group under its long serving Director General Norman Kipping, a former civil servant who exploited his Whitehall contacts to embed the Federation in the centralized policy-making system.

This centralized, metropolis-dominated mode of government was disastrous for small business, because its historical strengths were at the local level. Some of the evidence of the revitalization of small-business political activity that we have already noted reflects the partial dissolution of this centralized system. The interest-representation system itself has been opened up by two important developments. The first is the rise of political 'entrepreneurs' prepared to invest time and skill in organizing for sectors that hitherto were weakly represented: the story of the FSB told by Jordan and Halpin (2003, 2004) is a story of precisely that kind of successful entrepreneurship. The second is the way changes in 'hard' and 'soft' technologies have made it easier to mobilize interests outside the old centralized, metropolitan world. 'Hard' technology refers to the development of technologies like those in communication (mobile phones and the Web) which make group mobilization easier because they cut the cost of communication and make rapid coordination and mobilization easier. 'Soft' technology refers to the spread of innovative methods of group organization, allowing hitherto poorly mobilized groups to learn from more effective ones: learning about such possibilities as blockades, mass lobbying of Parliament, tactical use of electoral strength, use of the techniques of fund-raising, and membership network creation. The case of the fuel protests noted above shows how both of these influences helped create this striking example of the mobilization of small-business people in agriculture and road haulage (Doherty et al. 2003). The fusion of hard technologies of electronic communication and soft technologies of campaign innovation is also well illustrated by the many alliances at local level between small retailers and various kinds of radical environmentalists campaigning against large-retail developments. Web sites maintained by campaigning groups like Corporate Watch document the range of campaigns at any one time, put groups in contact with each other, and provide a central source of advice on both the practicalities of campaigning and the technicalities of planning law (see, e.g., Corporate Watch 2008).

This account paints a fairly benign picture of the impact of technological and institutional change on small-business interests – benign, at least, for those who wish more effectively to mobilize the sector. But there are other sides to this story of change which have more unsettling consequences. Our account of the decline of the old, centralized, London-focused lobbying system is also an account of the growth of a more competitive system of interest-group mobilization. The capacity of any interest to defend and promote itself depends critically on how it operates in this competitive world; it is not just a matter of having the resources, but also of using the resources in a struggle with other interests who may have very different policy priorities. The new hard and soft technologies, and the partial dissolution of the old centralized system, have not only advantaged small-business interests, but have also advantaged a wide range of groups and movements, some of whom are competitors with business. As we saw above from the example of campaigns against big-retail developments, it may be possible for some small-business interests to create alliances with movements – like environmentalists – against big-business interests. But these alliances are necessarily contingent and opportunistic, and their effectiveness and stability depends heavily on the political skills of interest-group leaders and the particular patterns of competition between different interests that exist at any one time, or in any one locality.

In short, small business now operates in a very different environment of representation from that which existed as recently as thirty years ago. This is a tougher environment. It is tougher because many of the influences that have broken open the old closed system of representation have not only made it easier for small business to mobilize, but have also had the same effect on the wider group system, and thus facilitated the rise of groups that compete with, or may even be opposed to, small-business interests. The point returns us to one of the main lessons of this whole book: that businesses of all kinds operate not just in competitive markets, but also in competitive systems of lobbying – competing both with each other and with non-business interests.

Two important institutional developments show the ambiguities and un-certainties which now surround the politics of the small-business sector in the United Kingdom. They both reflect the partial dissolution of the old central-ized system of government and interest representation: on the one hand, in the last decade, there has been a substantial devolution of authority to make policy in matters critically affecting small-business interests to new governing systems in Wales and Scotland (and, less completely, in Northern Ireland); on the other hand, there has been a substantial transfer of policy authority, and business lobbying, outwards to the institutions of the EU.

It might be natural to assume that, since the old metropolitan system was unsympathetic to small business, devolution represents a move to its advan-tage. We have little more than a decade of experience of how the devolved systems work, too brief a time to observe trends, let alone systematically assess those trends. There certainly has been institutional adaptation: the FSB, for instance, now has a separate Scottish organization and a Scottish policy unit. But the most systematic study of the impact of devolution on the business system conducted under the 'Devolution and Constitutional Change Pro-gramme' of the UK Economic and Social Research Council suggests that, while there has been indeed some institutional adaptation by small-business organizations, the impact of devolution on the power of small business has been limited: business politics in the devolved systems still reflects the distri-bution of power in the wider UK system (Wood et al. 2005). Indeed, there is one important way in which devolution may have strengthened the hands of big business: it encourages the devolved authorities to compete with each other for inward investment. Thus, in 2008, Aberdeenshire County Council turned down an application by the US developer Donald Trump to build the largest golf complex in the world on the Aberdeenshire coast. The Scottish Executive in Edinburgh then called in the application for review, on foot of an offer by the Northern Ireland First Minister to host the complex in County Antrim. Subsequently, the Executive confirmed approval of planning permission for Trump's scheme, not only in the face of opposition from the County Council, but also in the face of campaigning by environmental groups like the Royal Society for the Protection of Birds (Carrell 2008; Cramb 2008). We thus cannot assume that, because the devolved systems cover a smaller territory than UK-wide institutions, small business will receive a more favourable hearing. We also know that big business has geared itself up to operate as a lobbyist on the devolved governments. For instance, the Retail Consortium – which in London has consistently acted as the voice of the largest retailers – has replicated its organization in Scotland in the form of the Scottish Retail Consortium. And we know from case studies cited earlier – for instance of London – that merely putting the focus of policy making nearer the local level does not at all guarantee small-business influence.

The impact of the rise of the EU in economic government is similarly ambiguous. As we saw in the preceding chapter, the policy process in the EU often greatly advantages large corporations, and makes it very difficult for small- and medium-sized enterprises to enter that process. The Commission, the hub of policy proposals in the EU system, has a well-documented preference for dealing directly with the largest firms, since they provide a readily identifiable, and manageably small, population of institutions with whom to consult and bargain. Above all, they possess in abundance the currency most valued in Brussels: specialized information (Coen 1998, 2007; Broscheid and Coen 2003). More impersonal characteristics of the EU policy process help reinforce this bias favouring corporate giants. A well-known feature of Brussels-based policy making is the sheer complexity of the process. Monitoring policy proposals, tracking them through the system so as to influence the details as they evolve, and managing their implementation, including where relevant their transposition into national laws, involve investing large amounts of specialized resources – notably of specialists in both the policy process itself and in the substantive areas where policy is being made. Here again lies one of the obvious sources of big-business strength; unless they create institutions for collective action, small- and medium-sized enterprises are at a disadvantage.

Nevertheless, Europeanization can in some circumstances be exploited by small business. In their comparative study of the energy and the telecommunications sectors, Coen and Héritier (2000) identify a number of developments that counteract the power of the big battalions. In at least some sectors, such as telecommunications, EU policy, because of its liberalizing tendency, has encouraged the entry of small firms, thus multiplying the number of

Box 5.2 Small business and politics: the case of Japanese farmers

The case of farmers in Japan illustrates both the conditions under which a small-business sector can exercise extraordinary power over policy and the conditions under which that power can be chipped away. Japanese farms are predominantly small enterprises. Land reform after military defeat in the Second World War created huge numbers of tiny holdings (Babb 2005). There were about six million farms, and the average size was (and remains) just over three acres – barely a smallholding by British or American standards. But this created a powerful, cohesive army of voters: in 1950, 47 per cent of electors were in farm households (Mulgan 2005: 265). Farmers also developed, through a single national agricultural cooperative, a highly effective institution of interest representation enjoying close relations with the public bureaucracy. From the early 1950s, they also emerged as the bedrock of electoral support for the LDP, Japan's dominant party. The result created one of the most regulated, privileged, and protected small-business sectors on earth. Production of domestic rice – the staple food – was protected from external competition by a tariff of 700 per cent. The vast Japanese public system of credit allocation ensured the supply of an almost endless stream of cheap credit to the LDP's agricultural clients (Calder 1993: 107–8, 111). A powerful Ministry of Agriculture treated small farmers as preferred clients, and acted as their sponsor and defender in bureaucratic struggles over policy. Three sources of changes have now chipped away at this power; they are illuminating because they echo themes about the foundations of business power that crop up repeatedly in these pages. First, structural change: Japan has been transformed into an urban, industrial society. Farm holdings remain tiny, but numbers employed in agriculture show an inexorable decline, which has affected the electoral muscle of farmers: by the new millennium, farm household voters were down to 7 per cent of the electorate (Mulgan 2005: 265). Most farmers were part-time and the sector was finding it difficult to attract young entrants from a now predominantly urban Japan. Second, there were changes in political institutions. Until 1994, the electoral system magnified the power of farmers by drawing constituency boundaries so as to ensure over-representation of farm interests: it took five times as many urban as rural voters to elect a Diet (Parliament) member. The electoral law of that year greatly increased the weight of urban voters, and thus gave the LDP an incentive to put efficient production and cheaper food above the interests of small farmers. This links to the third important influence – globalization – and the trade diplomacy to which it gives rise. In trade liberalization talks under the umbrella of the World Trade Organization, Japanese manufacturing stands to make significant gains, but a price for this liberalization is the opening of hitherto protected Japanese markets in food: with a wealthy population of 127 million, the country is a rich prize to food exporters like the United States. Under the reforming Prime Minister Junichiro Koizumi (2001–6), there was particular pressure to liberalize in order to advance trade rule negotiations (Mulgan 2005: 276–83). But the outcome of these pressures also shows how entrenched interests can resist, and how historically created sources of power can survive the passing away of the original conditions that created them. The power of small farmers is being chipped away, not destroyed. Though numbers are falling, and the electoral system is reformed, the electoral power of farmers is still significant, in part because some bias favouring farm voters remains in the electoral system. As the LDP shifted in favour of urban and industrial interests, its party opponents tried to take advantage of the shift by courting the discontented farm vote. The historical entrenchment of pro-agricultural interests in the bureaucracy also remains, making it difficult for reformers to move from mere pronouncements favouring reform to practical implementation.

actors engaged with the policy process. One result of this has been also to create a range of specialist-representative trade associations for 'niche' markets. To some degree also, small-business interests have benefited from acts of interest creation and identification by policy elites. For instance, the Commission, conscious that it needs to break from its heavy reliance on consultation with large firms, has sought to create 'fora' – forums for targeted sectors and industries – which consciously try to incorporate small-business voices (Coen and Dannreuther 2002). There nevertheless remains a basic problem in small-business representation in the EU, neatly summarized by Coen and Dannreuther: divergence of interests, inability to set agendas, and a proliferation of fragmented institutional voices (ibid.: 127). In short, the fundamental problems of small-business interest representation at national level are replicated at EU level.

The United States: small business in a benign environment?

Examining the political role of small business in American politics immediately reveals some striking contrasts with the UK case. All of these suggest that small business has a more influential political voice in the United States. The differences begin with the historically shaped political culture. Any discussion of the role of American small business is inseparable from the legacy of Populism, which, as we saw in Chapter 2, was in part a revolt by small proprietors against the perceived power of big-business institutions, notably the large-financial conglomerates that were believed to control monopolistic trusts. The ideological assumptions that underlay Populism have persisted as important features of American political culture. They consist of both a suspicion of 'big' business and an idealization of the character of the small entrepreneur. In a national survey of 2004, for instance, 45 per cent of respondents thought big business had 'a negative influence on the way things are going'; the corresponding figure for small business was only 12 per cent. Unsurprisingly, responses to the suggestion about a positive influence mirrored this: 38 per cent thought big business had a positive influence; 78 per cent thought the same for small business. Again unsurprisingly, these views reflected views about the comparative power of business sectors: 7 per cent thought big business had too little influence, while 58 per cent thought small business had too little influence (Dennis 2004: 11–13). This snapshot is representative of a more enduring pattern. As Levitan and Cooper put it in their survey of business politics over a quarter century ago: 'Defending small business is, like motherhood, always popular with the voters' (1984: 40; see also Mitchell 1997: 42–3). Here then is a striking contrast with the cult of 'bigness' which, we noted earlier, so dominated the United Kingdom for much of the twentieth century.

The central place of values that idealize the small-business proprietor may also help explain another important source of strength of the sector in the United States. Although we shall see later that there are important differences of interest between small and large enterprises in particular sectors, like retailing and banking, the heart of small-business ideology – scepticism of government and a belief in the primacy of the individual entrepreneur – is strikingly common across the range of all business sectors. Smith summarizes his review of the evidence as follows: 'Several major studies of the opinions held by business owners and managers during the twentieth century have found them to be, on the whole, conservative' – meaning, in the American setting, that they are hostile to government intervention in economic life (2000: 55–6). In short, the ideology that unites small business is also the ideology that unites small business to big business.

This congenial cultural climate may help explain another distinctive feature of American small business: its high propensity to political activism. Polling evidence shows that small-business proprietors are more likely than the population at large to vote, to run for public office, and to hold local office (National Federation of Independent Business 2005). There is also some limited evidence that small business is particularly prominent in movements of the Christian Right which have been so influential in American politics in recent decades (Burris 2001). Contrast that with the picture of a withdrawal from political activism that we noted in the case of small business at the local level in the United Kingdom.

This high propensity to participate may help explain another contrast with UK small business: the superior organizational capacity of the small-business lobby in the United States. Small business has been, and remains, a key component of some of the leading national peak associations that speak for business. Two of the most important of these are the National Association of Manufacturers (NAM) and the US Chamber of Commerce. The former was founded in 1895 from a mix of protectionist and anti-union motives. Claiming a membership of 14,000 companies, as well as 300 specialist associations, as its name suggests it has been historically strongest in the manufacturing sector, and indeed markets itself as the voice of those in America who manufacture things, as distinct from providing services (National Association of Manufacturers 2007a, 2007b). The US Chamber of Commerce, which we encountered in Chapter 3 as the largest and best-funded of all business-representative associations, also incorporates large numbers of small-business associations, as well as individual firms. One distinguishing mark of both the NAM and the Chamber of Commerce is that they place a high value on adopting positions that reflect a consensus of the views of their members. Although there has been a tendency for officer posts in the Chamber of Commerce to be occupied by those from large firms (Levitan and Cooper 1984: 18), it really does seem that the Chamber, in particular, has tried to adopt positions that unify its big and small business membership.

Unfortunately, the common result of this, as Smith (2000: 14) shows, is that often anodyne statements please *neither* small nor big business. This lack of clear identification with the sectional interests of small firms is what creates the space for the growth of bodies that do more distinctly specialize in acting as the voice of small enterprise. Two are especially important. The National Federation of Independent Business (NFIB), founded in 1943, is by far the larger. It claims a membership in excess of 600,000, with especially heavy predominance of firms from the retail sector and from construction. It truly is an association dominated by small firms: over 50 per cent of its members have five or fewer employees, and to keep it that way it presently caps membership dues at $5,000 per annum – an obvious attempt to avoid the danger of big-firm domination to which the Chamber of Commerce is vulnerable (National Federation of Independent Business 2007: 4). The Federation lays particular emphasis on its procedures for solving the notoriously tricky problem of creating an agreed position on policy issues: it ballots all members on major issues and then adopts the majority view as its lobbying position. The National Small Business Association, founded in 1937 in the Midwest, claims a membership reach of only 150,000 but, partly to redress this weakness, pioneered the innovation of small-business 'umbrella' organizations (like the Small Business Legislative Council) that are designed to address particular issues or items of legislation (Levitan and Cooper 1984; National Small Business Association 2007).

American small business, therefore, has a benign public image, is politically highly active, and is well organized. But these characteristics do not guarantee influence. The best testimony to the influence of small business lies not in resources and organization, still less in claims to influence from the partisan source of the organizations themselves; it lies in the way the policy process has been shaped to protect the interests of small business. Here, the record of the small-business sector is mixed.

Historically, key legislative initiatives were indeed designed to hinder the ability of big corporations to compete with small enterprises. Two striking examples are in banking and in the retail sector, where the consequences of important laws passed in the inter-war years still help shape the structure of these respective sectors. The McFadden Act (1927) prohibited banks from establishing branch chains across state lines, and compelled federally char-tered banks to observe the different laws on branching enacted by individual states. These laws have varied. A minority, principally in the South and Midwest, have forbidden all but 'unit banking', where no branches are permitted at all. A majority of states have permitted branches, but with varying, often complicated, geographical restrictions. The effects of American branching laws on industrial structure are obvious. The McFadden Act delayed the development of a nationwide retail-banking system, while restrictive state branching laws perpetuated the existence of a large population of small banks. These branching laws were the product of a distinctive political history. Banks were at the centre of two of the most enduring conflicts in American political life: that concerning the balance between state and federal power, and that between agrarian interests (who were usually also debtors) and the interests of modernizing capitalism. They fuelled the great Populist agitations referred to several times in these pages (see Moran 1984, 1991 for the banking connection). In the wider retail sector, an important structural legacy was left by the Robinson–Patman Act of 1936. The Act sought to inhibit the market power of large retail chains by limiting the discounts which they could extract in bulk buying contracts from suppliers. The point was to prevent giant chains using their market power in price competition with small retailers (Bean 1996: 17–36).

These signs of the policy weight of small business continue to the present day. Within the Federal Government, there exists the Small Business Administration, which was founded in 1953 but which can trace an ancestry back to institutional initiatives in the 1920s. Its loan portfolio makes it the largest single public backer of business in the nation, and its programs now include financial and federal contract procurement assistance, management assistance, and specialized outreach to women, minorities, and armed forces veterans (Small Business Administration 2006a). Perhaps even more important, the agency mission is overwhelmingly directed to advocacy of the interests of small business, an advocacy reinforced by the weight of the two Congressional committees who oversee its operations. Both committees are highly receptive to small business lobbying. The political sensitivity of the Administration's operations are illustrated by the fact that its head resigned in 2006 following criticism of the adequacy of the response to the plight of small business in New Orleans in the wake of Hurricane Katrina.

There is, in short, convincing evidence that the political health of small business in the United States is much more robust than is the political health of small business in the United Kingdom: it operates in a more sympathetic culture; its lobbying organizations are better supported and better organized; its interests have been more elaborately protected by key pieces of legislation; and it has institutional advocates embedded in both the Federal Administration and in Congress. But despite this contrast, there is nevertheless a striking parallel with the British experience: whatever the official or popular philosophy, the twentieth century was the century of big business in America. Big business has been remarkably successful at circumventing attempts to restrict its market power, and in particular remarkably successful at circumventing laws and regulations designed to protect the position of small firms. At the root of this observation lies a simple fact: all interests, including business interests, operate in a competitive political environment, and what crucially matters is not just what resources they have at their disposal, nor even what laws they manage to put on the statute book, but how they employ those resources in competition with rival interests. From the start of the twentieth century, as Chandler's histories make clear, it was in the United States that many of the characteristically modern forms of the big-business enterprise were pioneered: 'from the 1880s to 1914...unprecedented capital accumulation in the new capital-intensive, scale-dependent technologies helped to propel the United States into a position of world leadership' (1997: 63). Indeed, Populism and the cult of the small entrepreneur was less a sign of the political strength of small business than of its weakness: a response to recession, the loss of control over markets, and threats from the exercise of political and market power by newly emergent corporate giants.

Structurally, therefore, the development of the American economy has been anything but a story of the dominance of small enterprises; America was a pioneer of the modern giant multinational corporation, and gave it a benign home. Indeed, many of exemplars central to the ideology that celebrates small-business enterprise have suffered serious decline. Two well-documented examples are as follows: in the American farm sector, where despite the myth of small-scale agrarian capitalism, there has been a long-term decline of precisely the kind of family-owned farms celebrated by that myth (Hoppe and Banker 2006: 34–5); and in retail, where despite the mythologizing of the family-run (Ma and Pa) general store, the last thirty years of the twentieth century saw a huge surge by retail giants. The extraordinary advance of Wal-Mart – which by the turn of the millennium accounted for nearly a sixth of the retail grocery market in the United States – stands as a symbol of the power of aggressively discounting giant retailers (for a case study of Wal-Mart, see Box 4.3, p. 76).

If the Robinson–Patman Act were truly effective, then a phenomenon like Wal-Mart should not exist. It is a firm whose giant stores now dominate numerous American communities, a domination made possible by aggressive price competition that uses bulk buying power to squeeze suppliers. (Box 4.3, p. 76, shows it has now spent over a decade trying to replicate this success in the United Kingdom.) This is precisely the kind of aggressive discounting which the 1936 Act was designed to prohibit. Yet, Wal-Mart has been able to use the legal resources it can command to create a jurisprudence of antitrust that interprets Robinson–Patman in a way quite compatible with its business practices (Bianco and Zellner 2003). Likewise, for all the efforts of the Small Business Administration, and successive policy initiatives, to discriminate in favour of small firms in federal procurement, Federal spending is heavily skewed in favour of small numbers of giant enterprises. Over the last two decades, there has been a trend, indeed, for consolidation into larger conglomerates in the key procurement area of defence contracting: 'In the early 1990s, defense contractors joined forces in several mega-deals that reduced the number of the industry's aircraft makers to three from eight; tactical-missile manufacturers declined to four from 13' (Merle 2003).

How has this state of affairs come about? There are three answers: the problems of small business in competing with rival business sectors, the success of big business in shaping the jurisprudence of business regulation, and the success of big business in using market innovations to circumvent regulations designed to protect the position of small business.

The first answer takes us back to the competitive character of interest-group politics in a democratic political system: outcomes are not just the product of the resources and organization of small-business interests, but of how these match up to those of other interests. Here, the historical and contemporary weight of organized big business has been extraordinarily impressive. As we saw in Chapter 2, the original critical episodes at the beginning of the twentieth century which led to the sudden creation of giant enterprises were not just the result of the operation of impersonal market forces, but were also the product of strategic manoeuvring and political lobbying by critically placed political actors and entrepreneurs (Bowman 1996: 13–18; Roy 1997: 3–20). Much of the superficially impressive organization of small business since then has been a kind of damage limitation exercise in the face of the sudden rise of the giant enterprise. These giants have embedded themselves successfully in the American state and in the American-lobbying system. Two very striking examples occur in policy domains where the scale of public procurement (and therefore spending) has been huge: defence and health. In both, a network of well-organized lobbies, cultivation of patronage, and distribution of lucrative public sector contracts and of lucrative private sector appointments has secured a huge slice of procurement business for a small number of giants.

The second answer directs us to the practical implementation of those legislative and other regulatory measures that were designed to protect the market position of small business. Struggle over these measures obviously did not end when the law was passed or the regulatory decision enunciated. In an economic culture where litigation is a key instrument of struggle for advantage in markets, all important legislative and other regulatory measures are continually tested in the courts, with affected interests using every possible substantive argument, and every possible judicial arena. In some instances – such as the fate of the giant tobacco firms documented in Derthick's study of tort actions arising from the damaging health effects of smoking – the impact of continuing political struggles in the courts was to create a public relations disaster for one section of big business, the tobacco giants (Derthick 2005). But in the case of the regulatory restrictions on competition in antitrust law, big business has been able successfully to challenge many of the restrictions in the courts. The jurisprudence of antitrust, especially since the onset of the new age of globalized competition from the 1970s, has favoured the ambitions of big business against the anti-competitive protections erected to defend the interests of small firms. Summarizing the totality of jurisprudence as well as regulatory interventions by the Justice Department, Bowman concludes that the Department 'has been able to imprint its own interpretation on judge-made law to enforce a new direction in antitrust policy... enforcement affecting mergers has swung sharply in favor of the presumption of freedom of contract by redefining or loosening restrictions on corporate combinations' (1996: 180). Nor is this too surprising. While individual giant firms have had bruising encounters over antitrust, success in this domain depends on resources which big business has in abundance: a wealth of money to hire the best legal teams and pursue issues endlessly through the courts, and a position well-embedded in Federal policy-making elites.

The success of big business in shaping the jurisprudence of antitrust links to the third reason for the limited impact of measures like McFadden and Robinson–Patman. Not only has big business been adept at using its resources to challenge the restrictions formally and to create alliances against them, it has also proved remarkably adept at their circumvention by market innovation. For example, it would be possible to write the history of the banking industry in the United States in recent decades, and in particular the history of retail banking, largely in such terms. Faced with prohibitions on the creation of cross-state banking networks, ambitious market actors responded with institutional and technological innovations designed legally to circumvent the rules. Institutions not classed as banks (like retail giants with chains that cross state boundaries) entered the markets, offering bank equivalent services in-store. Ingenious alternatives to a conventional 'branch' likewise allowed the creation of cross-state networks, and incidentally created lucrative business for lawyers arguing in the courts the meaning of a bank 'branch'. Credit-card consortia pioneered national networks of electronic cash machines (ATMs) which allowed customers many of the facilities of a nationally organized bank system (see Moran 1984 for some examples). The American retail-banking industry still does remain strikingly fragmented, when compared for instance with its UK counterpart. The existence of numerous small banks is indeed a tribute to the residual impact of the protections offered by legislative prohibitions on cross-state banking competition: there are still more than 10,000 banks in the United States, even after the carnage of the great financial crash of 2008. But the institutional and technological ingenuity displayed by the largest banking operations has meant that the attempt to keep the giants out of cross-state markets has in the new millennium largely failed. Indeed, the Riegle-Neal Interstate Banking and Branching Efficiency Act of 1994 repealed large parts of McFadden, allowing full nationwide banking across the country, regardless of state law. The repeal was in part a recognition of how far market innovation had effectively circumvented many of the original McFadden provisions.

We saw in the United Kingdom that it proved especially hard to estimate small-business influence in local and regional economies, if only because of the sheer diversity of local circumstances. The issue is naturally made more complicated still in the case of the United States by an obvious consideration: the much greater diversity of local, regional, and state conditions, whether we are speaking of the political, the economic, or the cultural. A large literature on community power has produced diverse findings about the extent of business influence generally, and it seems a fair, and unsurprising, summary to say that the extent to small-business influence varies greatly from community to community. Vidich and Bensman's classic study (1960) of small-town politics and society based on fieldwork conducted more than fifty years ago does suggest that the government of much of small-town America was historically dominated by owners of small enterprises – one might say by a 'shopocracy', to use a characterization employed in the UK case. However, the most recent influential literature on urban growth coalitions in the United States suggests that, whatever might be the case in small-rural communities, in the most economically dynamic and ambitious cities, power configurations seem to mirror the dominant finding from recent studies of the most important city and regional political systems in the United Kingdom: that in critical areas where attempts are being made to build coalitions to regenerate urban economies, the tendency is for big business rather than small business to dominate. This seems to be the main finding from the literature inspired by the original work on urban growth coalitions (Molotch 1976; Logan and Molotch 1987; Stone 1989). Indeed, the study of the way big business dominates policy making in Croydon in the United Kingdom cited earlier was one of a series of comparative studies, including the United States, which reported similar findings of the marginalization of small business across different national jurisdictions (Phelps et al. 2006). The single most important reason for this finding seems to be that economic regeneration, in creating urban growth coalitions, involves the attempt to 'globalize' local and regional economies: to tie the economy to some global networks and to create a niche for the locality in global markets (Rast 2001; Paul 2005). It is hardly surprising that this should then favour globally organized corporate giants. Of course this phenomenon is hardly new: the building of markets historically in cities like Chicago (the subject of Rast's study) likewise involved integrating the local markets with global-trading patterns. Indeed, it was this very process which helped give rise to the original small-business revolt that spurred the rise of Populism.

Box 5.3 The organization of the small-business lobby: the UK FSB and the US NFIB compared

---

Comparing the practicalities of campaigning by small-business lobby groups not only tells us a lot about the groups themselves, but also a lot about where the locus of power lies in making policy about small business in the two national systems that are the focus of this book. The FSB is the most important lobby group for small business in the United Kingdom; the NFIB is the largest national body representing small business in the United States. Their tactics and organization differ in a number of important ways. Easily the most significant is the differential attention paid to the legislature in the two countries. The case of the FSB is easily described in this respect: the account of its activities that it provides on its web site almost entirely neglects either chamber of the Westminster Parliament (http://www.fsb.org.uk/). That neglect reflects a realistic estimation of the low capacity of backbench members of the Westminster Parliament to influence the details of policy affecting small business. The legislature in the Westminster system is used only for 'fire brigade' campaigns – that is, campaigns that are mounted when all other means of lobbying have failed. For the US NFIB, by contrast, politics matters – and, in particular, electoral politics matters. A member of the US Federation is provided with a constant stream of information about elected officials. In 2008 alone, there were twenty-seven separate items of news related to the Congressional and Presidential elections of that year posted on the NFIB web site (National Federation of Independent Business 2008). They included a profile of the new Congress elected in November of that year; two items designed to advise members on how to get out the vote; an election day checklist of things to do; an item identifying key Congressional races that involved issues perceived to affect small-business interests; endorsements of individual candidates perceived to be friendly to small business, against opponents perceived to be hostile or less friendly; and a special briefing on the role of health finance reform in the campaign, since there is a long-standing belief that an extension of employer-funded systems of health insurance will load costs disproportionately on small business. In short, what the comparison indicates is that, even making allowances for the fact that we are examining evidence for a year in which there took place Congressional elections, the small-business lobby in the United States is much more involved in, and exposed to, competitive democratic politics than is the small-business lobby in the United Kingdom. A second major difference between the two organizations also reflects contrasts in the political environment. Although the UK Federation has an impressive list of regional office addresses, these are merely linked to organizational email addresses. An attempt by me to telephone these offices merely resulted in calls being transferred and then terminated. By contrast, the US Federation has offices in each of the fifty states, with named, identifiable contacts in each state and details of the people and personnel resources of each state headquarters office. Nor does this necessarily reflect differences in the efficiency of the two organizations; it reflects the fact that, while important decisions affecting the interests of small business are made at state level in the United States, no similar decentralization exists in the United Kingdom. Significantly, the only important exception to the picture of a centralized UK structure for the FSB lies in the offices established in the devolved governing systems of Wales and Scotland set up in 1998.

The setting of small-business politics in the United States is therefore strikingly different from that of the United Kingdom: there are obvious contrasts in the scale and diversity of both national systems, in their institutional arrangements, in the cultural setting of the two business systems, and in the organizational capacities of the respective small-business lobbies in the two countries. All the more remarkable, then, that there are such similarities in the actual capacities of the two national small-business communities to exercise power.

Political innovation and political weakness in the small-business sector

It is easy to see that the politics of small business in the two systems compared here share a story of decline. Powerful structural forces in the national and global economies are working against small-business influence in politics. But there is another side that should also be emphasized: the story on both sides of the Atlantic is also one of political renewal and innovation. Small business, we have seen, faces what Olson (1965) a generation ago identified as a key problem in the mobilization of any interest: the collective-action problem contained in the difficulty of persuading individuals to invest their energy, time, and money in political action without the guarantee of any individual payback. What is remarkable about the history of small business in the last generation is the extent to which political and institutional innovation has been designed to solve this problem. We saw that in the case of the United Kingdom, there have been determined attempts to build reward schemes that can deliver sufficient selective benefits to entice people into membership. As a result, the organization of small-business interests is much healthier than it was a generation ago. Likewise, there is evidence that small business, precisely because it faces acute problems of distilling a coherent 'interest' out of the highly varied market locations of its constituencies, has been spurred to innovate so as to overcome these problems of coherence: the balloting innovations pioneered by small-business groups in the United States allow them to adopt clear positions built on documented membership opinion. These contrast strikingly with the often anodyne and stilted responses of better known and connected peak associations, like the US Chamber of Commerce or the CBI, condemned to try to find some lowest common policy denominator when faced with a tricky, divisive issue. Likewise, small-business organizations have been adept at using innovative interest-representation techniques: at the utilization of the professional lobbying industry, at innovative forms of mass action, at using the latest 'soft technology' in solving problems of group formation, and at forming opportunistic alliances with other local campaigning groups.

Small business on both sides of the Atlantic is thus united by a recent history of political innovation. But this common history is itself the product of another commonality: political weakness in the face of competing interests, both elsewhere in the business community and in other domains of civil society. Political innovation is a sign of weakness, not of strength. We shall see in the next chapter that some of this weakness is due to the changing connection between parties and business interests.

6 Business Politics and Party Politics

Business, parties, and democracy

The connections between business politics and party politics take us to the heart of two key issues in the study of business politics under liberal democracy. The first concerns the relationship between democratic politics and business power. Parties are key institutions in the selection of political leaders in liberal democracy. In the two nations we are considering here, election to political leadership is virtually impossible without possessing a party label and identity – though the meaning of the label, the nature of party identity, and the importance of party organization in the election struggle all differ greatly in the two countries. In all theories of liberal democracy, elected leaders are supposed to have a decisive influence over the policies that are actually pursued by government. How far this theory can be put into practice in the face of modern business power is, as we know from earlier chapters, critical to the viability of capitalist democracy. The issues were laid out in general terms in Chapter 1. But since parties are central to democratic politics, we need to look more closely at the detail of how parties and business interests are connected. Bluntly, how dependent are parties on business interests; and to the extent that they are dependent, what are the grounds of this dependence, and how is it changing? The answers we give to these questions affect our view of whether democratic government is compatible with the exercise of power by business.

This first issue might be simply summarized as 'how far do parties have to rely on business support?' The second issue might be summarized equally crudely as 'how dependent is business on parties?' Political parties are important to the representation of business interests – that much is accepted virtually right across the political spectrum. But how important, and how and why modes of representation differ – across time and space – are open to dispute. We know from previous chapters that there has been a long-term growth on both sides of the Atlantic in the specialized resources and institutions of representation available to business – peak associations, trade associations, and lobbying firms. How has this rise in specialization affected the party–business connection? The roles of parties in electoral competition are very different on the two sides of the Atlantic. What effect do these differences

Box 6.1 Influencing the mood music in the European Parliament: the European Business and Parliament scheme

The influence of the European Parliament in economic policy making has been considerably strengthened in recent years, notably as a result of the Maastricht Treaty of 1992. The result has been greatly to increase the amount of lobbying in the Parliament by business interests (Bouwen 2002, 2004). But more important than special interest lobbying for business is the creation of a culture of sympathy and cooperation between legislators and enterprises. This is the purpose of the European Business and Parliament scheme – an initiative at the European level that has long been established in national parliaments. Despite the title, it is also open to officials of the EU other than those working in the Parliament. Established in 1997, it signs firms up to a scheme involving a range of activities: company attachments for Parliamentarians or officials; issue-based programmes, in effect brief courses providing over-views of particular sectors and their problems; and Parliamentary attachments for business executives from participating firms. It explicitly disavows lobbying, and all participants sign up to a code that commits them not to use contacts for that purpose. The collective benefits for business are nevertheless clear. As the sponsors of the scheme say, it can

Facilitate the understanding of major legislative and economic issues; provide a forum for frank and open dialogue protected by its internationally recognized Code of Principles; operate on the basis of participants sharing experience and learning from one another; serve all sectors and size of business within national economies; assist all political parties and groupings in Parliaments; enable business people and parliamentarians to understand the demands and constraints on each other. (International Association of Business and Parliament 2007: 6)

But we have frequently seen in this book that collective benefits are not enough. What might be in it for an individual enterprise? That is well illustrated by the case of one of the largest participants, the multinational British American Tobacco (BAT). As a glance at the health warning on any cigarette packet will show, tobacco firms face an uphill battle lobbying in the EU. BAT tries to ameliorate this hostile environment by offering the following choices of secondment, of a length between a few days or a few weeks:

1. BAT international headquarters in London (Globe House): a secondment to Globe House would allow insights into the development of global and regional strategy and the interaction between headquarter and the end market organisations 2. End market organisation (commercial): a secondment to one of the BAT end market organisations would allow insights into implementation and execution of strategy under real life conditions. The secondment could comprise an office part as well as days in the field with the sales force. This allows good insights into the marketing practises of BAT. 3. Factory: a factory secondment would give insights into the manufacturing of cigarettes. This could be of particular interest as here the impact of various elements of product regulation would be visible. (EBPS 2008*b*)

The company also offers issue-based programmes (in effect short courses) on topics like Corporate Social Responsibility, Responsible Tobacco Marketing, and Harm Reduction: To-bacco and Public Health. It is obvious why a tobacco firm would find this an attractive alternative to conventional lobbying. But the problem of getting other businesses to commit to the fostering of this culture of sympathy is illustrated by the wider experience of the scheme. Only thirty-one firms are listed in membership (though they include some multi-national giants like BP and Ericsson). The problem is unlikely to be the financial cost: the top annual subscription is €15,000, falling to (1,000 for a small firm. But the scheme demands the commitment of something much scarcer: management time. The annual commitment envis-aged is 'three to four sessions, including round-tables or parliamentary inquiries with MEPs. Annually two to three times hosting MEPs or senior officials of the Parliament on company attachments or business fellowships' (EBPS 2008*a*). The sponsors describe these demands on executive time as 'not significant'; companies might think otherwise.

have on the way parties represent business interests? The most up to date research on political parties suggests that there have been big changes in recent decades in party organization and in the relationship between parties and civil society. What have these changes done to business representation? All these questions are addressed in what follows.

Business and party politics in the United Kingdom: the rise of a business-friendly party system

Understanding the contemporary connections between business and parties in the United Kingdom has to start with understanding the history of those connections. Even when parties were not much more than Parliamentary factions, in the eighteenth century, the factions were nevertheless connected to important sets of economic interests in the wider society (Namier 1929). The shaping of the modern party system turned on the changing relationship between business interests and politics. In 1846, Sir Robert Peel laid the foundations of modern Conservatism when, in a famous reversal of policy, he embraced free trade in agriculture. This split the Conservative Party that had hitherto been aligned with the protection of domestic agriculture from foreign competition. Peel's famous 'U-turn' was designed to attract the rising new interests of industrial capitalism that wanted cheaper food through free trade. It caused a half-century of instability in party alignments as factions manoeuvred to represent the new business interests created by industrialism. It took a generation for the party system to stabilize, but by the closing decades of the nineteenth century the relationship between business interests and the party system was marked by two settled features: business relied heavily on party for representation, because specialized interest representation was still in its infancy; and both main parties – Conservative and Liberal – in the Westminster Parliament were business friendly, albeit with their roots in different business sectors and with different views over how tactically best to defend those sectors.

The First World War transformed this state of affairs, creating a new pattern that lasted until virtually the end of the twentieth century. At the outbreak of war, the Liberal Party controlled the Westminster Parliament, having won three general elections in succession. But differences over the conduct of the Great War bitterly divided the Party. In the first General Election after the War, in December 1918, David Lloyd George, the leading Liberal of his generation, led a Conservative-dominated coalition to electoral victory. What was left of the Liberal Party was virtually destroyed as a Parliamentary force. A new Labour Party tied closely to the trade unions replaced the Liberals as the main voice of radical reform in Britain. The Conservatives emerged as not only the dominant electoral force for most of the twentieth century, but also as the dominant party speaking for business interests (see Cowling 1971). From the 1920s to the 1980s, the configuration of the party system closely followed the configuration of the wider economic system: Labour was allied to workers organized in trade unions; the Conservatives were allied to business.

Another major consequence of the Great War affected business–party relationships more indirectly, but still profoundly: business, as we know from Chapter 3, developed its own specialized institutions of representation. The formation of the FBI in 1916 marked the first sustained attempt to organize a nationwide business 'peak association'. Its foundation was accompanied by the formation of a competing body that represented the interests of small manufacturers (the National Union of Manufacturers) and was soon followed, in 1919, by the formation of a national organization for employers, the British Employers' Confederation (Blank 1973; Middlemas 1979). In the immediate aftermath of the War, the City of London also organized behind the Bank of England to manage its interests. In short, as the party system was reorganizing its relationship with business, the business community was reorganizing its relationship with the party system: it was creating institutions of representation that could function independently of party, and could allow the voices of business to be heard regardless of which party was in office.

One reason these alternative institutions were needed was that the Conservative Party after 1918 could never function as the straightforward instrument of business. There were three reasons for this, and all are worth highlighting since all still complicate business–party relations. First, there was often no agreement on what constituted the interests of business, or the best way tactically to advance them. A good example is provided by policy on trade unionism. There have been deep differences within business, and within the Party, over whether unions harmed business interests or advanced them by establishing a stable and cooperative workforce. In the 1920s, the 1950s, and again in the 1980s, this issue divided business, divided Conservatives – and divided Conservatives from business (Harris 1973; Marsh 1992; Lockwood 2005). Second, the Conservative Party that became the dominant party of business had to operate after the First World War in a new electoral environment – one where, for the first time, most working class adults had the vote. It thus had to manage electoral politics in such a way as to achieve majorities in elected bodies like the Westminster Parliament. If the wishes of voters and the interests of business differed, the Party could only achieve electoral success by creating programmes that were more than just aligned to business interests. Third, while the Conservatives were the main business party from the 1920s to the 1990s, they did not quite have a monopoly of that role. Even in that era, the Labour Party was not always hostile to all business. Only a minority in the Party ever took seriously the commitment in the Party constitution to abolish private ownership of the means of production. On selected occasions – such as speeches to the annual Party Conference – Party leaders might play to the gallery by using anti-business rhetoric, and Labour rarely had successful big-business figures in its ranks. But over the seventy-year period from the 1920s to the 1990s, the Party believed – and practised the belief – in a mixed economy of public and private ownership; the differences with the Conservatives, and within the Labour Party itself, were about the content of the mix.

The 1990s saw a sea change in the pattern of business–party relations that had persisted since the end of the First World War. In that decade, Labour, after sustained electoral failures, abandoned even the formality of the commitment to 'socialism'. In 1995, the Party constitution was amended to replace the 'socialist' Clause 4 by one that commended 'the enterprise of the market and the rigour of competition'. That was part of a wholesale remaking of 'New Labour' designed to reinvent the Party as a business-friendly institution (Coates and Lawler 2000; Coates 2005). This inaugurated a new era in the relationship between business and parties. From the 1920s to the 1990s, the Conservatives had not been seriously challenged as the main business-friendly party. But since the 1990s, the Westminster Parliament has been dominated by two such parties – a return to the state of affairs that last prevailed before the First World War. As was the case in pre-First World War Britain, only some minority parties are seriously hostile to business. But of course the structure and operations of party institutions, and of business institutions, are now very different from those of a century ago. We have not simply recreated the world before 1914. Recasting the Westminster party system in a 'business-friendly' shape nevertheless has brought a number of changes.

Perhaps the most important is that the terms of partisan controversy have been reshaped. Not only has the Labour leadership abandoned any rhetorical or symbolic hostility to business, it has also accepted most of the 'business-friendly' policies that were introduced by the successive Conservative Administrations that ruled Britain between 1979 and 1997. These have included laws governing industrial relations that greatly weakened trade unions, at least in the private sector; cuts in personal taxation rates that benefited the highest paid in business; cuts in corporate taxation; deregulation of competitive practices; large-scale privatization; and the introduction of new business opportunities in the public sector by outsourcing of production and service delivery.

The transformation in the Labour Party's policies towards business was itself the product of a larger policy sea change, one that affected the relations between business and the wider Westminster party system. Important areas of economic policy that had once been furiously contested between the parties now ceased to be so. As a result, many issues which business had depended on the Conservative Party to manage just disappeared off the agenda of partisan, democratic politics. A glance back over the political history of the last thirty years or so helps make the point. Business no longer needs to convince the parties of its felt need for trade union reform. It no longer has to convince the parties of the undesirability of extending public ownership: on the contrary, it now has two dominant parties, at least in Westminster, who compete to offer policies of deregulation and privatization. Not even the cataclysmic banking crisis in autumn 2008 could shatter this consensus. The Labour Government was forced by the crisis to take ownership stakes in the major banks. But despite the claims of some of its radical supporters that this revived trad-itional socialist policies of nationalization, the government has been insistent that the measures are short term and that it will intervene only minimally in the management of the banks. There will be no return to large-scale nation-alization or party intervention in regulated industries. In short, the agenda of democratic politics has changed, so as to remove from the partisan arena many issues that were once threatening to business interests. (As we shall see in the next chapter, however, there have also been other shifts that have introduced new issues which business finds threatening.)

This change in the partisan policy landscape has been accompanied by a shift in the *institutional* relationships between business and the main West-minster parties – a shift much to the benefit of business. The Conservatives, both in opposition and in government, had long been open to business influences, as they sought to tap business expertise and business support – hardly surprising in the party that was historically the main business-friendly party in the state. But under the Conservative Governments 1979–97, and since then under New Labour, parties in office have stepped up considerably their reliance on business figures. For instance, a study of the numerous task forces used by New Labour in office to tackle policy problems showed that 25 per cent of members were identifiable with private producer interests (firms or trade associations). The comparable figure for trade unions was 2 per cent (Barker et al. 2000: 27). Griffiths' comprehensive study (based on a snapshot in 2007) of 187 quasi-government bodies (examples are as various as the Bank of England and the Arts Council) showed that there were only thirteen which did not have a businessperson on their board (Griffiths 2009: 209). A striking symbol of this conscious 'business-friendly' stance was contained in one of Gordon Brown's first acts as Prime Minister in 2007. He established a 'Business Council' to 'Examine the progress the Government is making to improve the business environment in areas critical to the future of the economy' and to 'Advise the Government on its policies and priorities'. (BERR 2008*b*). The Council not only includes CEOs of some of the largest UK firms (such as Tesco), but also one of the leading figures from the Private

Equity Industry, a sector that has for some years been strongly criticized by Labour's traditional allies in the trade unions.

The new world of business-friendly party politics is therefore marked by distinctive assumptions about policy and distinctive institutional connections. It is also marked by a further distinctive element that can be summed up in one word: money. In the era between the 1920s and the 1980s, when the Conservatives were the main business-friendly party, their opponents often pointed to the importance of business finance in the party. But in fact, in this era, business money was comparatively unimportant for either Labour or the Conservatives. In the Labour Party, the dominant institutional funder was the trade union movement. The Conservatives had an even more powerful money-raising machine. They built up their individual membership so successfully that by the early 1950s they were a mass movement with over 2.8 million members. Individual subscriptions, and the fund-raising activities of well-organized constituency parties, were the keys to Conservative wealth (Pinto-Duschinsky 1981: 126–54). Indeed after the Second World War, the Party introduced reforms that prohibited wealthy parliamentary candidates from donating to their constituency party – traditionally a means by which rich business people in effect bought a Conservative nomination (Pinto-Duschinsky 1981: 129–30). Thus, if anything, over time, the Conservatives reduced the influence of business money in the Party.

The huge Conservative membership was itself a sign of something wider: the period from the 1920s to the 1960s was the great age of the party with a mass membership. This gave the parties some financial independence from business. In the case of the Conservatives, it meant that business contributed only a minority of total party funding. But more generally, it cut the cost of politics, and therefore the need for outside funding, because the mass membership provided an army of free labour around which the dominant style of political campaigning was built: face-to-face contact with voters through intensive house-to-house canvassing and well-attended public meetings during elections campaigns.

The decline of the mass party, especially in the last thirty years, has fundamentally altered the arithmetic of party finance, and changed the relations between parties and business. From the late 1960s party membership fell, until by the 1990s neither major party could claim more than about 250,000 members – a figure that continues to fall, and seems destined to stay at a low level. (Party membership records are very unreliable, but Labour's membership is probably now at about 170,000.) We need not speculate here on the reasons for this decline, except to note that it is long term, rooted in fundamental social and political changes – and therefore probably irreversible. For the parties, a major source of funding, and of free labour, has therefore disappeared. Campaigning styles also changed, with a growing reliance on expensive market research and advertising (Lees-Marshment

2001). By the new millennium, the two dominant Westminster parties were spending in excess of £35 million on general election campaigns (the figure for the 2005 campaign). More than half of this was on advertising and market research (Electoral Commission 2007).

In short, the parties over the last thirty years have developed a greatly increased appetite for money that they cannot satisfy from their traditional non-business sources. They have partly satisfied this appetite with state funding, but public money is presently limited mostly to contributions in kind (e.g. free political party broadcasts) or support for policy research and for the operations of the parties in Parliament. The result is that we have entered a new age of party dependence on funding from business; and as a result, entered also an age of scandals and attempted regulation of business finance of parties (Grant 2005). The Election and Political Parties Act 2000 was passed after a series of revelations about the sources of – mainly Conservative – business financing in the early 1990s. But in 2006, a new set of scandals engulfed both the Conservatives and New Labour when it was revealed that both parties had developed means of avoiding declarations of business support, principally by soliciting (non-declarable) loans rather than donations. The episode produced a long investigation which resulted in a decision not to bring any prosecutions, but which was sufficiently embarrassing for the government to commission a review of funding from a retired senior civil servant (for the subsequent report, see Phillips 2007). That review recommended an increase in public support subject to putting a cap on total expenditure – a recommendation that is not presently implemented because both big parties are mired in financial difficulties and heavily reliant on business donors.

The last quarter-century has therefore seen the Westminster system of government dominated by two business friendly parties: the agenda of partisan politics at Westminster has removed many issues that were troublesome to business, the parties in government have turned to business figures in making appointments to the huge network of patronage appointments, and the two big parties have been forced increasingly to solicit financial donations from business.

Does this mean that business now dominates the party system? Any such conclusion needs to be tempered by four cautionary points. The first is that long-term changes have come over the nature of both business and political careers, and these changes have driven a wedge between party life and business life. A couple of generations ago it was quite common to combine a political career with a business career, and even for leading figures in business to occupy a seat in the House of Commons (Haxey 1942: 32–59). But the demands of politics have now turned a political career into a full-time occupation, in which the ambitious must specialize from an early age if they are to succeed (see King 1981 on this and on its consequences). In business too, there is much more specialization. Even non-executive directors now have significant responsibilities; the phenomenon of the leading politician who could sit on a board of a big company and simply act as an adornment on the headed notepaper is coming to an end. Thus, the kind of informal unity that used to link the Conservative elite to the business elite is now much weaker. There used to be a kind of organic connection between business and, especially, the Conservative Party, with powerful informal networks linking the two; but political relations now have to be much more formally organized than in the past. The relations between the Conservatives and small business provide a further illuminating example of this change, as we saw in the previous chapter. The collapse of Conservative Party membership at local level has greatly weakened one of the most important interest connections in British politics, a connection that had endured for over a century up to the 1970s: that between small local businesses and the Party.

A second change in the party system has also made the representation of business interests more problematic. In the discussion thus far, we have referred to relationships with the two dominant 'Westminster' parties. As recently as thirty years ago that would have been enough to describe the totality of parties. But the party system in the United Kingdom now is much more diverse than hitherto. To influence the Westminster leadership of Conservative and Labour is far from the same as influencing all the parties. Transfer of the locus of policy making to the EU means that party organization in the EU adds an extra dimension to party politics – and a very different dimension (Hix et al. 2006). Domestically, the creation of devolved systems of government in both Scotland and Wales has created increasingly distinctive party systems – and ones that are in important respects less business compliant than exists in Westminster. In both Scotland and Wales, the Conservatives are now a marginal political force. Labour in Scotland and Wales not only retains a leading position, but also many of the traits of 'Old Labour' hostility to business that were eradicated by New Labour in Westminster in the 1990s. In Wales, Plaid Cymru, the nationalist party, at the time of writing a member of the governing coalition, has inherited much of the radicalism of traditional socialism, especially its suspicion of big business. Even in local government party systems, and therefore systems of local control, are much more fragmented than was the case when the two giants of the age of mass parties, Conservative and Labour, virtually monopolized control at local level: independents, and even significant Green representation, are some substitute for the disappearance of 'Old Labour' hostility to business. Thus, while Conservative and Labour elites in Westminster are much more respon-sive to business interests than in the past, the wider party system is more difficult for business to control, because it is more fragmented and diverse than when the two big Westminster parties dominated the whole UK political system.

A third development, this time involving the party elite in Westminster, should also make us cautious of picturing the party system as simply overwhelmingly business friendly. The system of business–party relationships that existed a generation ago was often informal and far from transparent. Business and party leaders moved in a club-like world – often indeed centering on elite 'gentlemen's' clubs in London's West End (see Sampson 1965 for a contemporary portrait of this world). Policy favours, even contracts, could be quietly delivered without serious danger of public scrutiny. Paradoxically, the new age of party reliance on business finance has made much more difficult the process of returning financial support with policy favours or positions in public life. The party financing scandals led to the establishment of the Committee on Standards in Public Life in 1994. The Committee's successive reports have produced a revolution in the system for appointment to office in important public bodies like the regulatory agencies; appointments now have to be made in a much more open and competitive way than was the case in the past. In addition, the rules on the allocation of government contracts have become more formal and transparent (a good sense of the long-term impact of the Committee on transparency and accountability can be gauged from its successive reports at http://www.public-standards.org.uk/index.html). The cumulative impact of EU procurement policies has also shifted procedures in the direction of greater transparency and accountability (Dimitrakopoulos 2008: 58–75). Often desperate attempts to circumvent these new controls have simply led to disaster: scandals that have damaged the leadership of parties and damaged individual business figures. Even the effort to deliver worthless favours – such as a seat in the House of Lords – in return for financial support has proved a source of serious difficulty for all concerned. The Phillips Report referred to above came about because of a media campaign, and a long police inquiry, which tried (unsuccessfully) to track down a connection between contributions to the Labour Party and appointments to the House of Lords, a 'cash for peerages' scandal.

A final reason for caution in viewing the party system as business friendly is that, while the main parties now produce sycophantic rhetoric favouring business, they are unreliable and faithless friends. This is because parties are in business for votes, and it is the belief that seeming business friendly will bring votes that has reshaped the party system in recent decades. But precisely, because the business–party connection is just instrumental, party politicians will turn on their business 'friends' if it seems opportune to do so. A good example was provided in 2007 when a number of heads of leading private equity firms (including a member of the Prime Minister's new Business Council) were publicly mauled by the House of Commons Treasury Select Committee (House of Commons Treasury Select Committee 2007). The mauling occurred because the MPs perceived that private equity firms

---

Box 6.2 'Clientelism' and party–business relations in Ireland: Charlie Haughey loots business and the public purse

---

An important form of party–business relations across the democratic world is summarized as 'clientelism'. At its heart is the idea of exchange: the party as patron delivers goods and services (contracts, jobs, and favours) to clients in return for support (votes and money). The Republic of Ireland provides one of the best-documented accounts of the corrupt exchange of money and favours. For over a decade, judicial tribunals (see especially Moriarty 2006) investigated a network principally centred on the corrupt exchange of money by individual politicians in return for favourable decisions over land development applications – the impact of which was to enrich developers. The most sensational concerned the leading Irish politician of his generation, Charles Haughey (Taoiseach – Prime Minister – 1979–81, 1982, 1987–92). He was revealed to have received gifts totalling 8.5 million sterling equivalent from a wide range of leading business figures. Haughey was only the grossest and greediest of a number of corrupt politicians. Corrupt business–party relations are not unknown in the two systems that form the main cases in this book. The critical question that the Irish case focuses us on is, therefore, not the fact of corruption, but why corrupt relations between parties and business develop on such a huge scale. The Irish case suggests three possible explanations:

- An *agent-centred* approach stresses the character of individuals, such as the greed that marked Haughey as a personality. Since Haughey was only the most extreme instance of corruption, the explanation is summarized in the proverb 'a fish stinks from its head': in other words, corruption at the top seeps downwards. In small, highly centralized societies like Ireland, the influence of single individuals can be disproportionate to their number. An obvious difficulty with this reliance on the malign influence of one individual, however, is that it has problems explaining the timing and scale of the corruption.
- A *cultural* approach sees the origin of the problem in engrained features of the culture of clientelism, and the decay of that culture. At the heart of clientelism is indeed an exchange: the politician uses the resources of the state to distribute favours in return for various forms of support. On this interpretation, the great burst of Irish corruption in party–business relations only magnified what was engrained already in the culture of Irish business and political life. The boom in corruption can then be traced to cultural change in Ireland over the last generation, notably the decay of cultural restraints – such as the impact of Catholic ethics – on this engrained system of exchanging support for favours: the period covered by the corruption boom is the period when Irish society saw a steep fall in religious observance and other traditional practices. This cultural explanation, however, begs an important question: Why should these restraints have been so rapidly discarded?
- An *economic* approach offers the possibility of answering this question. At the root of the great cultural transformation in the Republic in recent decades has been an economic revolution that transformed the country from one of the poorest to one of the richest in the developed world. This was accompanied by a building boom. In this boom, a key source of enrichment has been a set of decisions formally controlled by public officials, including elected officials: zoning or rezoning land for building development in a hitherto largely agricultural country. Huge fortunes have been made, in particular, by the development possibilities opened up through the expansion of the Dublin metropolis. An approach that stresses the enrichment offered in a booming economy helps explain why the engrained culture of clientelism took such a spectacularly corrupt turn in the closing decades of the twentieth century.

were easy game, since media reporting had pictured them as tax-avoiding parasites. They were also easy game because, unused to public performance under aggressive Parliamentary questioning, they were incompetent: the head of their trade association, the British Private Equity and Venture Capital Association, resigned after the trauma of the public hearing (Arnold 2007). A key condition of keeping party politicians on the business straight and narrow depends not on controlling the politicians directly, but on controlling the wider public reporting of, and public perceptions of, business behaviour. If business loses control of these public perceptions, it loses its party friends – an experience that we shall see below repeated in the United States. Just how hard controlling media reporting and public perceptions can be is something we will explore in the next chapter.

A party system that is fragmented, dominated by two business-friendly party elites, and with a growing appetite for business money: superficially, the UK system is starting to resemble that in the United States. How far this superficial appearance corresponds to reality we shall now examine.

The United States: regulating the party–business connection

Critical changes have come over the US party system in the last few decades and these have greatly altered the relationship between the parties and business interests. But the significance of these changes can best be appreciated against the background of larger historical and cultural features of the American relationship between business and politics. Of these, two are particularly important: the kind of link existing historically between the party system and organized economic interests, and the particular cast of the system of business regulation in the United States. As we shall see, the two have interacted in recent decades, in the process deeply affecting the regulation of the way business can finance parties and politicians.

It is a truism that the American party system has historically been better designed for the defence of particular interests than for the promotion of the kind of broad class coalitions that characterized British politics for most of the twentieth century. This sectionalism made it comparatively easy for individual industries, or even individual businesses, to penetrate the parties, and even to capture individual parties, especially at state and local levels. But it has proved comparatively hard to establish the parties as distillers and defenders of a general business interest, in the manner achieved by the Conservative Party in the United Kingdom for much of the twentieth century. The national programmes of American parties in particular have been remarkable for their lack of coherence. This bias towards the defence of particular interests, at the expense of creating coherently integrated programmes, links to the single most historically important feature of the party system: it has been geographically and institutionally decentralized. State, and even local, parties and their elected representatives enjoyed high autonomy from national organization, and indeed in the case of the elected representatives from the party organization at any level. This meant that the parties took their ideological and interest 'colouring' from localities and regions. Particular state parties were close to particular industries, or even to powerful business dynasties. This diversity persists, hardly surprisingly in view of the size and complexity of the economies of the biggest states. Studies by the Center for Public Integrity (2008) of the outside interests declared by state legislators show that the configuration of ties follows the configuration of the state economy: thus, the largest source of outside ties in Texas is oil and related industries; in California the computing industry leads; and in Kansas the leader is crop production and related industries.

As these examples show, the fact that the parties were loose coalitions of diverse interests did not mean that they were hostile to business; on the contrary, it made easier than was the case in the UK party control by *sectional* business interests. There certainly were, also, ideological differences both within and between the two dominant parties across the twentieth century, and these involved issues central to the interests of business. Since the New Deal – the details of which we discussed in Chapter 2 – the Democratic Party in both Congress and the White House has been more likely to promote policies involving closer regulation of business than has the Republican Party. But nothing in these differences menaced the fundamental interests of the business system, in the way that the Labour Party seemed to do on occasions in the United Kingdom. Both the Democrats and the Republicans were overwhelmingly business-friendly parties, though often friendly to different parts of business, and often with different views about how to translate this generalized friendly stance into immediate policies.

The historically established relations between business and the party system were thus heavily shaped by the nature of party politics and party organization. The parties nationally were 'empty vessels': they had little control over candidates and office holders, and their programmes were assemblages of the views and interests of many factions. (The quoted phrase is from Katz and Kolodny 1994.) Locally, and in some cases across whole states, particular industrial interests could capture a whole party or even the whole party system: a small state like Delaware, for instance, has been extraordinarily susceptible to the Du Pont (chemicals) dynasty (Cohen 2002). This has turned the politician into a kind of entrepreneur, bidding for support, including financial support, from a range of interests, including business interests. That state of affairs gave particular enterprises, industries, and even sectors considerable leverage in the party system, and leverage over the behaviour of politicians once elected to office; but it also made the party system a kind of vessel into which the main conflicts of interests *within* the business community were poured.

Critical changes in the character of the party system in recent decades have affected these historically engrained features. They have made parties and politicians more dependent on the support, especially the financial support, of business, and have simultaneously prompted the increasing regulation of party–business relations. It is this latter development that has exposed party–business relations to the full force of the culture of the American system of regulation.

Three changes in the character of the party system have been particularly important. First, the parties have declined in significance as institutions in civil society. American parties never had memberships in a British (or other European) sense; rather, they had cohorts of local activists. But even this tradition of local activism has weakened. Most campaigning now rests not on the mobilization of voters by face-to-face contact with activists, but on campaigns managed through the mass media and (increasingly) through electronic means. The decay of local party life has also coincided with a decline in popular attachment to parties: the proportion of the population identifying themselves as Democrat or Republican has fallen over the long period since the 1960s (for a summary of the evidence, see Green 2002).

The second change is that there has been a sharp increase in the extent to which competition for office is candidate centred. This is particularly true at the crucial party candidate selection stage. Recall that, despite the decline in party identification, a party label is still a virtual precondition of election: to get into Congress it is necessary to run as a Democrat or Republican. The key to nomination in the system of party primaries lies in the perceived qualities of individual candidates – and in the manipulation of perception, especially through mass marketing. Thus, the historical role of the politician as a kind of individual entrepreneur bidding for the support of sectional interests has been magnified, because success in the primaries depends on building – and financing – a candidate-centred organization. Money – in large amounts – is thus critical to establishing the credentials of most aspirants for significant electoral offices.

This in turn connects to the third major change, and brings us directly to the issue of the modern connection between the party system and business: the shift away from party focused grass roots campaigning to candidate-focused campaigns heavily reliant on mass media communications, advertising and marketing has produced stunning increases in the costs of running for elective public office. The extreme case is provided by the Presidency, where total expenditures by all candidates probably doubled between 1996 and 2004, and where a serious candidate for 2008 in the primaries alone probably had to get hold of $100 million. But even for Congressional elections costs are rising way beyond inflation: for instance, Congressional candidates participating in the November 2006 raised 30 per cent, and spent 36 per cent, more than in the previous 2004 Congressional cycle (Federal Election Commission 2006). Even for city-wide office, like Mayor of New York, winning has demanded (see below) expenditure of nearly $70 million.

These developments hold the clue to the changing relationship between the parties and business, for business is of overwhelming importance as the source of this money. It is overwhelmingly important because it is the major controller of economic resources in the society and because it is the most intensively organized interest grouping: as we know from systematic studies of the interest group universe discussed in Chapter 3, business interest groups dominate the pressure group universe (Schlozman and Tierney 1986; Baumgartner and Leech 1998; Derthick 2005). American partisan campaigning is founded on business finance.

There is nothing novel in the fact of reliance on business. Historically, there was comparatively little to regulate the financial relationship between political parties and business interests, beyond the normal criminal law, and even that was probably ineffective. In this unregulated world, business could finance and bribe (the two activities often being indistinct) at will. In the first age of plutocratic capitalism, politicians could be fairly easily bought. In his history of the 'Robber Barons' – of the great capitalists like Carnegie and Rockefeller who transformed the American economy in the second half of the nineteenth century – Josephson documents how 'every industrial group and every great monopoly was almost directly represented in the political councils of the nation' (1962: 347–8). In 1896, McKinley's successful Presidential campaign was financed by levying assessments on corporations (Lehne 2006: 162). But the last three decades have ushered in a new age of scandal and regulation, as the system tries to cope with the increased reliance of party politicians on financing from business interests.

Scandal and regulation are connected, and they help explain the entanglement with the wider culture of the American regulatory system. The first modern regulatory measure dates from the Federal Election Campaign Act of 1971, and is best understood as part of the great wave of new social regulation – the burst of regulatory intervention in corporate affairs that originated in the 1960s. (This new age of regulation is described in more detail in Chapter 7.) The passage of the 1971 legislation, which was accompanied by no obvious means of enforcement, was almost immediately succeeded by a development familiar in other areas of the new regulation: the revelation of abuses and consequent scandals, this time brought to light as part of the Watergate affair that eventually toppled President Nixon in 1974. Watergate was only distantly connected to party finance by business, but the ancillary revelations uncovered a world of covert financing of party politicians by often shady business figures. These financial dealings were symptomatic, however, of the changes alluded to earlier – the growing reliance by candidates and parties on business finance due to increasingly expensive campaigns. The most important consequence of this was that in 1974 Congress amended, to strengthen, the 1971 law. More important still, it introduced a characteristically American weapon of enforcement – a regulatory agency, the Federal Election Commission (FEC). The aim of Congress in establishing the new system was to organize campaign financing through a system of Political Action Committees (PACs). These were designed to limit the scale of corporate contributions (since PACs could only gather contributions, fixed by quite modest ceilings, from individuals) and to make the system fully transparent by requiring detailed reporting of accounts to the FEC.

In the intervening decades, this regulatory system has taken on entirely unsurprising characteristics – unsurprising, at least, to any observer of American business regulation. The system of controls has been subjected to ingenious circumvention, both by donors trying to influence candidates, and candidates and parties trying to raise money. Most of this ingenuity has gone into regulatory avoidance: that is, the legal circumvention of the rules by employing smart lawyers to dream up ways of contributing that circumvented regulatory barriers. Some has gone into evasion: that is, illegal contributions and straight bribery. What were intended to be the key institutions in regulation – the PACs – are in reality estimated to account for only about one-third of all political funding (Hopkin 2005: 46). For nearly thirty years after the introduction of the new system in the mid-1970s, a great deal of ingenuity went into creation of 'soft' money, so named because it could escape regulatory restrictions both as to amounts and to uses. Soft money circumvented the ceilings by being dedicated not to the campaign of a single individual, but to other uses that could nevertheless affect an electoral outcome. The parties themselves could use it for purposes (such as organization and communication) that were an almost direct substitute for candidate support. Soft money was also widely used in issue-based advocacy: in expensive media campaigns opposing or promoting particular policy options. The scale of these soft-money campaigns not only represents important corporate interventions in partisan campaigns, but can also virtually directly substitute for campaign financing where candidates are clearly publicly aligned for or against a particular issues. An idea of the possibilities is provided by the following summary of what has been allowable:

(1) communications by a corporation to its stockholders, executive or administrative personnel and their families or by a labor organization to its members or families on any subject; (2) nonpartisan voter registration and get-out-the-vote activities by a corporation aimed at its stockholders and executive and administrative personnel and their families or by a labor organization aimed at its members and their families; and (3) the establishment, administration and solicitation of contributions to a

separate segregated fund (commonly known as a political action committee or PAC or SSF) to be utilized for federal election purposes by a corporation, labor organization, membership organization, cooperative, or corporation without capital stock. (Whitaker 2004)

In short, soft money has numerous political uses for business. In the words of Hansen and her colleagues: 'The flow of finance from the business sector to political parties and candidates is far larger than from all other interest group sectors combined.... The practice of American politics floats on business financial flows' (2004: 421–2).

The system of PACs has undergone significant change in the more than thirty years since the original regulatory arrangements were introduced, and it has done this because clever (and sometimes dumb) modes of avoidance and evasion have been developed both by party politicians and by business donors. The single most important reason for this history of circumvention is that the system cannot deal with the underlying cause of this party–business link: the rise in the cost of seeking and maintaining political office. The long history of circumvention prompted an equally familiar response when Congress passed the Bipartisan Campaign Reform Act 2002. This banned 'soft-money' donations to the parties, but it has now taken its place in the succession of regulations circumvented by smart lawyers and accountants. In the aftermath of 2002, the most successful of the circumvention devices were '527' donations, a new source of soft money based on exploitation of an esoteric tax-exemption clause: between 2002 and 2004 alone, '527' contributions doubled to $405 million (Rauch 2005). The institution at the centre of this history of circumvention, the Federal Electoral Commission, has behaved like a typical federal regulatory agency. Faced with ingenious (and sometimes crooked) institutions, it has tried to block the loopholes in the system by increasingly elaborate measures, and it has resorted to adversarial legalism to punish those who break the rules. Between 1980s and 2006, it imposed penalties exceeding $50,000 on 225 violators, and it was escalating its enforcement activity as time went on: total penalties in the first half of 2006 alone exceeded those of any full preceding year (Federal Election Commission 2007).

All this adversarial, legalistic regulation rests on an important assumption: that the scale of business financing of parties and candidates actually does impart a systematic business bias into the party system. On this, the research is inconclusive. A large literature has debated the impact of PAC contributions, chiefly because the reporting rules mean that data sets are easily available to academic researchers. The balance of evidence suggests that these donations do not produce much measurable policy benefit, or at least the findings are so notoriously contradictory and incommensurable that it is virtually impossible to make sense of the literature (Baumgartner and Leech 1998: 129–36). PAC donations seem to be motivated by the narrowest interests of industries and even firms, and the contributions are typically designed to try to secure some competitive advantage, often at the expense of other firms or industries (Milyo et al. 2000; Hart 2001; De Figueiredo 2002; Fellowes and Wolf 2004). In other words, they are as likely to be designed to damage other business interests as to damage the opponents of business. One of the most striking signs of this is what is usually called the incumbent effect: at the Federal level, in Congress for example, PAC contributions are heavily weighted in favour of incumbents, simply because of the calculation that they can do most benefit – or damage – to a firm or an industry, regardless of the wider ideological outlook of that incumbent. Incumbents in Congress can be particularly useful in the pursuit of sectional interests, for they have the potential to manipulate the small detail of regulatory or tax rules – complex, technical issues that are unlikely to be the subject of wide public interest or partisan debate, but that can make a big difference to the bottom-line. Indeed, a main conclusion of Smith's research on the political power of the US Chamber of Commerce is that business finds it hardest to control high profile, salient issues that turn on the wider interests of the whole of business, precisely because these are most likely to attract public attention, to be the subject of partisan controversy, and to force elected officials to adopt public positions; and easiest to manipulate the fine, technical detail of policy (Smith 2000: 20–30).

The effectiveness of PAC donations is also limited precisely because they are so transparent; that, after all, is why academic researchers track them so obsessively. Politicians have to be wary of trading particular policy concessions for particular inducements. The purpose of raising campaign finance is to win elections; and if candidates are damaged because they are shown to be the captive of particular interests, that destroys the point of taking the money in the first place. Offering a quid pro quo – support for a sectional business interest in return for a contribution – is dangerous in a world where well-organized public interest groups like the Center for Public Integrity (2007) publicize these contributions. In short, what might crudely be called the *public* bribery model of relations between business and party politicians is not a very convincing account of how business turns money into influence over party politicians.

This still leaves a variety of other ways of converting corporate money into influence. In a relentlessly adversarial regulatory system, corruption is obviously one rational tactic, since it hides things from regulators. The scale of corruption is nevertheless limited by two obvious factors: morality and the fear of being caught. There have been corruption scandals in recent decades, and these are in a long tradition of crookedness linking politicians and business. The most important recent episode was the Abramoff affair, where a number of Congressional careers were ended, and one Congressman jailed, for accepting illicit payments. However, it is perhaps symptomatic that Abramoff was a lobbyist not for a major corporate interest, but for Indian tribes. (There was some business connection through Indian gambling interests on reserved lands: for the comprehensive journalistic investigation, see Schmidt et al. 2006.) It is probable that the fear of being caught deters most large corporation from crude corruption, at least in domestic politics: as we saw in Chapter 4, the very salience of giant firms means that they face considerable problems in managing their reputations. More characteristic may be the world shown by the collapse, due to fraud, of the energy conglomerate Enron in 2001. The collapse revealed massive financial contributions both via 'soft money' and PAC donations to key figures in the Bush Administration and to leading Republican and Democratic congressmen. It also revealed efforts by Enron to try to influence appointments to federal regulatory bodies that oversaw industries where Enron was active, and efforts to lobby senior figures in Congress and the Executive to influence tax and regulatory policy to the company's advantage. The way Enron was able to use its local base in state and sub-state politics in Texas to influence Federal policy may also be indicative of how corporations can turn local influence into national policy influence through control over local political leaders who also perform on the Federal stage. Nevertheless, Enron is probably an extreme case, in the sense that it was a grossly fraudulent enterprise (which most businesses patently are not) and in the sense that its 'friends' stretched right up to President Bush. In fact, all Enron's expensively acquired political 'friends' deserted it when the fraudulent pack of cards collapsed in 2001 (Mclean and Elkind 2003). The significance of Enron probably lies in the way it illustrates how the smaller worlds of state politics can often escape the kind of scrutiny to which operators in Washington are subject, and in the way it shows how local political cultures can shape business–party relations. For instance, an analysis of the Federal Justice Department's annual reports on its investigations into state-level corruption, covering the decade up to 2006, showed that three southern states – Louisiana, Mississippi, and Kentucky – topped the corruption league (Corporate Crime Reporter 2007).

The totality of the evidence so far indicates that the appetite of candidates for money is so great that enormous ingenuity goes into circumventing any regulatory limits to business finance. But on the critical question of how far all this money translates into business power, the evidence indicates that attempts to trace direct connections between business power and campaign financing probably simultaneously *overstate* and *understate* the impact of business money on the behaviour of party politicians.

They *overstate* the importance of the connection, especially at Federal level, in looking for some very direct reward – for instance, through support via votes in Congress favourable to a particular interest – resulting from contributions. Indeed, it is doubtful if corporations expect much by way of a direct benefit of this sort. Publicly declared campaign contributions are best conceived as analogous to advertising or insurance. Within the totality of the corporation's resources, they are comparatively trivial; but like advertising and insurance, the money is spent because nobody is quite sure what damage to corporate interests might be caused if it were not.

But accounts that seek to link financing of candidates and parties directly to favours *understate* the impact of business on parties and candidates, because they neglect the context in which this flow of money takes places. The context is one where businesses have structural advantages in the struggle to influence elected politicians. Two kinds of advantage are particularly important.

First, the huge rise in campaign costs over the last generation has turned campaigning for office into a plutocratic activity. As we saw earlier, even for comparatively modest office candidates need to have access to huge sums, and for Presidential candidates these sums are stunning. The only individuals with the resources to personally finance such campaigns are those with business fortunes. There are indeed some striking recent examples of this. In 2001, for example, Michael Bloomberg, hitherto a billionaire Democrat, won the mayoral electoral contest in New York City as the Republican candidate. Although campaign rules set limits to the contributions that any candidate could accept from any single source, Bloomberg circumvented these by the simple device of spending his own money, over $69 million, in the contest. In the 1992 and 1996 Presidential elections, the Texas billionaire, Ross Perot, running as an independent candidate, secured 19 per cent (1992) and 8 per cent (1996) of the popular vote, the former the largest vote for a third-party candidate since before the First World War. Of course as the example of Perot shows, immense expenditure does not convert into electoral victory: Perot spent $60 million of his own money in the 1992 campaign without coming within sight of success. Being super-rich therefore cannot guarantee election to public office. But it does allow plutocrats like Bloomberg to run independent of campaign finance constraints if they are willing to spend their own money. It also means that the enormous expense of fighting the successful primary campaigns that are the necessary condition of securing a party nomination can only be met by the personally super-rich or those who can attract rich backers. Candidates for public office thus either need personal wealth or access to supporters with that wealth. The corporate rich are the most important source of such fortunes, and the richest have become immensely richer in recent years. For the new 'working rich', as Folkman et al. (2007) dub them, donations to candidates are a drop in the ocean. A system where business finance is the key to campaigning thus creates a very different kind of incentive system for politicians from that existing in countries where – as was until recently the case in the United Kingdom – parties could raise their resources from institutional interests other than business, like trade unions, or from the activities of a numerous mass of supporters. The expense of running for high electoral office has, certainly, stimulated innovations in fund raising which can reduce this reliance on money from the corporate rich. Aspirants for Presidential office in 2004 and 2008 used the Internet to solicit

Box 6.3 Regulating business money in the parties: a study in contrasting national regulatory styles

There is substantial evidence that there are contrasting styles of regulation in different nations. In Chapter 7, we discuss this in terms of the general character of business regulation in the United States and the United Kingdom (see Vogel 1986; Kagan 2001). The contrast is between an American system that has traditionally been highly juridified and adversarial, and a British system that has sought to avoid legal controls and tried to work cooperatively between regulators and regulated. These differences, though declining, remain important and are well illustrated by how the two nations have gone about a key regulatory task that is central to this chapter: controlling the financial relations between parties and business. The contrast starts with different histories. The United States has nearly a thirty-year head start in applying the law to these relations. As we have seen from this chapter, the first significant legislation was passed as the Federal Election Campaign Act of 1971 and the key regulatory agency, the FEC, was established in 1974. The corresponding UK legislation was not passed until 2000 (the Elections and Political Parties Act) that also established the UK regulatory agency, the Electoral Commission. The FEC and the UK Electoral Commission operate with very different styles. The American agency has an established history of both shaping regulations and of resorting to the law to enforce its mandate. As we note in this chapter, between the 1980s and 2006, it imposed penalties exceeding $50,000 on 225 violators, and it was escalating its enforcement activity as time went on (Federal Election Commission 2007). The Electoral Commission has been much more low key in its approach. It defines its mandate indeed in more than regulatory terms, interpreting its role as encompassing political education and encouraging citizen participation in parties and elections (Electoral Commission 2008*a*). The enforcement style of the Electoral Commission, notably its hesitation to use legal sanctions, is well illustrated by its statement in its latest Annual Report – a very short passage in a report otherwise concerned with more promotional matters:

As a result of our investigations, we made two referrals to the Metropolitan Police. Another case, which involved the acceptance of an impermissible donation, was not referred to the police and as the sum was voluntarily forfeited we did not need to apply to the courts for a forfeiture Order. We have developed a close working relationship with the police and prosecuting bodies, which will form the basis of more formal protocols going forward. (Electoral Commission 2008*b*: 6)

By contrast, the most recently available annual report from the FEC is dominated by enforcement issues. It includes a detailed 'enforcement profile' and shows that over 300 legal cases were 'closed' during the year. The 'laws and regulations' section of the US Commission's web site has over twenty subsections detailing laws, regulations, and Commission guidance on party financing. The contrasting cases show, however, the pressures for convergence between the two systems. The Electoral Commission's traditionally 'British' regulatory style has drawn criticism which is slowly pushing it in a more legalistic direction. The most notable criticism has come from the Committee on Standards in Public Life in its review of the workings of the Commission (Committee on Standards in Public Life 2007). The Commission's new corporate plan, unveiled in 2008, is designed to respond to that criticism by an increasing emphasis on its enforcement role and by calling for more statutory powers (Electoral Commission 2008c). But the Committee on Standards in Public Life mounted a more fundamental critique of the culture of the commission, reflecting differences over the extent to which the regulatory system for political parties should move in a move adversarial direction. How far these differences will be resolved in favour of the adoption of a style of regulation that resembles that of the FEC remains to be seen.

small donations from large number of citizens. The 2008 Democratic nominee Barack Obama raised most of his funds for the primary campaign in this way: in a single month, January 2008, he raised $28 million, out of a total income of $32 million, through separate small Internet donations (Mosk 2008). But this kind of financing is only available to a small number of candidates with high national visibility, and it cannot yet generate sufficient cash to make even an Obama independent of business support: by the time he was campaigning as Democratic nominee, Obama was turning to sponsorship by rich investors like Warren Buffet (Luo and Drew 2008).

The second kind of business advantage can be understood by realizing that the relationship between elected politicians and business is embedded in the wider system of business lobbying described in earlier chapters. Influence does not primarily depend on getting pledges out of politicians at election time. Corporate interests we know, dominate the lobbying system in the United States. Politicians are not only, or even primarily, influenced by business at the moment when they seek to raise campaign finance, but are, whether in the White House, in Congress, in the Mayor's office, or in the Governor's mansion, also the object of unremitting and intense lobbying. Periodic corruption scandals reflect the fact that politicians and the lobbyists for business interests live in the same networks and are constantly exchanging things: not just money for favours, but also advice, information, and even arguments about the substantive merits of policy proposals.

What this observation means is that estimating the influence of business interests in the parties is more than a matter of working out the significance of short-term campaign financing, or understanding the institutional role of business in the life of the party. It is also a matter of setting these features into the wider character of the lobbying system. Conveying this understanding is an important purpose of the next chapter.

The travails of business-friendly parties

It is obvious that, while the historical relations between business interests and the party system have been very different in the United Kingdom and the United States, they have been reshaped in quite similar ways in recent decades. The most important source of this reshaping lies less with business and more with secular changes in party systems and campaigning modes. These changes, the party system literature indicates, are indeed not confined to Anglo America, but represent secular changes in the party systems of the advanced liberal democracies (for an overview, see Webb et al. 2002). Parties are in decline as institutions in civil society. They are becoming, in the language used by Katz and Mair (1995), 'cartel' parties: organizations with low levels of active support in the wider society, surviving by forging close connections with other elite institutions in the state and the economy. As they have declined, so they have been forced to abandon many of the mass-based modes of campaigning, and have professionalized their campaigning to fit their elitist, cartel status.

A consequence of this has been, on both sides of the Atlantic, a sharp rise in the cost of campaigning, as the parties lost their armies of free labour (activists and members). In the United Kingdom, in addition, those active members were themselves important sources of finance. The ensuing hunt for money, however, has taken different forms in the United States and the United Kingdom. In the United Kingdom, the parties still generally control access to elective office, and still control the bulk of campaign spending. The result has been to throw the parties as institutions close to business interests, and to inaugurate a new era of business-friendly party politics in the United Kingdom. In the United States, the historical 'business-friendly' party system has further disintegrated, strengthening the importance of candidate-centred politics. The need to market these candidates has resulted in astronomical increases in the dependence of candidates on business finance. It is this shift to plutocratic politics which is the most striking feature of the link between American parties and business interests in recent decades – a shift which has also inaugurated a new age of scandal and regulation.

The rising importance of business finance thus lies behind a development common to the United States and the United Kingdom: the increased regulation of parties, notably of party finance and notably of party finance raised from business. Although the timing has been different, it is striking that both systems have acquired state regulators (the FEC in the United States and the Electoral Commission in the United Kingdom), both with a duty to regulate party finance. While the styles of national regulation of party finance differ (as they do in regulation more generally), the forces driving regulation are remarkably similar, and they are driving the systems in the same direction. The driving forces are circumvention of the rules by business and the politicians, affliction with periodic scandals, and the consequent creation of ever more elaborate systems of rules and of their enforcement. Party–business relations have thus become entangled in the wider regulatory politics of the business community. This wider regulatory politics is a main theme of the following chapter.

7 Business, Politics, and Society

Understanding the cultural setting of business

This chapter returns us to an argument which loomed large in Chapter 1: that to understand the political position of business we need to know more than the narrowly institutional arrangements under which business operates. In Chapter 1, we surveyed some of the most important competing theoretical positions about business power. What is striking about these is that they differ not only in their views of the institutional capacity of business to exercise power, but also offer competing views about the nature of the wider social and cultural context of business institutions. Evidently, it is not possible to have a theory of the power of business without having a view about its wider social and cultural setting. The purpose of this chapter is therefore to examine some of the competing wider views, and to assess what they can tell us about business politics in the United Kingdom and the United States.

Three accounts here provide a framework for the chapter. All derive from sweeping theories of the nature of modern capitalist society; two are derived from theories – Marxism and pluralism – that were sketched in Chapter 1.

The most striking Marxist accounts can be called Gramscian, after perhaps the single most important Marxist theorist of the last century, the Italian Antonio Gramsci (1891–1937). Gramsci puzzled at a great problem: Why were hierarchies and inequalities, which he believed to be unjust so readily, accepted by their victims? His answer was that holders of social resources – notably economic resources – were able to use those resources to shape the hegemonic (dominant) belief systems of society in their favour (Gramsci 1971: 11–12, 245–6; Jones 2006). The idea of hegemony has deeply influenced modern Marxist understandings of capitalist society. The values of business are commonly argued to be hegemonic in the sense that key features of the business system – the right to appropriate property to private ownership and to allocate resources by market exchange – are accepted more or less instinctively, as if they were part of the natural order of things. The great power of business does not lie therefore in its ability to shape particular policy decisions by lobbying or by control of parties, but in the way a hegemonic ideology guides what both policy makers and the mass of populations think are the right ways to order economic life.

Gramsci attributed a key role to intellectuals in the creation of hegemonic ideologies. Intellectuals operated in elite institutions like the press and universities, and helped form cultural values. They are also central to our second great account, derived from the work of Joseph Schumpeter (1883–1950). Schumpeter's view of business under capitalism has much in common with accounts offered by Marxists. He stresses the dynamic, ever changing character of the capitalist system: it is a restless social phenomenon where 'creative destruction' (Schumpeter's famous phrase) leads to the constant replacement of enterprises by competitors. But a more fundamental destructiveness derives from the culture of the capitalist order. Capitalism swept aside older social forms like feudalism because it was founded on a culture of scepticism and rationality; it ruthlessly exposed the frailties of those older social orders and of their legitimizing ideologies. But this sceptical and rationalistic culture does not disappear with the triumph of capitalism. On the contrary, it intensifies. The very success of capitalism produces strata of intellectuals who in turn sceptically scrutinize the legitimacy of the institutions of capitalism itself – of business institutions – thus demystifying their claims to authority. This produces a cultural setting which is increasingly hostile to business institutions and to the spirit of enterprise in a free market – a very different vision from that of Gramscian hegemony. The 'hegemony' that is shaped by intellectuals results in a climate hostile to business enterprise.

Both Gramsci and Schumpeter agree in picturing advanced capitalist systems as converging in their dominant cultural traits. But they differ in their account of what capitalist systems converge upon: for Gramsci, the convergence is on a culture where business enjoys a dominant, legitimizing ideology; for Schumpeter, convergence consists in the progressive erosion of the ideologies that support the business system.

But what if there is no obvious tendency to convergence? Suppose the cultural and social context of business under advanced capitalism is just contingent on many different conditions – like the particular historical period or the particular national setting? Readers will recognize that this is a relative of a general theory discussed in Chapter 1: pluralism. We already know from earlier chapters that institutions and policy in our two countries are very different. Why, then, should not the social and cultural settings of business be very different? Why should they not reflect a plurality of influences: different institutional settings, different national historical experiences, and different sectors and industries? These three accounts – Gramscian, Schumpeterian, and pluralist – give us a framework to examine the two national experiences.

Box 7.1 Civil society groups and the regulation of business lobbyists in the EU

In June 2008, the European Commission, faced with allegations that business lobbying in Europe was excessively powerful, introduced a voluntary register for lobbyists. But this has failed to appease civil society groups critical of business power in Brussels. In October 2008, a much tougher model of registration was proposed by an alliance of three groups: the EU Civil Society Contact Group, the EU consumers' organization BEUC , and the Alliance for Lobbying Transparency and Ethics Regulation (ALTER-EU), a transparency body (EurActiv 2008). Three features of this episode are revealing. First, the Commission and big business are now in an almost permanently defensive mode in justifying their relationships: the Commissioner responsible for the voluntary register, in rejecting the alternative model, nevertheless conceded that the Commission's model was provisional and that its effectiveness would have to be reviewed after its first year of operation. Second, the alternative model of registration and monitoring is patterned on that in the United States – the system which has been most marked by an adversarial, confrontational model of regulating the business lobby. We know that business lobbies in the EU are influenced by American models and tactics; this example shows that civil society lobbies critical of business exhibit the same pattern of cross-Atlantic learning. Third, and most important, the campaign on the regulation of lobbyists shows the existence of a dense network of civil society groups at work within EU institutions, attempting to combat the power of business lobbies. The EU Civil Society Group was founded in 2002. It brings together environmental campaigning organizations like Greenpeace International, Birdlife International, Friends of the Earth Europe, and Bankwatch Network. The last is particularly instructive of the way civil society groups critical of business are replicating the success of business in multiplying 'niche' action groups: the contact address for Bankwatch Network is c/o Friends of the Earth Europe (EU Civil Society Contact Group 2008). The BEUC (European Consumers' Organization) is one of the longest established lobby groups in Brussels (tracing its origins back to 1962). It now has in membership forty-one independent national consumer organizations drawn from some thirty European countries. It acts, in its own words, as a kind of 'embassy' in Brussels for the consumer lobby. And as the range of national members indicates, it is not confined to organizations from EU member states, but covers also members from applicant countries and from the EEA – membership of which encompasses the twenty-seven members of the EU plus Iceland, Lichenstein, and Norway (BEUC 2008). The ALTER-EU is a coalition of over 160 civil society groups, trade unions, and public affairs firms concerned, in its own words, 'with the increasing influence exerted by corporate lobbyists on the political agenda in Europe'(Alter-EU 2008.). The mere existence of these groups in itself of course demonstrates nothing about the effectiveness of civil society critics of the business lobby in the EU: it is perfectly possible that large national coalitions of such groups suffer the same problems of cohesion as are suffered by business groups. But the existence of such groups reminds us of an elementary but critical point that has recurred many times in the pages of this book: lobbying is a competitive business. What matters is not the existence, or even the resources, of an organized lobby: the critical factor is how effectively an interest operates against its competitive critics. The dense network of civil society groups at EU level shows that business lobbies have to operate in such a competitive and critical environment. In estimating the likely success of a firm's products in the marketplace, we would not just focus on the strengths of those products, but we would also compare them with the attractiveness of rivals. Likewise, it only makes sense to estimate the power of a business lobby by comparing it with the workings of its political rivals.

The United Kingdom: the transformation of a hegemonic order

We know from our discussion in Chapter 2 that the critical historical feature of British business was that it created the first industrial society, and that this society was based on the principles of capitalism. In Chapter 2, we also described the way this historical feature helped shape the wider social and cultural setting of business, so we need here only briefly summarize that historical context.

The first great modern industrial capitalist enterprises had emerged by the middle of the nineteenth century. The social and cultural setting of this business system was immensely favourable to business autonomy and privilege. Most of the population was excluded from government, which was the preserve of oligarchies dominated by the traditional aristocracy, its clients, and some allies from manufacturing itself. Culturally, this was a society where there was deference to social hierarchy, especially to hierarchy backed up by property ownership.

In this setting, the most successful enterprises in finance and manufacturing enjoyed great autonomy and privilege. Business regulation meant self-regulation. In the City of London, this meant that the markets controlled their own affairs. But we also know from Chapter 2 that even when the state created regulatory laws – for instance, in health and safety for the workplace or environmental pollution – those laws were implemented in a business-friendly fashion. And we also know from Chapter 2 that this regulatory culture persisted well into the twentieth century.

Did this mean that business values and institutions were hegemonic? Far from it, for autonomy and privilege were bought at a price. Here lay the cultural weakness of business interests. The price was that, while business ruled in its own spheres, like the regulation of the enterprise, it was weak and excluded in other key social spheres, and was often culturally marginalized. That weakness and marginalization particularly affected manufacturing enterprise. Two instances are particularly important. First, there is convincing evidence that the wider culture, especially the culture of elite institutions in British society, was unsympathetic to the life of business, especially the business of manufacturing. For most of the twentieth century, the elite universities, which trained governing and business leaders, declined to teach many 'vocational' subjects, and as lesser universities climbed the ladder of prestige, they sloughed off their vocational origins. Within business itself, professions like law, and the life of City banking and stock broking, enjoyed more prestige than manufacturing. Thus, the manufacturing sectors that had created British world supremacy were actually often disdained by educational elites, by governing elites, and by elites in finance (Nettl 1965; Wiener 1981/1998; Barnett 2001).

A second weakness flowed from this wider social and cultural subordination. The central state had little influence over the daily life of business; but business, especially manufacturing, had little influence over some of the key policies of government. The civil service and political elite in Whitehall and Westminster had small experience of business life, and were dominated by individuals educated at elite universities with little interest in vocational education. The history of British economic policy for the first three quarters of the twentieth century shows that the core of economic policy making – in 10 Downing Street, in the Treasury, and in the Bank of England – had priorities very different from those of fostering manufacturing competitiveness. These elites were more concerned with the management of national prestige and with the conduct of economic policy as an instrument of national prestige. A well-documented example is the way the management of sterling was designed to advance wide strategic objectives in foreign policy, and was insensitive to the effects on the export competitiveness of British manufacturing industry (Strange 1971; Pollard 1992).

The cultural legacy therefore bequeathed to the enterprise in Britain is complex and contradictory. There undoubtedly was a kind of Gramscian hegemonic regulatory ideology, which lasted well into the second half of the twentieth century. It consisted in the widespread assumption that business was the best regulator of its own affairs. This endowed business with great control over the daily life of the enterprise. But the price of this was the exclusion of business from many key policy-making processes in central government and the pursuit of economic policies that were damaging to the interests of the enterprise, especially of the manufacturing enterprise.

Much of this has been described in the past tense because, as we shall now see, the social and cultural settings have greatly changed in the last quarter century. That change has occurred is undeniable; but we shall also see that there is room for debate about whether change has strengthened or weakened business interests.

The mid- and later 1970s were critical years in reshaping the setting of business in British society, as they were critical in reshaping much else about Britain. A great crisis of the British economy, already one of the weakest in the advanced capitalist world, was sparked by the wider international economic turmoil caused by oil price rises in the wake of the Arab–Israeli War of October 1973. That in turn signalled the end of a 'long boom' across the advanced capitalist world that had lasted virtually for twenty-five years, and the end of the boom brutally exposed the weaknesses of the British economy – and the international uncompetitiveness of much of British business. The crisis, and the conclusions from the crisis drawn by governing elites in Britain, produced important changes in the governing culture. Although the changes are mostly associated with Thatcherism in the 1980s, there had already occurred a more general cultural shift in the late 1970s even before the ascendancy of

Thatcherism. This shift accepted important elements of the 'anti-business culture' thesis. It accepted that there were 'too few producers' in the words of an influential critique of the time (Bacon and Eltis 1976). It accepted that the public sector was too unproductive and too large, that institutions like universities and schools needed to connect more directly to the needs of business, and that public policy needed likewise to be more closely geared to the needs and wishes of business.

This new policy agenda shaped much of what government did in the 1980s. Leading figures in the new Thatcher Administration, such as Sir Keith Joseph, the most important intellectual influence inside the Cabinet, were deeply influenced by the 'anti-business culture' argument and by the argument that the 'industrial spirit' of enterprise and innovation was undervalued (Denham and Garnett 2001). The 'Thatcher Revolution' tried to reshape British culture and British institutions in a business-friendly fashion. Though Thatcherites would have been horrified by the comparison, one could say that they were attempting to create a new Gramscian hegemony. The results were, however, mixed in their impact on the power and privilege of business.

Some results plainly did advantage business, especially big business. Labour market policies in the 1980s tilted the balance of power in the workplace towards business: they greatly reduced trade union power by a mix of legislative change and policy initiatives, and they greatly strengthened the hands of business managers. In a series of high-profile struggles between employers and powerful unions – notably in coal mining and in newspaper printing – the government successfully used employers as auxiliaries in battles that destroyed traditionally powerful unions. An ambitious policy of privatization shrank the public sector to the benefit of the private sector: the domains of private business thus greatly expanded. The government's policies also helped produce a wider cultural shift in what remained in the public domain. The language and culture of business were introduced into the daily operations of institutions of the public sector, like health and education. Broader economic policies, such as the reduction of taxation rates on corporate earnings and on the highest income earners, were also designed to reward business elites.

Most of these changes began under Mrs Thatcher's Premiership after 1979, but they were continued under her Conservative successor John Major (1990–7). More important still, none of the key Thatcherite reforms were reversed under New Labour which ruled in Westminster after 1997: there was continuity in respect of industrial relations law, privatization, taxation, and the introduction of business interests and concepts into the public sector (Coates and Lawler 2000; Coates 2005). As we saw in the last chapter, New Labour has been determined to present itself as a business-friendly party. In short, for over a quarter of a century now, determined attempts have been made by governing elites in Britain to reinforce business domination. We are seeing the attempted creation of Gramscian hegemony – the attempt to establish a culture where business domination seems part of the natural order of things.

The success of these changes is, however, limited by three factors: the effects of other policies associated with the revolution of recent decades, the effects of changes in the wider regulatory environment of the business system, and the effects of cultural changes in Britain only indirectly connected with the actions of either government or business. We examine each of these in turn.

Some important 'by-products' of the policy revolution have proved destructive of the traditional sources of business hegemony. Business self-regulation had its roots in a deferential and pre-democratic Britain. Recent decades have seen grave damage done to these very institutions of self-regulation. They were transformed in their traditional heartland, the City of London, into something very different: a system of regulation managed by a publicly accountable agency, the Financial Services Authority, which administers an increasingly complex set of rules, based on law. The great financial crisis of 2007–9, which began with the nationalization of Northern Rock, and culminated in the partial nationalization of most of the biggest banks, has subjected the financial regulatory system to even more regulatory controls. The regulation of the most economically sensitive professions – commercial law, accounting, and auditing – also witnessed persistent corrosion of the structures of self-regulation. The hegemonic ideology of self-regulation – where it was instinctively assumed that business had an unchallenged right to control its own affairs – has thus been weakened. If business now wants self-regulation, it has to argue the case (Moran 2007: 67–94). After the near collapse of the banking system in the autumn of 2008, it finds this case increasingly hard to make.

Parallel changes have come over another part of that traditional hegemonic ideology, the part that stressed the importance of practising 'business-friendly' regulation in cases, like safety at work, where the state and the law were historically present. The evidence from a wide range of domains – environmental regulation, health and safety at work, and pollution control – paints a consistent picture: domains once regulated informally and cooperatively with business are seeing a shift to more formal, legally based, systems of regulation where there is much more emphasis on business compliance with externally prescribed rules (ibid.: 131–8).

One reason for these developments can be traced to a well-documented paradox of Thatcherism: it simultaneously dismantled some state controls but reinforced others. Gamble's characterization (1994) of Thatcherism as involving 'the free economy and the strong state' catches this: reforms involved the attempt by the state actively to redesign civil society so as to promote the free market and achieve greater national competitiveness. This produced not only institutional change, but also a change in regulatory style, as the central state became more aggressive and activist in the way it dealt with business interests. The simple division of labour that once existed – where business controlled its internal affairs and central government ran economic policy – broke down. Wilks's work on a key area of regulation – competition and merger policy – has documented this shift. This is how he contrasts the two landmark pieces of legislation governing competition and monopoly, separated by a period of fifty years. He begins with a reference to the law of the late 1940s that first established a system of control over monopoly, and then contrasts it with the regime at the end of the twentieth century:

the 1948 Act catered to the voluntarism, the self-regulation, and the accommodative arm's-length relationship between government and industry that permeated the political economy of the 1940s. The 1998 Act creates a more formal and legally objective framework for industry. It provides didactic guidance rather than the cooperative exploration that underlay its 1948 predecessor. (Wilks 1999: 322)

This formal shift has also been accompanied by a much more activist pursuit of firms that breach competition law, coupled with the imposition of historically unprecedented penalties. In 2007, British Airways lost several senior executives, and paid fines in excess of £270 million to the Office of Fair Trading (OFT) and the US Department of Justice, when it admitted attempts at fare fixing (Done et al. 2007). (At the time of writing, criminal charges are also in progress against some of the former executives.) In June 2008, the OFT raided the offices of two bank giants – Barclays and Royal Bank of Scotland – in search of evidence of price collusion. The case of competition policy also highlights an additional source of change: the rise, in the case of the EU, of a business regulator with very different traditions and expectations from those that dominated UK policy domestically. Wilks again has documented the rise of the European Commission (through DGIV, the competent regulator) to what he calls the 'most effective antitrust regime in the world.' (Wilks and McGowan 1996; Wilks 1999: 300; Wilks and Bartle 2002). In 2007, the EU scored a notable victory over a corporate giant when Microsoft agreed to comply with its finding (backed by a ruling of the European Court of Justice) that it must lower prices and allow competitors access to its technology. Compliance from Microsoft came after a struggle lasting several years, and involved the imposition of fines totalling nearly €800 million on the corporation (Buck 2006; Bounds and Dixon 2007).

From the 1980s, therefore, business in Britain faced a policy environment very different from that which had been historically dominant: one where many assumptions about the right of business to control its own affairs were now open to challenge. These changes, we have seen, can be traced in part to the way the attempt to rebuild the UK economy demanded a more interventionist regulatory system, and partly to changes – like the impact of the EU – which independently reshaped the institutional environment of business life.

To this must be added the third factor identified above: wider cultural changes that affect perceptions of the legitimacy of the business enterprise. This goes to the heart of the problem of business power, for the most important part of the policy revolution of recent years has not been institutional, but cultural: to create a society where business values are hegemonic. Political elites evacuated many historically important positions precisely with this aim in mind: we have seen that New Labour abandoned many of its historically established policies and accepted those – such as restrictions on union power and privatization – introduced in the Thatcherite revolution.

But this transformation in *elite* culture was not matched by what a Gramscian might expect: a corresponding change in the wider civil society. On the contrary, as elites moved in favour of business, the wider society actually increased its hostility. There are several striking instances of this. In the 1970s – at the moment when the attempt to create a more business-friendly environment began – the main institutional opponents of business, the trade unions, were consistently evaluated unfavourably in polls of the population at large. But after thirty years of business-friendly policies, evaluations have altered significantly. Now, it is big business that is viewed as untrustworthy and lacking in social conscience by a majority of the population (Glover 2006; Moran 2006).

Moreover, while it is indeed the case that an important counterweight to business – trade unionism – has been greatly weakened, new institutional critics of business have become important. Some of these are creations of recent decades, like the environmental groups such as Friends of the Earth that inflicted the damaging defeats documented in Chapter 4. Some are traditionally conservative institutions that until recently could be relied on to support business elites. Thus, the social stance of the Catholic Church – a traditionally reactionary institution – has been radicalized in recent decades. Some are established charities, like the large-aid charities, which have widened beyond charitable relief to policy advocacy (Moran 2006). Alongside this mix of old and new critics stands a more diffuse world of radical action against either business as a whole or against particular industries. The campaigns mounted by these groups span a wide range. Some have engaged in violent attacks on whole sets of institutions, as was the case with anti-globalization protests in the City of London in June 1999 (themselves part of a set of protests in other leading cities). Some have involved campaigns against individual businesses that were either directly violent or worked on the borderline of legality. In Britain, opponents of the use of animals in experiments have conducted a sustained campaign against leading pharmaceutical companies and the academic research institutes to which they are linked. Some campaigns against business involve peaceful lobbies – often allied to traditional institutions like churches – that target the sourcing, the employment, or the trading practices of individual corporations; some, like part of the animal rights movement, have involved serious illegality.

These institutional developments are inseparable from some wider cultural changes in the environment of business. One critical development concerns media treatment of the enterprise. Business practices and institutions, notably those in financial markets, have been 'mainstreamed'. In other words, activities that were once only reported in specialist outlets, mostly in the printed media, are now a staple of mainstream news: of newspaper reporting and of programmes in the broadcast media. (The rise of 'mainstreaming' is a phenomenon shared with the United States, see Clark et al. 2004). Scrutiny of big business – often connected to criticism of its employment and trading practices – has increased. (In the United States, we shall see below a similar development in allied media, also widely available in Britain: the development in film and television of a genre of successful productions which are critical of business practices.) It is possible that this increased media exposure, often of a hostile kind, helps explain the cultural shift identified earlier: the change in public perceptions of business, especially big business, and the development of an institutional world which is critical of the practices of large corporations.

It will be plain that developments over the last three decades have produced complex changes in the social and cultural setting of the business system and of the individual enterprise. It is indeed the case that we have been witnessing the attempt to develop a 'Gramscian project' by governing elites. Institutions and groups that traditionally criticized business in Britain – notably in the Labour Movement – have been marginalized. But there is no Gramscian hegemony. On the contrary, the story is very mixed as far as business is concerned. An older hegemony – one that privileged self-regulation and was deferential to business interests – has passed away, to be replaced by a very different system of legally based regulation.

But if a Gramscian account does not fully convince in the case of Britain, neither do the developments described here vindicate the interpretation we might derive from Schumpeter: of a culture reshaped by intellectual elites into hostility to the market order. Indeed, some of the confrontations between individual business and state agencies derive from a determination on the part of the latter more aggressively to enforce market competition: that is part of the story of the role of the Office of Fair Trading in prosecutions of firms like British Airways. Elite opinion shapers have been deeply divided. Many elite commentators have been among the cheerleaders for neo-liberalism and deregulation; others have been highly critical of big business. And, in a manner that a Marxist might expect, capitalists in competition with each other have turned out to be a highly damaging 'hostile brotherhood': the price-fixing case against British Airways documented above was supported by a competitor, Virgin Airlines, which 'blew the whistle' on a price-fixing

---

Box 7.2 Lobbying a corporation about its marketing practices in the developing world: Nestlé and the baby milk campaigns

---

Nestlé is a Swiss-based multinational, one of the longest established multinational corporations (1866). It produces what brand researchers identify as one of the top ten iconic global brands, Nescafe (Sklair 2001: 86, 120–1). It has also been the subject of one of the longest, best-organized campaigns by civil society groups aimed at controlling corporate marketing practices in the developing world. The campaign centres on the marketing by Nestlé of dried baby milk. Campaigners claim that it is nutritionally inferior to mothers' milk. They also claim that unscrupulous marketing practices mean that mothers in developing countries are persuaded unnecessarily to use the milk, and that low levels of literacy also mean that mothers cannot understand the instructions that would make the milk safe to consume. The campaign has pioneered many of the methods now used by civil society groups against multinationals. It began in the 1970s with a German campaign that led to a libel suit by the company (see below). The first coalition (INFACT – Infant Formula Action Coalition) was launched in the United States in 1977. Now, through the International Baby Food Action Network, it covers groups in over 100 countries. It has proved remarkably sophisticated in lobbying international health organizations, and was the driving force behind the formulation in 1981 by the World Health Assembly of the International Code of Marketing Breast-Milk Substitutes. This Code has proved to be the crux of the case both for and against the company. Two other features of the campaign are notable. First, it has spread from a single focus on Nestlé to a wider concern with multinational food marketing practices in the developing world. Second, it has proved adept at using the Web to publicize and propagandize: see for instance the web sites of INFACT (http://www.ibfan.org/) and of Baby Milk Action (http://www.babymilkaction.org/). It is, however, hard to know how much significant impact this has had on Nestlé's fortunes. On the one hand, global consumer polls show it to be one of the most boycotted brands on earth, alongside Coca Cola and McDonald's (Tren 2005). On the other hand, the diversity of its products means that, for ordinary consumers, identification for purposes of boycott, beyond obvious icons like Nescafe, is difficult. What is without doubt is that the campaign has produced a drastic change in the political tactics used by the company, and this change is emblematic of a wider shift in corporate political strategy. In the 1970s, Nestlé reacted aggressively. The original libel action was brought by the company against its critics. But the favourable court judgement was so hedged round with judicial comments and qualifications that it amounted to a Pyrrhic victory. As was the case with another famous libel action by a multinational against critics (McDonald's), it served more to create sympathy for critics. Now the company concentrates on trying to convince consumers, governments, and civil society groups that it does indeed comply with the International Code of Marketing Breast-Milk Substitutes, and that any failures to observe the code are due to actions of local employees, who are suitably disciplined. It also invests heavily in reputation management strategies, such as corporate philanthropy in the developing world. The fact that the campaign is so long established thus allows us to observe the evolution of corporate strategies in the face of the growth of critics in civil society. The most striking feature of Nestlé's behaviour is the way it confirms the argument of this chapter. The company began with highly adversarial, confrontational tactics, but its behaviour is now marked by a much more subtle understanding of how difficult issues can be managed in the media, and by the way it plainly appreciates that the baby-milk issue cannot be dealt with in isolation, but has to be integrated into a wider strategy of corporate reputation management. How successful in the long run this strategy will prove we simply cannot tell. The story is still unfolding. Civil society groups have also proved increasingly sophisticated, especially in dissemination and mobilization, and have proved remarkably tenacious in pursuing the company over more than three decades.

approach; and the EU case against Microsoft was prompted in part by lobbying on the part of some of the Microsoft's competitors who wanted to improve their competitiveness against the software giant (Done et al. 2007).

The United States: between Gramsci and Schumpeter

In earlier chapters, notably in Chapter 2, we discussed the social and cultural legacy of American business, terminating our discussion at a moment in the 1960s when, most commentators agree, important changes took place in the environment within which business had to operate. Here, we briefly recall the terms of the legacy before turning to that new environment.

Any national society and culture is bound to be shot through with contradictory traits. The United States is no exception, and these contradictions, we can recall, ran through the historical experience of American business. On the one hand, a variety of historically established features contrived to give the business system a hugely favourable environment, endowing it with more prestige than that enjoyed by business in Britain: there was no preceding aristocratic culture to offer an alternative social hierarchy or an alternative to commercial values; with the North's victory in the Civil War, the foundations were laid for a system of industrial capitalism that gave enormous wealth, prestige, and political prominence to large enterprises and to the figures who created them; America's emergence as a world superpower during and after the Second World War was bound up with the global expansion of American big business. On the other hand, the very disruption associated with these massive economic and social changes had prompted the original development of Populism. This grew out of an agricultural culture of egalitarianism; it celebrated the small and the local – in business and politics – against the large and the national. It crystallized in suspicion of both 'big government' in Washington and 'big bankers' on Wall Street.

These two traditions – those that place business at the centre of cultural and society, and those that view its manifestation in large organizations as a malign interest to be controlled – hold the key to what has happened historically to the long-term social and cultural setting of business; and we shall see in a moment that they continue to shape the experience of business in American society. Viewed with the benefit of hindsight, the two decades after the Second World War look like a golden age of business culture. The New Deal had successfully stabilized American capitalism: from the early 1940s, the American economy began a sustained period of growth that spread mass prosperity. The large corporation had learnt the techniques of mass communication and persuasion sufficiently well to create 'the corporate soul', in Marchand's (1998) phrase: in other words, to endow the corporation with a perceived personality that transcended mere economic calculation and that established it as an important and benign institution in American life. The emergence of the United States as the world's leading economic and political power conferred on American business, and especially on the large corporations that dominated the world economy, enormous prestige, and self-confidence. The confidence this produced was exemplified by the remark of Charles Wilson, the head of the giant General Motors Corporation, that 'what was good for the country was good for General Motors and vice versa.' (Wilson actually made the remark in 1953 at his Senate confirmation hearings on appointment as Secretary of Defence under the new Presidency of Dwight Eisenhower – an administration that recruited a large number of leading business executives.)

In short, it seemed for a period that the historical tensions between two views of big business – as exemplifying the dominant values of American life or as threatening the core values of American society – had been resolved in favour of the former view. But experience since then has shown that, on the contrary, these contradictions remain intense. The contradictions and tensions have reappeared, often in a highly explosive way.

There are five signs of this, and they are discussed here in turn: a change in the character of business regulation, a related intensification of a tradition of adversarial legalism, a rise in lobbies surrounding the giant corporation, a long-term shift in public opinion, and a shift in the outlook of some parts of elite opinion.

CHANGING CHARACTER OF REGULATION

The change in the character of business regulation dates from the era of the 'new social regulation', whose origins most observers trace back to a few years of hectic legislative activism in the late 1960s and early 1970s, when Congress passed measures governing environmental, workplace, and consumer protection (Eisner et al. 2006: 37–9). This new era of regulation had a number of distinctive features. The most important, as the name suggests, is that it involved a widening in the range of regulatory tasks. The regulatory agencies of the New Deal, and before, had essentially been concerned with instances of market failure: for instance, with combating attempts by business to 'rig' competition or, as in the case of the Securities and Exchange Commission, with regulating honesty and openness in financial markets. Now a whole new set of agencies and laws appeared that attempted to control the social dimensions of business: health and safety in the workplace, discrimination in employment, control of the environmental impacts of economic activity, and protection of consumers at the point of purchase. The changes also involved an important shift in principle: whereas traditional 'market failure' regulation had focused on the control of individual firms, the new social regulation now involved the regulation by general principles of whole sectors and markets. It applied general proscriptions or injunctions to business life, and attempted to narrow the range of bureaucratic discretion in implementing regulation. In doing this, it helped intensify adversarial legalism.

INTENSIFICATION OF ADVERSARIAL LEGALISM

A considerable body of work has established that American 'adversarial legalism' (Kagan 2001) is distinctive: that is, businesses in the United States have been much more likely than their counterparts in the United Kingdom (and elsewhere in Europe) to be subjected to civil or criminal sanctions or indeed to meet contesting parties in court. The sheer scale of the new social regulation strengthened this culture. Stewart has summarized the important changes that consequently came over both the procedures and culture of American business regulation:

After 1960, Congress created many regulatory programmes – most notably health, safety, environmental, and anti-discrimination programmes – that apply to many or all industries or employers. Faced with the necessity of regulating very large numbers of firms, agencies shifted from a case-by-case adjudication (the traditional procedure for making and enforcing regulatory policy) to adoption of highly specific regulations of general applicability.... At the same time, the large number of firms and industries affected, and the conflicts of interest among them, made negotiated solutions more difficult. (1988: 107)

CORPORATIONS MORE AGGRESSIVELY LOBBIED

The rise of legal adversarialism is in turn connected to another development: the practice of 'lobbying the corporation', in Vogel's phrase (1978). Corporations, we know from earlier chapters, are formidable lobbyists; but as the giant corporation has become increasingly recognized as a powerful 'visible hand' in social allocation, it has itself become the object of well-organized lobbying. Perhaps the most striking feature of the political life of the large American corporation in the last generation is the extent to which institutions in the wider civil society have increasingly directed their efforts at trying to shape its internal decision making. The plethora of groups varies along a number of dimensions, particularly in radicalism, in methods used, and in their history. Some are well-established institutions that for long had little interest in affecting corporate behaviour, but which have now developed precisely such an interest: two very good examples are the established churches, which traditionally were quiescent in their dealings with corporations in which they often had substantial investments, but which have now almost universally become more assertive; and some long-established environmental groups, like the Sierra Club (Eisner 2007: 46–7). To these recently active established groups, we should add a range founded in the last three decades that lobby the corporation, and are inspired by a diversity of ideas: environmentalism, consumerism, feminism, and pacifism, to name only four (Berry 1999). What is more, the evidence is that the growth in the number of advocacy groups seems to have been disproportionately concentrated among non-business organizations (Skocpol 2003: 145).

We should not imagine that all these attempts to lobby the corporation are radical, or anti-capitalist, in intent. Some indeed do spring from quite fundamental opposition to key features of advanced capitalism: the most obvious examples include the anti-globalization alliances and some of the 'deep-green' environmentalist groups that see the corporation as an agent of a destructive and humanity threatening industrialism. Some, like many church groups, are much more piecemeal in their demands. Some, indeed, such as stockholder activism groups, share with corporate elites the quite conventional aim of extracting the maximum in shareholder value from corporate operations; they just want executives to pursue those aims more ruthlessly. That does not, however, make them easier to deal with: on the contrary, since their focus is often on details of everyday corporate activities, such as the remuneration of top executives, rather than grand critiques of the whole corporate order, they make quite immediate demands for changes in the policies of individual enterprises.

MORE HOSTILE PUBLIC OPINION

The rising population of groups lobbying the enterprise seems to be connected to a wider change in the environment of the large corporation, one which has already cropped up a number of times in earlier pages. It seems that there has occurred a sea change in the last generation in popular attitudes to the corporation, and that the change involves greater popular hostility. All generalizations about public opinion have to be made with caution, and the caution needs to be redoubled when we are making generalizations about trends, especially about trends that cover a long time period. It nevertheless really does seem to be the case that this change has occurred. (We may gain further confidence from the fact that it resembles a trend already identified in the case of Britain.) When we go back as far as we can safely go – to opinion polls dating from the 1960s – the image of big business seems to have been increasingly damaged. Giant corporations are decreasingly trusted, and there is a decreasing belief that their activities contribute to the common good. What is more, there is also now a striking contrast between public perceptions of large corporations and small business – with the latter gaining much higher approval ratings (Vogel 1996: 271; Dennis 2004: 11–13). In other words, the established historical pattern originating in Populism seems to have reasserted itself. The revelations surrounding the collapse of financial institutions on Wall Street in the autumn 2008 strengthened this revival of the Populist tradition.

MORE HOSTILE ELITE OPINION

It is possible that this long-term shift in public opinion is linked to the fifth and final development summarized here, though whether as cause or effect is hard to determine: a change in the character of the opinions of some elite groups to an outlook which is more sceptical about the market order in general, and big corporations in particular. Business, especially big business, retains powerful instruments of mass communication, and we shall see in a moment how it uses these to defend its position. But there are at least two signs of the development of attitudes critical of big business, and in some instances of the market order, in elite institutions of American society.

The first is connected to a major institutional development of the last generation: the huge expansion of the system of higher education. Universities are highly diverse places, and the American university system, partly because of its size and because of the complex mix of private and public institutions that it encompasses, is particularly diverse. But universities – in part because of the genuine protection provided by the system of academic tenure – are significant centres of criticism of big business and the market order. This has been true historically, but two developments are new: the critical turn taken in large parts of the academy in the 1960s which provided important intellectual foundations for the new social regulation (Eisner et al. 2006: 37–8), and the sheer scale of the university system which has made it as central to American society as is the corporation. The elite American university perhaps comes closest to Schumpeter's vision of an institution that fosters groups able sceptically to interrogate the pretensions of business institutions and the market order. Take the case of Yale University, one of the leading elite institutions. Yale's greatest political scientist of the last half century, Robert Dahl, turned after the 1970s from a defender of American pluralism to a sustained critic of the corporation (Dahl 1961, 1985). His colleague Charles Lindblom produced the most influential book of the 1970s which argued that fully developed democracy was incompatible with corporate capitalism (Lindblom 1977). And at the other end of the time scale, his Yale colleague James Gustave Speth published in 2008 an influential book arguing that capitalism as it now operates is incompatible with environmental sustainability – or even human survival (Speth 2008).

The second sign of the growth of elite hostility to business concerns the institutions of the mass media. Berry has documented the considerable change in the tone of media, especially television, reporting of business since the 1960s (Berry 1999: 119–30; Berry and Wilcox 2008). In part, the change connects to a feature we have already identified – the 'mainstreaming' of business reporting, so that it is no longer confined to specialist media but is a staple of main headline news. This has coincided with the onset of an age of scandal in business life, in which much business reporting is concerned with the critical reporting of the conduct of business life, the exposure of 'scandals' and the aggressive interviewing of figures who speak on behalf of business. In turn this has been influenced by the activities of groups identified above – the new lobbyists of the corporation who, naturally, try to pursue their case via the mass media.

One of the oddities of the rise of this culture of criticism of big business in the mass media is that, in the case of television, it is commonly transmitted by companies that are themselves part of giant enterprises. A similar paradox can be seen in another important area of cultural criticism, the creative film industry. Hollywood has a long history of making outstanding movies informed by a populist critique of the wickedness of big business, especially of big finance: that is a theme of a classic like *Citizen Kane* (1941), a bleak account of the corrupted life of a tycoon based on the life of the controller of the Hearst newspaper empire; and *It's a Wonderful Life* (1946), where the fate of a small town is pictured as imperilled by a wicked banker – an exercise in pure Populism. In recent decades, this critical tradition has been renewed. The ideological foundations of many hit films that have nothing overtly to do with big business nevertheless convey powerful messages critical of the business order. A particularly significant example from the world of adult cinema is provided by one of the great classics of the 1970s, the Godfather movies (especially part I, 1972, and part II, 1974). In these films, criminality is viewed as exemplifying an American way of business success, and the Mafia pictured as a corporate venture fundamentally like any other. Some of the most striking lines from the movies – 'nothing personal, just business' – have entered the language. And in a development paralleling the changes in the reporting of business news, a considerable mainstream market has developed for films that expose the allegedly antisocial activities of big business: they include hits like *Wall Street* (1987), an attack on the culture of big finance; *Super Size Me* (2004) an attack on McDonald's, an enterprise that has suffered media criticism over a long period; and *The Smartest Guys in the Room* (2005), which gleefully exposed the culture that led to the collapse of the Enron Corporation (for Enron see also the discussion in Chapter 6). Many films critical in this way have been made by small independent moviemakers, but they typically depend for commercial success on the willingness of large corporations to distribute films that contain hostile anti-big business messages: *Super Size Me*, for example, was given its television broadcast in North America by MSNBC, a joint venture of two corporate giants, Microsoft and NBC.

But while the cultural context in which big-business operates has become more difficult in the last generation, this is not the whole story. An obvious qualification is that the institutions we have described above as displaying hostility are pluralistic in their structures and cultures. American universities not only foster critiques of the business order and advocates of stricter regulation, but also provide important service functions – through their research and teaching – for big business. Yale not only produces critics of capitalism like Lindblom and Speth, but also graduated the two Bush Presidents (1988–92 and 2000–8), pillars of the American corporate order. The pluralism of American intellectual life also means that – especially in departments of economics and in law schools – universities produce powerful advocates of neo-liberalism and of market deregulation. The (University of) Chicago school of economic theory, which deeply influenced public policy from the 1970s on, is a good example. (Though this did not mean that academic advocates of deregulation did what big business liked: the great economist Alfred Kahn, during his tenure as head of the main federal agency regulating the airlines, dismantled cartels in the face of opposition from the big airlines, dismissing aeroplanes as 'marginal costs with wings'; McCraw 1984: 22.) Likewise, the growth of a newly adversarial style in reporting of business affairs has been matched by another kind of adversarialism: the development of channels – the most famous of which is probably the Fox News Channel, the largest of the cable news subscription channels in the United States – which are closely aligned to the business priorities of their owners and which overtly produce propaganda for the market order.

The rise of this new pro-business adversarialism is connected to a set of developments within business institutions, some of which we have touched upon in earlier chapters. Three are particularly important. First, we know from earlier chapters that there has been a transformation in the sophistication of business lobbying in the last generation – a development that plainly responds to a much more competitive lobbying environment and to a much more questioning cultural setting for business. The sophistication has partly consisted in improving the quality of the specialized lobbying operations themselves, and in part in a realization that specialized lobbying alone is often ineffective: it is necessary to integrate this kind of lobbying with a more sustained attention to public perceptions of enterprises and brands, precisely because of the growth of scepticism among wider publics. Hence the convergence that we described in Chapters 3 and 4 of orthodox lobbying with corporate PR.

Second, we can see in the last generation a change in the way business, especially big business, manages the problem of collective action. This goes to the heart of trying to create a business-friendly culture, as distinct from advantaging one enterprise or industry. The transformation of big-business lobbying which we described in Chapters 3 and 4 catches this development. The formation of the Business Roundtable coincided with the development of a more difficult cultural environment for corporations. The shift from the 'personal' and 'informal' style of the old Business Council to the more professional and publicly active style of the Roundtable was a functional response to this new, more difficult setting. The impressive resources and professionalism of the Roundtable are tributes to the way big business rose to the challenge posed by a more hostile cultural climate.

But it is the third development that is most significant of all, for it addresses directly the problem of the growth of a more hostile cultural environment. Faced with a climate of hostility born of long-term shifts in public opinion and the growing sophistication of institutional critics of business, the business community has responded with an active campaign designed to influence opinion, especially opinion among elites and those capable of forming attitudes in the wider public. The best-documented instance of this is the 'think tank' boom: an extensive investment in think tanks designed to produce both research and advocacy favourable to business as an institution and to produce opinion favourable to the wider free enterprise system. Think tanks have sought to influence the general debate about the terms of economic policy and have sought to shape partisan political outcomes. Among the best known are the Heritage Foundation (established 1973) and the Cato Institute (established 1977), as well as longer established bodies that were revitalized from the 1970s, like the American Enterprise Institute (originally established 1943). The modes by which these different bodies work are varied. Some target the core of the intellectual elite by sponsoring substantial, well-researched monographs (historically the route followed by the American Enterprise Institute). Berry has shown that more recent creations have sought to shape everyday debates among intellectual and policy elites, for instance, by trying to place 'op eds' in places that are read by the influential, such as *The Wall Street Journal* (Berry 1999: 137–42). This tactic is plainly designed to combat the hostility in intellectual circles that Schumpeter forecast: or to put it another way, it is an attempt to create a Gramscian hegemony for the market order.

A growing body of academic work charts this 'Gramscian' project (for instance, Ricci 1993; Béland and Waddan 2000; Parmar 2005; Peck 2006). How successful the project has been is nevertheless debatable. It is undoubtedly the case that there have occurred, alongside the growth of public scepticism, a number of developments which have greatly benefited the business elite. They include the deregulation of markets, the growing emphasis on extracting shareholder value from enterprises, and a sharp increase

Box 7.3 How an Anglo-American giant responds to the challenge from civil society groups: the case of BAT

The tobacco industry is one of the most difficult to defend from critics in civil society groups because of the definitive link established a generation ago between tobacco consumption and a range of mortal diseases, notably forms of cancer. BAT is in the eye of the storm, as the world's second largest quoted tobacco company by market share, with brands sold in more than 180 markets. The business is by origin an Anglo-American enterprise, established in 1902 as a joint venture between the United Kingdom's Imperial Tobacco Company and the American Tobacco Company founded by the great innovator in cigarette production, James Duke. How BAT organizes its public face to counter the storm of criticism can easily be observed from its very informative web site (at http://www.bat.co.uk/). How it talks internally is nicely described in one of a series of annual reports on its performance in corporate social responsibility published by the Corporate Responsibility Coalition (CORE). (The ease with which CORE gained access to internal BAT documents incidentally highlights another aspect of the political life of the large corporation: as it is a bureaucratic organization which conducts its affairs quite formally, virtually nothing it says 'internally' can in practice remain confidential.) The range of the alliance formed by CORE indicates the scale of the challenge facing the company. It goes well beyond anti-smoking and public health organizations, representing more than 100 charities, faith-based groups, community organizations, unions, businesses, and academic institutions. Christian Aid and Friends of the Earth are members of its steering group. Two features of the BAT strategy revealed by its own documents are particularly striking because they illustrate key themes in both this chapter and in Chapter 4: reputation management and management by corporate giants of industry trade associations. But what is also remarkable about the strategy of reputation management is the pessimism of the company's documents, which mostly contain a set of rhetorical questions to itself. Thus, 'The question we need to ask is: Can the tobacco industry move itself ahead – fast enough and far enough – of the WHO (World Health Organization) agenda to enhance its reputation?'; and 'The most elusive part of the campaign . . . reputation management will require some searching discussion, solid research and hard business decisions' (quoted in CORE 2005: 10). In short, it is easy to identify the problem of reputation management, more difficult to solve it. Whether establishing university chairs or sponsoring musical events (two BAT tactics) can suffice is questionable. More tractable, because more institutionally specific, is the manipulation of a trade association. Manipulation of this kind, we have seen at several points in this book, is important because it identifies the narrow interests of a company with the more general interests of a sector. Hence, BAT speaks of using the International Tobacco Growers' Association (ITGA) as 'a "front" for our third world lobby activities'. In exactly the way described in our account in Chapter 5 of how large firms engage with trade associations, it speaks of using the ITGA to capture the 'moral high ground', and claims to have transformed the Association from 'an introspective and largely ineffectual trade association to a pro-active, politically effective organization.' Hence, it says, 'this is one way of getting value for our subs to the ITGA' (quoted in CORE 2005: 14–15). None of this guarantees success in BAT's lobbying activities, but it reinforces three critical points in making sense of how corporate giants respond to their wider social environment. First, for many industries political struggle is at the heart of their lives, and issues of production and marketing are secondary. Second, giant corporations are realistic and sophisticated in their view of the challenges that face them. Third, above all, what they do cannot be evaluated in isolation – effectiveness also depends on what the opponents and critics of business in civil society are doing.

in inequality as the rewards of the business elite have outstripped the pay of normal people. This last development is accompanied by an intellectual apparatus that ranges from the sophisticated to the primitive. The former include elaborate theories supporting the creation of incentives like stock options which have massively enriched parts of the business elite, and equally elaborate theories arguing that reducing personal taxation on the very rich creates incentives for wealth creation that benefit all society. The primitive include the crudest kind of 'boosterism', often promoted by the beneficiaries of the new inequality: an example is the self-adulatory publications of Jack Welch, former CEO of the corporate giant General Electric (see Welch and Welch 2005).

How far the rise of neo-liberalism and of massive enrichment of the corporate elite is significantly due to the shaping influence of business-sponsored think tanks is more uncertain. There are, as we have seen, spectacular instances of high-profile pro-business think tanks that have been created, or revitalized, in recent years. It also seems that the new think tanks designed to engage in partisan policy advocacy are more common on the libertarian 'right' than on the liberal 'left' (Berry 1999: 141). On the other hand, the wider population of citizen activist groups, which the libertarian think tanks are partly designed to counter, are overwhelmingly dominated by 'liberal' groups that promote active government and are critical of business (Berry 1999: 142–4). And the libertarian think tanks are, as we have also seen, working in a pluralistic elite culture where substantial parts of the intellectual elite – in universities and in the mass media – question the terms of the neo-liberal order.

From hegemony to pluralism

We can now review the fate of the three theoretical accounts with which we began, in the light of the evidence from our two cases. There is no doubt that at particular periods, in both our country studies, there has existed what can reasonably be called a Gramscian hegemony: in other words, a state of affairs where business power and privilege, and the market system, were thought more or less instinctively to be part of the natural order of things. Two particularly important periods are: the United Kingdom for much of the nineteenth and the first half of the twentieth century, when the right of business to regulate its own affairs was barely challenged; and the United States for a couple of decades after the end of the Second World War, when the giant corporation was able to picture itself as a benign institution in American life. It is also the case that in the last couple of decades, we have seen a determined attempt to recreate a Gramscian hegemony: to establish as an instinctively accepted fact of life that the market is the naturally best way to allocate resources and that empowerment and enrichment of a corporate elite inside the biggest enterprises is simply a necessity if the market order is to prosper. The generalizations offered in the preceding sentence apply to both the United States and the United Kingdom.

But the success of the Gramscian 'project' is limited both by what we can in summary call Schumpeterian influences and by the persistence of pluralism. In exactly the way we would predict from Schumpeter's work, there have developed strata of intellectuals – in universities, in the mass media, and amongst lobbying groups in civil society – critical of the market order and of the giant corporation. Nevertheless, nothing like the suffocating anti-market orthodoxy predicted by Schumpeter has arrived: the intellectual critics of the market order form a significant part of the policy chorus, but are neither the only voices, nor the dominant voices. This is precisely because the policy choir has, contrary to the expectations of both Gramscian and Schumpeterian theory, actually become more pluralistic in the last generation. There is a cacophony of voices to be heard in debates about the market order in general and about the practices of the giant corporation in particular. The swelling cacophony has something to do with the changing character of democratic politics – one of the themes of the next chapter.

8 Restless Democracy and Restless Capitalism

Economic change and the politics of business representation

'Restless capitalism' is the famous characterization of the economic system of advanced capitalism offered by Joseph Schumpeter: a ceaseless process of 'creative destruction', to use another of Schumpeter's vivid phrases, where sectors, industries, and firms are destroyed and displaced by competitors through competition and continuous innovation (Schumpeter 1943/1976). But democracy is also restless. Two mechanisms help produce this: democratic politics are, in part, about the representation of powerful interests, so they are bound to reflect the struggles originating in the creative destruction of a capitalist economy; and since democracy is itself a competitive system, the very process of democratic politics destroys or weakens some institutions and interests, and strengthens others. Thus, democratic competition is an accomplice of Schumpeter's creative destruction.

This final chapter is about the way restless capitalism and restless democracy combine, and about the consequences of this combination for the politics of the business system. We will see that some of the 'restlessness', both economic and political, is especially pronounced in the Anglo-American world; but the changes surveyed here are also present in the wider world of capitalist democracies. Restless democracy and restless capitalism raise issues that are both empirical and normative. They return us to some of the empirical questions that opened this book, notably about how we can best characterize business power in capitalist democracy, especially in the two systems that are the main concern of this chapter. But these empirical questions naturally connect with difficult evaluative problems. One of the most important reasons we need to arrive at accurate empirical accounts is that they affect the credibility of the claims made for democratic government. If business power does indeed limit the practice of democracy, then that finding must damage any normative defence of democratic politics. A defence of the moral superiority of democratic systems over other forms of government has to rest in part on the empirical claim that democratic politics can be practised in the presence of the giant corporation.

Box 8.1 Representing business in the EU: two strategies for collective action – Round Tables versus Grand Confederations

A recurrent theme of this book has been the tension within business between political action designed to protect the interests of the individual enterprise, and political action designed to protect the collective interests of the business system. We have seen that individual enterprises can try to resolve this tension, if they are sufficiently well resourced and sophisticated, by 'capturing' or even founding trade associations. That still leaves the problem of providing a collective voice for business. No Europe-wide party political movement has yet emerged (of comparable cohesion to nation-based pro-business parties) to do that job. The difficulty is peculiarly acute in an EU of 27 member states. Two institutional solutions to this problem have emerged. One we have already examined at a number of points, notably in Box 4.1, p. 62. That box described the European Round Table of Industrialists and summarized its main strengths and weaknesses: it encompasses the significant corporate giants in the EU, and copies the institutional innovation of the US Business Roundtable in demanding the active engagement of the most senior executives of member firms; but it manages to combine a heterogeneous membership with identification with a particular sector, big business, and a generally unpopular one at that. The alternative strategy is provided by the longest established business lobby group in the EU, Business Europe, which aims for a much more comprehensive coverage. It grew out of the *Conseil des Fédérations Industrielles d'Europe* (*CIFE*), founded in 1949, and was formally established as the *Union des Industries de la Communauté europé-enne* (*UNICE*) in March 1958, 'to track the political consequences of the community created by the Treaty of Rome' (Business Europe 2008*a*). It has from the start gone down a very different route from the highly personal engagement of the European Round Table of Industrialists. It is a grand European confederation: an organization which consists of members drawn from the most important national 'peak' business associations, both trade associations and employers' associations. There are presently forty national federations and confederations in membership. They include some of the national giants of business representation, such as the Confederation of British Industry and the Bundesverband der Deutschen Industrie. Given this range of members, it is not surprising to discover that Business Europe is engaged right across the spectrum of economic and social policy in the Union, and is engaged also in the international diplomacy of business. For instance, it convened a meeting of leaders of the most important national business federations in Paris on 7 November 2008 to discuss the world economic crisis. But the outcome of that meeting illustrates the problem of this level of collective action. When the leaders in Paris turned to a statement of what they believed in they were reduced to the anodyne: 'Private enterprise is the engine of the economy and will drive the recovery process. High ethical standards, risk and initiative taking, responsibility, accountability, sustanability [*sic*] are all essential values' (Business Europe 2008*b*). The platitudes are rooted in the institutional nature of Business Europe. It indeed includes the national big hitters like the CBI and the Bundesverband der Deutschen Industrie. But its 40 members also include bodies like the Employers' Confederation of Latvia. In other words, to the extent that it achieves its ambitions of comprehensiveness to give it legitimacy as the collective voice of European business, it incorporates also all the divergences and tensions that divide the interests of different sectors and different national business communities. None of the member federations and confederations depend on Business Europe for their EU level representation. All have offices in Brussels, and all are well networked in their individual national political systems. Thus, while the European Round Table of Industrialists has some problems of maintaining cohesion in the face of its members' diverse interests, its problems pale into insignificance alongside the delicacies of diplomacy entailed in getting the institutional members of Business Europe behind common positions.

As we shall see, it is demonstrably the case that in the last generation both capitalism and democracy have confirmed their 'restlessness'. Two critical questions therefore arise: what has change done to our empirical understanding of the connection between business and democratic politics; and what has it done to any normative defence of the viability of democratic politics in the presence of the characteristic institution of the capitalist system, the business enterprise? We begin by sketching the changing character of 'restless democracy', and what this has done to the political position of business; continue with an examination of the changes in business, and what these, conversely, have done to democratic politics; examine some of the normative implications of what we have found; and in the last section of the chapter come full circle, to the issues about similarities and differences between American and British capitalism with which the book began.

Restless democracy and business politics

Democracy is 'restless' for many reasons but, in advanced capitalist democracies, the restlessness may be summarized as the product of two kinds of competition: political competition, for office and for influence over public policy; and economic competition which creates changes in the patterns of interests that then struggle in the political arena.

Anglo-American democracy has been subjected to particularly important changes in recent decades. The 'democracy' that we understood in the Anglo-American world in the 1950s is not the democracy that we see now. Particularly important changes have taken place in some of the key institutions of democratic participation, in the way democratic political leaders have viewed the business community and in the kinds of policy outcomes produced by competitive democratic politics. Let us look at each of these in turn.

Institutional change is fundamental because it goes to the heart of the democratic political process: the means by which mass political loyalties are shaped, and mass political participation engaged. In respect both of loyalties and engagement, there have been profound shifts. The most obvious sign of this is the secular decline of the political party, historically the key institution that engaged the loyalty of citizens and shaped their participation in politics. In the United Kingdom, this has taken the form of a precipitous fall in the their membership: the individual membership of the Conservative Party, recall from Chapter 6, has fallen from over 2.8 million in the early 1950s to around 250,000 now; in the same period, Labour's individual membership fell from around 1 million to around 170,000. American political parties have no comparable category of membership, but there is convincing evidence that by other measures they have been losing their hold. In the United States, active engagement with parties is on the wane: readiness to identify with parties is in decline, and preparedness actually to turn out to vote for parties at elections is likewise in decline. We discussed this at some length in Chapter 6, so here we offer only a summary of change. Green, in a review of the evidence spanning the 1960s through the 1990s, describes things as follows: 'there seem to have been significant decreases in the identification with, and evaluation of, the major parties and the party system as a whole' (2002: 319). In turn the ability of parties to turn out the vote – the most important form of conventional political participation – has declined: turnout in American Presidential elections, for instance, fell from about two-thirds of the electorate to under a half between the 1960s and the 1990s (ibid.: 334). This finding is made more striking because it parallels party decline across a wide range of (otherwise often very different) European democracies (Mair and Van Biezen 2001) and indeed across the larger world population of capitalist democracies (Dalton and Wattenberg 2002). As in numerous other respects, the American Presidential election campaign of 2008 disrupted this pattern: the extraordinary enthusiasm generated by Barack Obama, the successful candidate, significantly raised turnout, to about 64 per cent of the eligible electorate – the highest for a generation. How far this is a single 'spike', and how far a reversal of a long history of decline, obviously only time can tell.

For the institutions and actors damaged by the long-term developments – the party elites that a few decades ago dominated political participation and political loyalties – they appear as signs of difficulty or even crisis in the functioning of democratic politics. But a more neutral way to understand change, and one that throws a revealing light on its implications for business, is to see it as the natural product of the competitive character of democracy. In the 'marketplace' for political loyalty and political participation, new modes and institutions have captured the attention of citizens, at the expense of parties. There has not been a retreat from participation, but rather a shift to new kinds of engagement. Here the evidence of similar patterns in our two cases – and indeed in other advanced capitalist democracies – is also striking. The arenas where participation is taking place are changing: there has been a move to public demonstrations, involving activities in 'public spaces' (marches, rallies, and direct action like blockades). These often challenge the established notion that participation and protest should be 'constitutional' – that is to say, should be channelled through the hitherto dominant institutions like the big political parties. There has also occurred growing individualization of political participation. That is, there has been a shift away from engagement with explicitly political institutions concerned with collective action, such as political parties and trade unions. By contrast, there has been a rise in activities that can be done individually: signing petitions; turning out for demonstrations and marches; and boycotting goods, services, and even whole countries.

This change to a more individual style of participation has not happened in an institutional vacuum. It is connected with the organization of new modes of political action. We can see that some kinds of 'individualized' participation can indeed happen spontaneously – in the manner of some demonstrations in public places, for instance. But it is equally obvious that most forms of individual action are only possible because some person, or institution, has created the opportunity for action. To be signed, petitions have to be drawn up; and most demonstrations, marches, and boycotts have to be organized. The key institutional development here is change in the world of pressure groups. Although we do not have robust long-term data, it does seem that there has been an expansion in the population of this part of the organized social world. It is true that observers like Putnam have traced in the United States a decline in associational activity, though even this is controversial, and it does not seem to be replicated in Britain (Maloney et al. 2000; Putnam 2000). More pertinently, in the world of organized pressure group politics, it seems that there has been a long-term growth in the number and membership of such groups. Many new groups have been created, and many old ones have prospered. There has been particular rapid growth in membership of leisure and cultural organizations, the most successful of which seem to be focused on the natural world, and are loosely called environmental organizations. There has been a boom in membership of long-established bodies concerned with nature (the Sierra Club in the United States, the Royal Society for the Protection of Birds in the United Kingdom) and in addition many new ones have been founded (Berry and Wilcox 2008). The creation of new groups in turn is linked to the spread of networks of groups that form 'movements' of various degrees of cohesion: the best documented are the women's movement, the environmental movement, and (more problematically) the anti-globalization movement.

As this last illustration shows, these developments have potentially important consequences for the shape of business politics, and some of these have cropped up already in earlier pages. They both potentially advantage and potentially disadvantage the business lobby.

One big advantage for business plainly arises from the character of party organization and partisan campaigning. A generation ago, the parties were labour rich organizations, and campaigning was a labour intensive activity. In the intervening years, the parties have substantially lost this resource. Partly in consequence, they now rely much more on mass media and electronic campaigning, and on professional probing of public opinion to shape party policies, by techniques such as focus groups. The decline of mass attachment has not only robbed the parties of a direct resource, but has also robbed them of a way of raising financial support, a problem magnified by the fact that the new ways of trying to gauge and shape public opinion generally require lots of cash. This is why on both sides of the Atlantic parties now increasingly rely on institutional sources of financial support. In part, this means state financing, but it has also involved soliciting the wealth of the super rich, or the support of large corporate backers. As a result, business has permeated the party system to an increasing degree in recent years – though with variable consequences for recruitment to elective office on either side of the Atlantic, as we shall see later.

The changing character of the pressure group system has also advantaged business. The multiplication of groups has been accompanied by the growth of a lobbying industry. There has been increasing professionalization of the lobbying process. In all this, as we have seen at numerous points of this book, business has considerable advantages, and it has exploited this new feature of modern democracy in important ways. It is a major client – indeed the major client – of the new lobbying industry: since it has big interests at stake in the policy process, it has the incentive to employ professionals, and it has the means to use their (expensive) services. Indeed, even within the largest firms, as we have also seen at numerous points in earlier pages, there has been a growing professionalization of the lobbying function.

These effects arise from the damage done to political parties by the processes of democratic competition. In the struggle to exercise control over the policy process, they have been partially displaced by professionally organized lobbyists and popularly based political movements. The contingent results include an increasing reliance by politicians and their parties on business finance, and an increasing tendency for special lobbies – where business is exceptionally well organized – to 'drive' policy processes.

This links to another big advantage that business has derived from the changing character of democracy. Parties have not only declined in the competition for institutional resources, but have also declined in the competition for ideas. Party ideologies – for instance those organized on a left right spectrum – decreasingly occupy a central place in shaping the expression of political preferences. The decline of party identity has allowed many new identities to influence policy preferences – such as those reflected in the rise of political movements like environmentalism. But perhaps the most important advantage accruing to business from this change has been the decline of parties as repositories of ideologies critical of business institutions and the business system. The single biggest example in these pages is provided by the case of the Labour Party in Britain, where New Labour in the 1990s reinvented itself as a business-friendly party. Business is now less likely to be confronted by critics in the political parties than at any time for nearly a century.

In summary, the biggest changes in the political system which have accrued to the advantage of business interests all turn on the changed character of political parties: their decline as agents of political identification, participation, and policy preference formation; and the rise of competitors to parties as sources of identification, participation, and policy innovation.

But these developments do not always produce benign outcomes for business. A number of problems have been created for the smooth exercise of business power by 'restless democracy'. The most important arises from the way newly successful competitors to political parties have created a social and cultural environment which is often hostile to business. As we have seen at numerous points in this book, notably in Chapter 7, the changes have helped transform the social environment of the firm and of the business order. This has had particularly important consequences for the kingpin of the modern business system, the giant firm. The proliferation of new kinds of group organizations, of new modes of lobbying, and of new policy concerns has helped create an increasingly sceptical, social, and cultural environment. In short, the challenges outlined in the preceding chapter are fundamentally the result of the transformed partisan environment within which business, especially big business, has to operate. Parties are more business compliant than they have been for a long time, but the worth of this compliance is much less than it has been for a long time.

These problems have been made acute by a development that has also recurred in these pages: it concerns the individualization of business lobbying, especially in the large corporation. By individualization, I mean the extent to which the large-business corporations have felt able to 'go it alone' in organizing their own lobbying. There is no doubt that this has transformed the effectiveness of business lobbying, and for the better as far as the individual corporation is concerned. But in many cases, as we have seen at numerous points in the preceding pages, it has also reduced the reliance of the individual corporation on institutions of collective representation, like trade associations, and has fragmented the business lobby. One of the themes of earlier chapters has been the extent to which the highly professionalized lobbying operations of business enterprises have been mobilized to counter the ambitions and interests of *other* business enterprises.

This very professionalization has another significant consequence, documented by Martin. As we saw in Chapter 4, she speaks of whole sectors and industries being 'stuck in neutral'. This is a metaphor for the problems faced by enterprises in forming a clear view of their interests, and acting upon them – mobilizing, in other words, the impressive resources at their disposal. They are stuck in neutral because the very professionalization of the lobbying function inside the firm has complicated the organizational and ideological process by which the enterprise recognizes and acts on its interests. The positions adopted by a firm have to be negotiated under the influence of professionals who themselves are subject to a wide range of ideas, not all of them originating in the business world. The development of professional roles inside firms concerned with the management of the firm's regulatory responsibilities

---

Box 8.2 The World Economic Forum: transnational planning body or the world's most lavish cocktail party?

A key theme of this and the previous chapter has been the significance of the rise in civil society of critics of big business, and of the way changes in the domestic organization of leading democracies have helped these critics mobilize politically. But big business has not been acquiescent in this development, and one of the most widely noticed developments has occurred on the level of global policy organization in the form of the World Economic Forum (WEF). The Forum's annual meeting in Davos is its public face – a globally publicized mix of public and private business and social meetings for the global economic elite. Is it part of a 'transnational planning body' that Robinson and Harris (2000) claimed had now developed for a new capitalist class? The public face of the Forum – the gigantic extended annual cocktail party in Davos – is only part of the story. As Graz (2003) documents, this is just the tip of the iceberg: the Forum is a well-resourced institution which runs all year round as a lobbying and intelligence institution for global business. Carroll and Carson (2003) show that the core of the WEF – the membership of its governing Foundation board – is drawn from a well-integrated corporate elite that is also prominent in other transnational groups, like the Bilderberg Group (discussed in Chapter 4). More elusively, but perhaps still important, there is a reputational effect: by contrast with more discreet bodies like Bilderberg, the Forum has managed to establish itself in the public eye as the representative of global business in a globalized economy. But three problems remain in showing that we are indeed looking here at part of a transnational planning apparatus. First, Carroll and Carson show that the small numbers of corporate leaders prominent at the heart of the WEF are not representative of the global economic elite: they are disproportionately drawn from a North Atlantic elite, which also dominates other transnational institutions. In short, the leadership is not truly global. Second, real doubts exist about how far common membership is translated into social and policy cohesion – typified by the difficulty of making sense of the annual meeting in Davos, which has become an increasingly diverse jamboree attended by a curious mix of individuals with real economic clout, invited figures from NGOs, some of whom are critics of global business, and narcissistic celebrities. The third and most serious difficulty concerns the policy meaning of the operations of the Forum. That its intelligence and policy commentary functions are important is well established. But how far it functions as a *planning* body for a global business elite is much less certain. As we have seen, it does not encompass the full range of that elite, though it does encompass an important part of its core, in the North Atlantic. As Graz shows, what it also does when it turns to substantive policy problems is to integrate the often very different policy preferences of different parts of the business elite. Moreover, since the number of business leaders involved at the core is quite small (the Foundation's Board has twelve members), it can be sensitive to the personalities and prefer-ences of highly assertive and able individuals. In short, the WEF may do exactly what it says on the tin: provide a forum. In other words, it may provide an important place where key members of the business elite can meet to debate, and sometimes to coordinate; but that is quite a long way from performing a sustained planning role.

---

is especially significant. These regulatory responsibilities impinge on every aspect of the enterprise. The professionalization of roles, notably those concerned with regulatory compliance, imports into the firm many of the views and policy debates that are in the wider social and ideological environ-ment of business. Thus, industries and sectors become 'stuck in neutral' because they themselves become arenas in the struggle to identify what actually constitute collective business interests. In Martin's words, summarizing her argument:

> The patterns of corporate deliberation investigated in this book give insight into a central feature of business interest representation – stalemate. Despite the popular view of big business as the Goliath of American politics, the large employers most likely to support human capital investment policies are weakly organized in most areas of policy. Although large corporations often dominate regulatory politics directly connected to their core production activities, they are less well equipped to act on shared social concerns. Lacking a forum for expressing collective interests, these companies are stuck in neutral, unable to generate positions in debates about broad collective, social goods. (2000: 5–6)

This last insight – that the firm itself is an internally complex institution in which views and preferences are by no means simple to work out – connects to a major theme to which we now turn: the changing character of the business system itself.

Restless capitalism and business politics

'Restless capitalism' is derived from Schumpeter's characterization of the capitalist economic order – the ceaseless process of 'creative destruction' involving the linked mechanisms of market-driven change and technological innovation (Schumpeter 1943/1976: 82–4; Metcalfe 2006). We know from our discussion in Chapter 7 that Schumpeter predicted that capitalism would destroy itself by its very achievements: it would dissolve the institutions and social bonds that underpinned the market order, and would be succeeded by some kind of socialist collectivism. At this point in the third millennium, the triumph of anything resembling socialism seems unlikely. But whatever the long-term accuracy of Schumpeter's prediction about a socialist future, there can be little doubt that capitalism's restlessness has been evident with a vengeance in the last generation: its power has been newly unleashed (Glyn 2006). The early 1970s were a well-documented watershed in the history of the capitalist order. In August 1971, the decision of the United States to abolish the convertibility of the dollar to gold signalled the beginning of the end of the Bretton Woods era of fixed exchange rates. The actions of the OPEC oil cartel in the wake of the Israel–Arab War of autumn 1973 resulted in a quadrupling of oil prices by the following year. Thus ended the 'thirty glorious years' of sustained economic growth in the advanced capitalist world. They were succeeded by an era of recession, unemployment, high inflation, financial crises, and drastic structural change as national capitalist economies struggled to come to terms with hard economic times.

This is the background to the new age of restless capitalism. Three particularly important changes are sketched here, for they impinge directly on the political position of business. In summary, they amount to a new age of globalization, a new age of turmoil in corporate structure and ownership, and a new age of inequality.

THE NEW AGE OF GLOBALIZATION

The age of globalization has recurred so often throughout this book that we need here only provide a summary. There is, true, contention surrounding this subject: about the very meaning of globalization; about how far the changes that occurred from the early 1970s were indeed historically novel, or only amounted to the recreation of an older pattern disrupted by the great wars of the twentieth century; and about just how truly 'global' were the institutions of globalization. But the most nuanced and comprehensive survey of what we know about the phenomenon concludes that 'accelerated globalization of recent decades has left almost no locale on earth completely untouched, and the pace has on the whole progressively quickened with time' (Scholte 2005: 119). Indeed, Scholte's conclusions are even more emphatic for he traces the changes over a period of fifty years, thus predating the collapse of the Bretton Woods order. The business enterprise, the key institution of restless capitalism, has been central to this experience – both as an agent of change and as the subject of change. To take two examples from Scholte again: the number of firms working simultaneously in several countries multiplied ninefold from the late 1960s to 2003; while one critical domain, finance, 'has shifted substantially out of the territorialist framework that defined most banking, securities derivatives and insurance business before the middle of the twentieth century' (ibid.: 105, 113).

THE NEW AGE OF CORPORATE TURMOIL

This new age of restless globalization is connected to a new age of transformation in corporate structures. Schumpeter's vision of capitalism indeed puts this kind of transformation at the centre of economic life: the famous image of 'creative destruction' is mostly about enterprise creation and destruction. Firms and sectors rise and fall as the result of ceaseless competitive struggle and technological innovation: whole industries and their corporate populations become obsolete, and are displaced by new institutions. We can see something of this technology-driven change in the emergence of globally prominent enterprises in recent years: Microsoft, Apple Computer, and Google are three examples of corporate giants who rose by exploiting new technologies. But there has also been another key aspect of change in structures that is particularly noticeable in the markets of the Anglo-American world: there has been almost ceaseless destruction, and reconstruction, of corporate entities. This is partly the result of Schumpeter-like competitive struggles and innovation in product markets, but it is also the result of pressures in financial markets. The pressures come from the trading of property rights in enterprises by stockholders attempting to maximize returns, from senior managers maximizing reward, and from financial intermediaries maximizing fee income from arranging the trades. Froud and her colleagues call this 'financialization': intermediation in financial markets produces unprecedented destabilization of enterprise ownership structures (Froud et al. 2006). Savage and Williams give some indication of the scale of upheaval as follows:

More than 70 of the FTSE 100 companies of the early 1980s no longer survive in the index and most of those giant companies have vanished to hostile takeover. Over the past twenty five years, giant companies in the UK and USA have spent as much or more in buying other companies as on fixed capital investment. (2008: 13)

Change on this scale has important consequences for the representation of business interests. In a Schumpeterian world of 'creative destruction', the struggle is not only economic, but also political. Firms and sectors will not just acquiesce in decline as more vigorous competitors appear; they will try to organize to defend their established positions not only by responding in markets, but also by political means. The history of regulatory change in key arenas, like financial markets, is precisely such a political history: interests within the markets threatened by competition from outsiders used their political muscle to obstruct change and to impose restrictions on competition (see, for instance, Vogel, S. 1996; Eisner et al. 2006). Rising interests, on the other hand, rarely rely just on market competition to succeed; they also try to mobilize political support to alter the terms of market exchange in their favour. In short, the process of creative destruction is an important source of division between business interests. A related issue, which in previous pages we have examined in studies of 'new' corporate giants like Google and Microsoft, is how new giants that have grown rapidly, often around creative and highly individualistic founders, adapt to the need to defend their interests in the world of professional lobbying.

The scale of financially induced institutional restructuring revealed in the figures cited above from Savage and Williams also entails important consequences for the stability and continuity of business representation. Giant firms with a long history develop distinctive political cultures: they establish modes of lobbying; they cultivate contacts; and they build up long-lasting networks, both in business communities and in policy-making communities. (Recall, in this connection, our discussion of the evolution of IBM as a political actor in Chapter 4.) They have also been important in representative associations, on occasion being the dominant influence over the life of those associations. But the patterns of upheaval seen in recent decades put into question precisely this picture of political continuity, institution building, and adaptation.

Financialization not only has consequences for the external face of the firm as a political actor, but also has consequences for power *within* the business enterprise. As we saw in Chapter 1, the most important theory of the distribution of power within the giant firm over the course of the twentieth century was developed by Berle and Means (1932). They argued that the rise of professional management coupled with the dispersal of ownership between numerous property (share) holders had tilted the balance of power in favour of managers. Out of this came a picture of large corporations as stable entities with a long-term existence – exactly what has been missing in recent decades. Part of the reason for this transformation to a more unstable world is a Schumpeter-like shift in competitive conditions. We can see this at a concrete institutional level in the disappearance of corporate giants who could not cope with the rise of global competitors in a world economy marked by an increasingly elaborate division of labour: the disappearance of corporate giants in the UK automobile industry is emblematic of the change. Part of the reason lies in the great institutional upheavals in corporate structures associated with another facet of globalization – the creation of corporate giants built to organize on a multinational scale, and recruiting their corporate leaders from a cross-national, cosmopolitan talent pool. These changes are also closely associated with the onset of the age of 'financialization' identified by Froud and her colleagues (2006). They mark the ascendancy of financial markets, especially in the markets for corporate ownership. Financial intermediaries have become critical agents in shaping and reshaping corporate structures; and the pursuit of returns in the name of maximizing 'shareholder value' has become a key determinant of the fate of the corporation as an institution. This is a world of business representation very different from that implied by the settled worlds of partnership between state bureaucracies and corporate bureaucracies pictured by a generation of studies written under the inspiration of Berle and Means (see, for instance, Shonfield 1965; Galbraith 1967/1972).

THE NEW AGE OF INEQUALITY

One of the most important outcomes of the developments in 'restless capitalism' summarized above is a sharp increase in inequality. Some of this growing inequality, while remarkable, is not surprising, for it is a predictable result of wider changes associated with the rise of a neo-liberal order in Anglo-America. Thus, we have increasingly convincing evidence of a decline in inter-generational social mobility, and an increase in income inequality – by some measures, in the United Kingdom, there is now a more unequal distribution than for half a century (Atkinson 2005). These trends are unsurprising because they can be traced to wider changes in policy and in labour markets: to cutbacks in many of the programmes that assisted mobility in the classic age of welfare state; and to changes in labour markets that have differentiated 'insiders' in stable employment from a workforce employed on temporary contracts, and poorly organized for collective representation. The neo-liberal policies pursued by all administrations in both the United States and the United Kingdom for nearly thirty years have thus been quite consciously designed to secure this increase in inequality, on the grounds that it is a necessary price to pay for an effectively functioning market order.

But if the wider context of social and economic inequality is unsurprising, a considerable puzzle is provided by what has happened to the distribution within business, and especially within the business elite. The trends are most marked in the United States, but are also apparent in the United Kingdom. There has been a huge increase in the income gap between the rest of the workforce and the very top of the corporate elite (documented in Erturk et al. 2005). One of the mechanisms creating this great surge in the enrichment of the corporate elite is the new financial engineering that has redistributed property rights in corporate entities. The best-known mechanism is the use of stock/share options to transfer enormous rewards to that elite. Financial engineering has created a new stratum of 'working rich': not only corporate executives, but also high-income financial dealmakers who are central to the trading of corporate property. The institutions of finance are, in the words of Folkman et al., 'organized for enrichment' (2007: 561).

The result of all this has been perhaps the greatest spate of enrichment for the business elite since the age of the 'robber barons' in the United States (see Chapter 2). Even quite modestly successful – and in some cases unsuccessful – corporate leaders have been able to extract huge personal fortunes from their enterprises. This scale of enrichment is a puzzle because it is hard to understand – and because hard to understand, hard to legitimize, to anticipate the dominant theme of the next section of this chapter. It seems to transcend individual corporate success: the kind of industrial construction associated with the 'robber barons', or the kind of exploitation of new technologies by the founders of enterprises like Microsoft or Google. It also seems to transcend the conventional case made for the liberalizing and deregulatory policies that were introduced on both sides of the Atlantic from the early 1980s. It is plainly linked to wider patterns of inequality but is a hugely magnified version of these patterns. And since it is taking place in rapidly changing systems of democratic politics, it needs to be accommodated to those systems. In short, 'restless capitalism' and 'restless democracy' have to find some way of living together. How they might do so is the theme of the next section.

Business, democracy, and legitimacy

The giant corporation is a dominant part of our lives. Even I, employed in a public university, nevertheless encounter it as a pervasive presence: I shop weekly for groceries in the store of a giant retailing multinational (Tesco), buy most of my clothes from another (Marks and Spencer), drive a car produced by a Japanese giant (Toyota), buy books online from a US giant (Amazon), download music from another (Apple), routinely use PC hardware produced by a multinational Japanese giant (Toshiba), and software developed by an American giant (Microsoft). I am entirely typical – save that the majority of readers will probably also be employed at some time in their working lives by a giant enterprise in the private sector,

This pervasive and dominant presence means that we are inclined to take the existence and operation of the giant enterprise for granted – as if it were a natural part of the social landscape. It is not. It is a special historical creation. The form it takes is the product of a particular historical conjuncture in a particular national setting. As we saw in Chapter 2, the corporation that emerged to dominate the American economy from the beginning of the twentieth century was the result of a distinct configuration of political forces. Likewise, the legal position, and the political position, of the corporate enterprise in the United Kingdom was the result of a very British configuration of influences.

These obvious points lead to one less obvious, and critical, conclusion: the corporate order is a politically negotiated order. It happens to be the case that in the two systems that are at the centre of this book, the political negotiation of the corporate order has to take place within the institutions of formal democratic politics. 'Formal' is used here because, as we saw in Chapter 1, there is considerable debate about how far democratic politics do indeed constrain business – or, indeed, how far business, especially the giant corporation, actually constrains democratic politics. Yet, whatever position we take on the big arguments about the extent to which corporate power and genuine democratic politics are compatible, it cannot be denied that the wider context of democratic civil society presents political challenges for the corporate order.

Those challenges have taken an odd, paradoxical form in the Anglo-American world in recent decades. On the one hand, in both the United Kingdom and the United States, the period since the early 1980s has been a golden age of business influence and privilege; but on the other hand, it has also been an age when business, and especially big business, has come under unique political pressure and been the object of popular discontent.

The sources of this golden age can be summarily expressed; some of them have already cropped up earlier in this book, and indeed in this chapter. In the last generation important sections of the governing elite that once were hostile to the corporate order have adopted a 'business-friendly' position. On both sides of the Atlantic, regardless of the formal political colour of those who held governing office, all governments have tried to be business friendly. They have produced tax, welfare, and labour market policies adapted to the perceived needs of the business community, and especially to the needs of the business elite. Most of the historic opponents of private enterprise, and especially of the giant enterprise, have been greatly weakened. Socialism – the most intellectually consistent criticism of the business order over the course of the twentieth century – has been gravely weakened as a domestic force in the United Kingdom, and as an international force. Labour unions on both sides of the Atlantic have seen their membership decline, notably in the private sector. Labour markets have been reconfigured to make it easier for managers to organize their labour force in the interests of business efficiency. And as we noted above, it has been a golden age of reward for the corporate elite – a gilded era of astonishing enrichment.

The paradox in this state of affairs lies in the following: this golden age of political influence, economic power, and individual enrichment for the business elite has also coincided with a renewed crisis of business authority – of legitimacy. Legitimacy matters because the business system is, among other things, a hierarchy of authority. Chandler's 'visible hand' allocates economic resources and cultural prestige. This visible hand only works because the hierarchies of business institutions are able to command assent. But any efficient authority system has to command more than assent, in the sense of bare obedience. This is what the idea of legitimacy is telling us. Legitimate authority can command obedience because those who are subject to it believe that it has some moral right to make a claim for obedience. This legitimate authority can thus be distinguished from the exercise of power in a prison camp or in a dictatorship; and this kind of legitimacy is a critical foundation of the efficient exercise of power. More telling still, the stability of the business system depends on a willingness on the part of the people at large to trust in the good faith, truthfulness, and public spiritedness of the business elite.

Despite all the political advantages which business has enjoyed for a generation, it is exactly this kind of legitimacy that is now lacking. A growing body of survey evidence, which has been examined in some detail earlier (see especially Chapter 7), shows that there has occurred a long-term withdrawal of popular trust in the business elite. To put it shortly, in the very period when political elites moved in its favour, the people at large moved against it. The evidence is remarkably similar on both sides of the Atlantic. We have quite robust survey evidence stretching over more than three decades that demonstrates convincingly a waning in public trust in, and approval of, business, especially the largest enterprises that are at the heart of the business order. It might be countered that, while this is serious, it is no more serious than the withdrawal of approval and trust which has been experienced by elites generally – and indeed, there is robust comparative evidence to show that something like that has occurred for many elites, such as political elites. But this brings us to the second sign of a legitimacy problem: business seems to have suffered disproportionately in this withdrawal of support and trust. There are indeed some elites – such as those in medicine, education, and religion – which still command very high levels of approval and trust; and there are others, such as those in politics and journalism, which are widely despised. The business elite is in the second category.

One possible reaction to this observation is: So what? After all, it has indeed been a golden age for the exercise of business influence. Critics may surround the corporation, but it seems to survive that environment of criticism in robust health. Indeed, alternative models of economic organization – such as cooperatives or mutuals – remain marginal, and indeed have been disappearing in key economic sectors, like finance. (The fact that many of the former mutuals were victims of the great 2008 financial crisis may reverse that trend.) Moreover, until very recently, the business order has, in the Anglo-American world, actually delivered – not just riches for the business elite, but also economic growth, rising employment, and macroeconomic stability. The social order created in the last couple of decades was marked by striking inequality, but it was also marked by features which, even as recently as the late 1980s, would have seemed marks of high economic success. And whatever the mistrust of business, there seems to be no popular support for any anti-business movements: on the contrary, leftist parties have reinvented themselves precisely because the historic alternative to the business system, socialism, was electorally unsuccessful and, in its extreme command forms, a byword for incompetence.

Yet, it is this very experience of benign economic conditions that must give pause for thought. One might have expected that a period when the business system was instrumentally successful would be one when approval of business institutions would rise. Yet the business system found it hard to generate legitimacy in the good times of the fifteen-year boom from 1992. Since the first banking crisis of 2007, these good times have come to an end, especially in the Anglo-American world. Legitimacy, which was hard to create in benign economic conditions, must now be created in new hard times, against the backdrop of the greatest financial crisis for at least eighty years.

The solution that one proposes to this problem of a legitimacy deficit obviously depends on what one diagnoses as its cause. For Schumpeter, for instance, the case was pretty hopeless. He believed that the root cause lay in the very character of the capitalist order itself, in the spirit of capitalist civilization: a spirit which was sceptical and interrogating, and which produced a stratum of intellectuals that ruthlessly dissected and demystified authority – first the authority of capitalism's predecessors, but then of the capitalist system itself. We have certainly seen something of this in the preceding chapter, in the way institutions like universities have been home to regulatory ideologies hostile to the business order. But Schumpeter expected a particular resolution: that capitalism would evolve into socialism as the economy became more planned, and as large corporations became like public institutions. The most influential accounts of capitalism in the preceding generation – Shonfield (1965) and Galbraith (1967/1972) – reproduced this faith in the rise of a new planned order. It is hard to have any such expectation now.

One potentially appealing alternative diagnosis – because it leads to some obvious remedies – is that business has brought down on its own head the legitimacy crisis by its greed and dishonesty. On this account, the root of the problem lies in the new age of inequality that we sketched earlier. The remedy must lie in the creation of a culture of corporate restraint: either self-restraint or restraint imposed by the state. These are the terms of political discourse that began to be used after the partial nationalization of big banks across the capitalist world in the crisis of autumn 2008. Yet, there are two grounds for being sceptical about this: one analytical and one historical. The analytical one is that we cannot answer the question: Just how much inequality is acceptable for the market order to function with a high level of legitimacy? That the market order requires, and generates, inequality, is not questioned by any observer. Why should the degree of enrichment of the corporate elite experienced in the last couple of decades have become unacceptable, when a high level of inequality has always characterized the business order? The historical difficulty is that it is not at all clear that we are indeed living in a new age of corporate rapacity. It is true that corporate scandals are common, but they are common in part precisely because standards expected of corporations have risen. The big corporation, in particular, is marked by much higher levels of probity and corporate governance standards than was its predecessor of even a generation ago.

The puzzle thus deepens: business becomes better at delivering the economic goods, and raises its standards of behaviour – and is increasingly distrusted and despised. What individual businesses do in these conditions is perfectly rational: they concentrate on managing their own reputations, and insulating themselves against the wider hostility to the business order. There is evidence that they do enjoy some success in this. The phenomena we have

Box 8.3 How the great financial crisis of 2007–9 changed business and politics in Anglo-America

One of the arguments of this book is that the idea of a single 'Anglo-American' model of capitalism is an oversimplification: historical development, patterns of regulation, party engagement with business, and the organization of interest representation for particular business sectors are often strikingly different in the two countries. But the great financial crisis of 2007–9 did show that markets across the Atlantic were interlocked, and it did reshape the connections between those markets and democratic politics. The crisis produced five important changes:

1. *It turned financial market regulation into a political issue once more.* For a quarter century, the notion that financial markets should be subject to light touch regulation, and should be kept free from political control (for which read: free from democratic politics) dominated the minds of market actors and public policy makers. After the crisis, all but the most zealous of free-market advocates came to the view that a considerable increase in political control over financial markets was needed.

2. *It strengthened adversarial regulation.* We have seen that adversarial regulation – the notion that the regulator should not trust the regulated and should use the weight of the law against them – was already a well-embedded tradition in American regulatory culture. The wave of American popular hostility against Wall Street in the autumn of 2008, when the plan publicly to underwrite the banking system's untradeable debts was produced by Treasury Secretary Paulson, strengthened this tradition. In the United Kingdom, after almost a generation when leading politicians of all main parties had celebrated the City of London as an emblem of British economic success that should be left to get on with its own business, both government and opposition now pledged to tighten legal controls.

3. *It nationalized whole parts of the financial system.* This was perhaps the most dramatic effect because it happened with such speed, usually under the threat of the collapse of leading financial institutions. In Britain, the first great event of the crisis occurred in September 2007 when the Treasury was obliged to take into public ownership a failing bank, Northern Rock. In the United States, apart from the 'nationalizing' of a huge volume of bank debt, two leading suppliers of housing mortgages were also taken into public ownership: the Federal National Mortgage Association, nicknamed Fannie Mae, and the Federal Home Mortgage Corporation, nicknamed Freddie Mac. These events dramatized how the wheel of policy had turned. Both Fannie Mae and Freddie Mac were originally public institutions created under President Roosevelt's New Deal as part of the attempt to cope with the last great global financial crash. They were privatized in 1968 at the start of the modern era of free-market triumphalism.

4. *It made politicians managers of the financial system.* The wave of nationalization was itself the sign of a wider shift: a huge increase in the importance of politicians in financial management. On both sides of the Atlantic, the ferocity of the crisis sucked governing politicians into the detail of managing markets: brokering mergers and takeovers to rescue failing institutions; extending the guarantees of protection to depositors in retail banks against the threat of collapse, to the point where the state was guaranteeing virtually all deposits in the system; and using treasury and central bank resources to supply the financial markets with liquidity to try to keep trading going.

5. *It ended the ideological dominance of the 'Anglo-American model' of capitalism.* The notion that the United Kingdom and the United States are part of a single model of capitalism is an oversimplification, but an oversimplification that exercised a powerful hold over the minds of business people and politicians in the two countries, who came to believe that it represented the model of the future for the rest of the capitalist world. After 2007–9, the idea that the future rested with lightly regulated financial markets where virtually all assets were turned into tradeable securities was little heard of again.

noticed in these pages reflect this adaptation: brand management, corporate public relations, and a whole sub-industry concerned with the burnishing of corporate reputation. Individual enterprises can build trust, and can even recoup trust after suffering scandalous revelations. Yet, this is a fragile foundation on which to build the legitimacy of a whole social order.

Business power and the Anglo-American model of capitalism

We began with questions about the power of business under capitalist democracy, and in particular with the question of how far we could characterize the United Kingdom and the United States as a distinctive model – inhabitants of an imagined community of 'Anglo-America', to use Gamble's language (2003: 83–107). Models of capitalism naturally entail more than accounts of patterns of business power: they stretch to the role of the state in economic management, to patterns of welfare provision, and to the government of labour markets. But at their core lies the political life of the business order: the way it deals with governments and with the democratic politics, and conversely, the way governments and politicians deal with the business order. A 'model of capitalism' is thus an economic image, but it is also a political image. Indeed, it is primarily a political image, for the economic patterns so often used to delineate the model – such as the character of corporate governance or of labour market organization – are shaped by the regulatory regime under which economic institutions operate. These regulatory regimes represent political choices: for instance, about the extent of state presence and about the style of state intervention should it take place. They often do not look like political choices, and are often not felt as political choices. The historical British preference for self-regulation, for instance, reflected a dominant regulatory ideology: in other words, it seemed to most of those concerned like a part of the natural order of things – the 'obvious', commonsense way to regulate markets. But it nevertheless did amount to a political choice – to marginalize the state, especially the state when it was under democratic influences. Judging and comparing the American and British varieties of capitalism is therefore not just a matter of focusing on economic structures, but also a matter of focusing on patterns of governance – both the internal governance of economic institutions and the way economic institutions interact with the wider governing institutions of society.

The recognition that any 'model of capitalism' is a political phenomenon gives us an important clue to how we can understand the links between business power, the capitalist system, and democratic politics in the comparison of the United States and the United Kingdom. And when we do this, what we see is a pattern of important historically established differences, some growing similarities; but no straightforward pattern of convergence on a common model.

It makes sense to begin with regulation, because regulation *is* critical for business, is a defining feature of its connection to the political system, and is central to any form of corporate governance. It is also part of the historically engrained differences between the two national systems. Throughout the book, we have seen how the political and legal contexts shaped very different regulatory regimes for business in the United Kingdom and the United States. American business experienced the law sooner, experienced it as a more comprehensive and pervasive influence, and experienced regulation as a highly adversarial contest between business and regulators. Despite the rise of a deregulation movement and the widespread employment of the rhetoric of deregulation, we have seen in previous pages that the essential features of this American culture have not been altered – indeed, in respect of adversarial legalism have if anything become more pronounced. This distinctive culture is, in essence, the product of a particular kind of historical connection between the institutions of business and the institutions of popular politics. The same is true of the very different British system: in essence, as we have seen, the state was marginalized and this marginalization persisted for much of the era of formal democracy over the course of most of the twentieth century.

If the most striking development in the United States in the last generation is the intensification of the culture of adversarial regulation, the most striking in the British case is the transformation of a system that was once very different from that of the United States. Business in Britain had accomplished something that was beyond the wit of American capitalism: insulating a great deal of business life from the institutions of democratic politics. It has lost that capacity to insulate. The passing away of the characteristic British systems of self-regulation, and business-friendly regulation, has certainly made the British system resemble in some very obvious ways that of the United States: it is now more shaped than in the past by legal regulations, it now involves more formal relations between regulators and regulated than in the past, and it is now more often characterized by an adversarial, punitive approach to en-forcement than in the past. It is tempting to describe this in the language of Americanization, and to identify the growth of a common Anglo-American regulatory culture. But the evidence of the previous pages suggests that growing similarity is actually due to distinctively British causes. The two great influences in the British system are the breakdown of the pre-demo-cratic regulatory regime and the growing influence of the EU. 'Convergence' in the sense of the two systems moving to a common point, or 'American-ization' in the sense of the diffusion of dominant American regulatory norms to the British system, is a small part of the story. Far from looking more and more American, the UK system, under the influence of the Union, is looking increasingly 'European' in its business regulatory culture: we only have to think of the role of the EU as a leader of regulatory change in the critical field of competition law to see that.

The story of regulation might be conceived as a story about how politics intervenes in the business system. But a similar picture of difference rather than similarity is revealed when we compare the more direct engagement of the business system with politics. The contrasts begin with the experience of different sectors of business. Small business is a much more effectively organized interest in the United States than in the United Kingdom. It operates in a particularly favourable cultural environment, identified in the public mind with many traditional American virtues. It has pioneered many innovative lobbying techniques and is able to exploit the institutional diversity of the American policy-making system. In all this, its experience is very different from that of small business in the United Kingdom, though there are some tentative signs in Britain of a revival of small-business political confidence and sophistication in the last couple of decades. If one ran a small business in one system, and then transferred it to the other, the experience of the political environment, and the possibilities of effective lobbying, would be very different.

A picture of enduring difference also emerges when we examine the experience of big business. Despite the new age of inequality and enrichment of the corporate elite, the political fate of the two national elites remains strikingly different. We already have a sense of that from the case of regulation, where the American corporate elite faces a much more hostile cultural and legal environment. In respect of the relationship with political parties, especially in respect of political recruitment, the picture is also different, though this time it works in favour of empowering the American corporate elite. Despite the generally more favourable climate historically for big business in British government, it has proved much more difficult in the United Kingdom than in the United States for the plutocratic elite to penetrate the political elite. Indeed, if anything recruitment to elite positions via election in the United Kingdom in the last generation has become more meritocratic, despite their financial difficulties: the political parties have resisted the kind of plutocratic colonization experienced in the United States.

In summary, there are powerful common features to the exercise of business power and influence in these two political systems; democratic politics is under great pressure from business power in both those cases, but very important differences remain. Democracy has problems accommodating to business power, but the difficulties, and the possibilities, remain highly contingent on national history, culture, and institutional setting.

BIBLIOGRAPHY

Albert, M. (1993). *Capitalism against Capitalism*. London: Whurr.

Alter-EU (2008). About Alter-EU. http://www.alter-eu.org/en/about-alter-eu accessed 5 November 2008.

Armstrong, K. and Bulmer, S. (1998). *The Governance of the Single European Market*. Manchester: Manchester University Press.

Arnold, M. (2007). Head of private equity body quits. *Financial Times*, 15 June.

Ashby, E. and Anderson, M. (1981). *The Politics of Clean Air*. Oxford: Clarendon Press.

Association of Foreign Banks (2007). Winter Newsletter 2007. http://www.foreignbanks.org.uk/newsletter/Winter07/AFBWinter07.pdf accessed 14 July 2008.

Atkinson, A.B. (2005). Top incomes in the UK over the 20th century. *Journal of the Royal Statistical Society, Series A*, 168/2: 325–43.

Babb, J. (2001). *Business and Politics in Japan*. Manchester: Manchester University Press.

—— (2005). Making farmers conservative: Japanese farmers, land reform and Socialism. *Social Science Japan Journal*, 8: 178–95.

Bache, I. and George, S. (2006). *Politics in the European Union*. Oxford: Oxford University Press.

Bacon, R. and Eltis, W. (1976). *Britain's Economic Problem: Too Few Producers*. London: Macmillan.

Barker, A., Byrne I., and Veall, A. (2000). *Ruling by Task Force: The Politico's Guide to Labour's New Elite*. London: Politico's.

Barnett, C. (2001). *The Audit of War: The Illusion and Reality of Britain as a Great Power*. London: Pan.

Bassett, K. (1996). Partnership, business elites and new forms of governance in an English city. *Urban Studies*, 33/3: 539–55.

Baumgartner, F. and Leech, B. (1998). *Basic Interests: The Importance of Groups in Politics and Political Science*. Princeton, NJ: Princeton University Press.

Bean, J. (1996). *Beyond the Broker State: Federal Policies towards Small Business 1936–1961*. Chapel Hill, NC: University of North Carolina Press.

Beer, S. (2006). Encounters with modernity, in R. Rhodes, S. Binder, and B. Rockman (eds.), *The Oxford Handbook of Political Institutions*. Oxford: Oxford University Press, pp. 693–715.

Béland, D. and Waddan, A. (2000). From Thatcher (and Pinochet) to Clinton? Conservative think tanks, foreign models and US pensions reform. *Political Quarterly*, 71/2: 202–19.

Bensel, R. (1990). *Yankee Leviathan: The Origins of Central State Authority in America, 1859–1877*. Cambridge: Cambridge University Press.

Berle, A. and Means, G. (1932). *The Modern Corporation and Private Property*. New York: Macmillan.

BERR (Department of Business Enterprise and Regulatory Reform) (2008a). Enterprise and Small Business. http://www.berr.gov.uk/bbf/enterprise-smes/index.html accessed 16 July 2008.

BERR (2008*b*). Business Council for Britain. http://www.berr.gov.uk/about/bcb/index.html accessed 16 July 2008.

—— (2008*c*). Statistics for Small Business. http://stats.berr.gov.uk/ed/sme/smestats2007-ukspr. pdf accessed 21 October 2008.

Berry, J. (1999). *The New Liberalism: The Rising Power of Citizen Groups*. Washington, DC: Brookings Institution Press.

Berry, J. and Wilcox, C. (2008). *The Interest Group Society*, 5th edition. New York: Longman.

BEUC (2008). Consumers on the European Stage. http://www.beuc.eu/Content/Default.asp? PageID = 855&LanguageCode = EN accessed 5 November 2008.

Bianco, A. and Zellner, W. (2003). Is Wal-Mart too powerful? *Business Week*, 6 October.

Bimbaum, J. (2005). The road to riches is called K Street: lobbying firms hire more, pay more, charge more to influence government. *Washington Post*, 22 June.

Birch, A. (1959). *Small Town Politics: A Study of the Political Life of Glossop*. Oxford: Oxford University Press.

Blackaby, F. (ed.) (1979). *British Economic Policy 1960–74: Demand Management*. Cambridge: Cambridge University Press.

Blank, S. (1973). *Industry and Government in Britain: The Federation of British Industries in Politics, 1945–65*. Farnborough: Saxon House.

Boddewyn, J. (2007). The internationalization of the public-affairs function in US multinational enterprises organization and management. *Business and Society*, 46/2: 136–73.

Bolton, G. (Chairman) (1971). *Report of the Committee of Inquiry on Small Firms*. Cmnd 4811. London: HMSO.

Bounds, A. and Dixon, L. (2007). Microsoft concedes defeat in EU battle, *Financial Times*, 22 October.

Bouwen, P. (2002). Corporate lobbying in the European Union: the logic of access. *Journal of European Public Policy*, 9/3: 365–90.

—— (2004). The logic of access to the European Parliament: business lobbying in the Committee on Economic and Monetary Affairs. *Journal of Common Market Studies*, 42/3: 473–95.

Bowden, S. (2000). Corporate governance in a political climate: the impact of public policy regimes on corporate governance in the United Kingdom, in J. Parkinson, A. Gamble, and G. Kelly (eds.), *The Political Economy of the Company*. Hart: Oxford, pp. 186–94.

Bowers, T. (2000). *Branson*. London: Fourth Estate.

Bowman, S. (1996). *The Modern Corporation and American Political Thought: Law, Power and Ideology*. University, PA: Pennsylvania University Press.

Braithwaite, J. and Drahos, P. (2000). *Global Business Regulation*. Cambridge: Cambridge University Press.

Branson, R. (2007). *Losing My Virginity*. London: Virgin Books.

Brickey, K. (2003). From Enron to Worldcom and beyond: life and crime after Sarbanes-Oxley. *Washington University Law Review*, 81/2: 357–401.

Broscheid, A. and Coen, D. (2003). Insider and outsider lobbying of the European Commission. *European Union Politics*, 4/2: 165–89.

Brown, E. (1979). *Rockefeller Medicine Men: Medicine and Capitalism in America*. Berkeley, CA: University of California Press.

Bryson, J., Keeble, D., and Wood, P. (1997). The creation and growth of small business service firms in post-industrial Britain. *Small Business Economics*, 9/4: 346–60.

Buck, T. (2006). Microsoft fined (Euro)280m over EU ruling. *Financial Times*, 10 July.

Burris, V. (2001). Small business, status politics, and the social base of New Christian Right activism. *Critical Sociology*, 27/1: 29–55.

Burt, S. and Sparks, L. (2001). The implications of Wal-Mart's takeover of ASDA. *Environment and Planning A*, 33/8: 1463–87.

Business Europe (2008*a*). History. http://www.businesseurope.eu/content/default.asp?pageid = 414 accessed 13 November 2008.

—— (2008*b*). Joint Statement by American and European Business Leaders. http:// 212.3.246.117/docs/1/CABCOIKBBDBHHPNPLKGPCFJAPDBW9DWGPY9LTE4Q/UNICE/ docs/DLS/2008–01921-E.pdf accessed 13 November 2008.

Business Roundtable (2008). About us. http://www.businessroundtable.org/aboutus/members. aspx accessed 30 June 2008.

Cain, P.G. and Hopkins, A.G. (1993). *British Imperialism: Innovation and Expansion, 1688–1914.* London: Pearson Longman.

Calder, K. (1993). *Strategic Capitalism: Private Business and Public Purpose in Japanese Industrial Finance.* Princeton, NJ: Princeton University Press.

Callan, E. (2007). Democrats to close tax door. *Financial Times*, 19 August.

Carosso, V. (1973). The Wall Street Money Trust from Pujo through Medina. *Business History Review*, XLVII/4: 421–37.

Carrell, S. (2008). 'World's best golf course' approved complete with 23-acre eyesore. *Guardian*, 4 November.

Carroll, W. and Carson, C. (2003). Forging a new hegemony? The role of transnational policy groups in the network and discourses of global corporate governance. *Journal of World Systems Research*, IX/1: 67–102.

—— and Fennema, M. (2002). Is there a transnational business community? *International Sociology*, 17/3: 393–417.

Carson, W.G. (1970*a*). Some sociological aspects of strict liability and the enforcement of factory legislation. *Modern Law Review*, 33/4: 396–412.

—— (1970*b*). White-collar crime and the enforcement of factory legislation. *British Journal of Criminology*, 10/4: 383–98.

—— (1979). The conventionalization of early factory crime. *International Journal for the Sociology of Law*, 7/1: 37–60.

Cater, D. (1965). *Power in Washington: A Critical Look at Today's Struggle in the USA.* London: Collins.

Center for Public Integrity (2007). About us. http://www.publicintegrity.org/about/about.aspx accessed 18 September 2007.

—— (2008). Our private legislatures. http://www.publicintegrity.org/projects/entry/292/ accessed 18 September 2007.

Chandler, A. (1977). *The Visible Hand: The Managerial Revolution in American Business.* Cambridge, MA: Belknap Press of the Harvard University Press.

—— (1990). *Scale and Scope: The Dynamics of Industrial Capitalism.* Cambridge, MA: Harvard University Press.

Chandler, A. (1997). The United States: engines of economic growth in the capital-intensive and knowledge intensive industries, in A. Chandler, F. Amatori, and T. Hikino (eds.), *Big Business and the Wealth of Nations*. Cambridge: Cambridge University Press, pp. 63–101.

Clapham, J.H. (1944). *The Bank of England: A History. Volume 1, 1694–1797*. Cambridge: Cambridge University Press.

Clark, G., Thrift, N., and Tickell, A. (2004). Performing finance: the industry, the media and its image. *Review of International Political Economy*, 11/2: 289–310.

Clarke, M. (1981). *Fallen Idols: Elites and the Search for the Acceptable Face of Capitalism*. London: Junction Books.

Clay, H. (1957). *Lord Norman*. London: Macmillan.

Coates, D. (2000). *Models of Capitalism: Growth and Stagnation in the Modern Era*. Cambridge, MA: Polity Press.

—— (2005). *Prolonged Labour: The Slow Birth of New Labour in Britain*. Basingstoke: Palgrave Macmillan.

—— and Lawler, P. (eds.) (2000). *New Labour in Power*. Manchester: Manchester University Press.

Coen, D. (1997). The evolution of the large firm as a political actor in the European Union. *Journal of European Public Policy*, 4/1: 91–108.

—— (1998). The European business interest and the nation state: large firm lobbying in the European Union and member states. *Journal of Public Policy*, 18/1: 75–100.

—— (1999). The impact of US lobbying practice on the European business-government relationship. *California Management Review*, 41/4: 27–44.

—— (2002). Business interests and integration, in R. Bulme, D. Chambre, and V. Wright (eds.), *Collective Action in the European Union*. Paris: Science-Po Press, pp. 255–72.

—— (2007a). Empirical and theoretical studies in EU lobbying. *Journal of European Public Policy*, 14/3: 333–45.

—— (2007b). *Lobbying in the European Union*. PE 393.266. Brussels: European Parliament, www.library.ep.ec accessed 18 September 2008.

—— and Dannreuther, C. (2002). When size matters: Europeanisation of large and SME business government relations. *Politique Européenne*, 7/1: 116–37.

—— and Grant, W. (2001). Corporate political strategy and global policy: a case study of the Transatlantic Business Dialogue. *European Business Journal*, 13/1: 37–44.

—— and Héritier, A. (2000). Business perspectives on German and British regulation: telecoms, energy and rail. *Business Strategy Review*, 11/4: 29–37.

—— and Willman, P. (1998). The evolution of the firm's regulatory affairs office. *Business Strategy Review*, 9/4: 31–6.

Cohen, C. (2002). *Only in Delaware: Politics and Politicians in the First State*. Wilmington, DE: Grapevine.

Committee on Standards in Public Life (2007). *Eleventh Report: Review of the Electoral Commission*. CM7006. Norwich: HMSO.

Competition Commission (2008). *Groceries Market Investigation Final Report*. London: Competition Commission, http://www.competition-commission.org.uk/rep_pub/reports/2008/fulltext/538_3_1.pdf accessed 10 November 2008.

Congress Watch (2002). *United Seniors Association: Hired Guns for Pharma and Other Corporate Interests*, http://www.citizen.org/documents/UnitedSeniorsAssociationreport.pdf accessed 22 July 2008.

CORE (2005). *BAT in Its Own Words*, http://old.ash.org.uk/html/conduct/pdfs/bat2005.pdf accessed 13 November 2008.

Corporate Crime Reporter (2007). Louisiana most corrupt state in the nation, Mississippi second, Illinois sixth, New Jersey ninth. *Corporate Crime Reporter*, 40, 8 October, http://www.corporatecrimereporter.com/corrupt100807.htm accessed 11 August 2008.

Corporate Watch (2008). Checkout chuckout, http://archive.corporatewatch.org.uk/pages/check_out_chuck_out/local_campaigns accessed 16 July 2008.

Cowling, M. (1971). *The Impact of Labour 1920–1924: The Beginning of Modern British Politics.* Cambridge: Cambridge University Press.

Cramb, I. (2008). Ian Paisley Jnr courts Donald Trump. *Daily Telegraph*, 1 March.

Curran, J., Rutherford, R., and Smith, S. (2000). Is there a local business community? Explaining the non-participation of small business in local economic development. *Local Economy*, 15/2: 128–43.

Dahl, R. (1961). *Who Governs? Democracy and Power in an American City.* New Haven, CT: Yale University Press.

—— (1985). *A Preface to Economic Democracy.* Berkeley, CA: University of California Press.

Dalton, R. and Wattenberg, M. (eds.) (2002). *Parties without Partisans: Political Change in Advanced Industrial Democracies.* Oxford: Oxford University Press.

Dannreuther, C. (1999). Discrete dialogues and the legitimation of SME policy in the EU. *Journal of European Public Policy*, 6/3: 436–55.

Davenport-Hines, R.T.P. (1984). *Dudley Docker: The Life and Times of a Trade Warrior.* Cambridge: Cambridge University Press.

Davis, A. (2000). Public relations, business news and the reproduction of corporate elite power. *Journalism*, 1/3: 282–304.

—— (2002). *Public Relations Democracy: Politics, Public Relations and the Mass Media.* Manchester: Manchester University Press.

—— (2007). *The Mediation of Power: A Critical Introduction.* London: Routledge.

De Figueiredo, J. (2002). Lobbying and information in politics. *Business and Politics*, 4/2: 125–9.

Dearlove, D. (2007). *Business the Branson Way: 10 Secrets of the World's Greatest Brandbuilder*, 3rd edition. London: Capstone.

Denham, A. and Garnett, M. (2001). *Keith Joseph.* Chesham: Acumen.

Dennis, W. (2004). *The Public Reviews Small Business.* Washington, DC: National Federation of Independent Business Research Foundation.

Department of Trade and Industry (2007). *Small and Medium Enteprise Statistics for the UK and Regions*, http://www.dtistats.net/smes/sme accessed 25 June 2007.

Derthick, M. (2005). *Up in Smoke: From Legislation to Litigation in Tobacco Politics.* Washington, DC: CQ Press.

Devlin, L. (1972). *Report of the Commission of Inquiry into Industrial and Commercial Representation, Chairman, Lord Devlin.* London: Association of British Chambers of Commerce and Confederation of British Industry.

Dimitrakopoulos, D. (2008). *The Power of the Centre: Central Governments and the Macro-Economic Implementation of EU Public Policy.* Manchester: Manchester University Press.

Doherty, B., Paterson, M., and Plows, A. (2003). Explaining the fuel protests. *British Journal of Politics and International Relations*, 5/1: 1–23.

Done, S., Kirchgaessner, S., and Peel, M. (2007). BA fined in global crackdown on cartels. *Financial Times*, 2 August.

EBPS (2008a). About EBPS, http://www.businessandparliament.eu/index.php?id=75 accessed 30 September 2008.

—— (2008b). British American Tobacco, http://www.businessandparliament.eu/index.php?id=86&cat_id=2 accessed 30 September 2008.

Eisner, M. (2007). *Governing the Environment: The Transformation of Environmental Regulation.* Boulder, CO: Lynne Rienner.

—— Worsham, J., and Ringquist, E. (2006). *Contemporary Regulatory Policy*, 2nd edition. Boulder, CO: Lynne Rienner.

Electoral Commission (2007). Regulatory Issues, http://www.electoralcommission.org.uk/regulatory-issues/gbcampaigns.cfm accessed 9 September 2007.

—— (2008a). Do politics, http://www.electoralcommission.org.uk/guidance/do-politics accessed 9 November 2008.

—— (2008b). *Annual Report 2007–8.* HC 936. London: The Electoral Commission.

—— (2008c). *Corporate Plan 2008–9 to 2012–13.* HC 491. London: The Electoral Commission.

Erturk, I., Froud, J., Johal, S., and Williams, K. (2005). Pay for corporate performance or pay as social division? Rethinking the problem of top management pay in giant corporations. *Competition and Change*, 9/1: 49–74.

EU Civil Society Contact Group (2008). About us, http://www.act4europe.org/code/en/about.asp?Page=2&menuPage=2 accessed 5 November 2008.

EurActiv (2008). Civil society demands more lobbying transparency, http://www.euractiv.com/en/pa/civil-society-demands-lobbying-transparency/article-176819 accessed 5 November 2008.

European Small Business Alliance (2008). ESBA then and now, http://www.esbaeurope.org/03BD0/About_Us/ESBA_Then_Now.aspx accessed 29 September 2008.

Fallon, G. and Brown, R. (2000). Does Britain need public law status Chambers of Commerce? *European Business Review*, 12/1: 19–27.

Federal Election Commission (2007a). Congressional campaigns spend $966 million through mid-October, http://www.fec.gov/press/press2006/20061102can/20061102can.html accessed 14 September 2007.

—— (2007b). FEC reports record civil penalties in first six months of 2006, http://www.fec.gov/press/press2006/20060713enforce.html accessed 14 September 2007.

Federation of Small Businesses (2008a). FSB in Europe, http://www.fsb.org.uk/data/default.asp?id=605&loc=policy accessed 29 September 2008.

—— (2008b). FSB: policy year and achievements 2008, http://www.fsb.org.uk/documentstore/filedetails.asp?id=400 accessed 29 September 2008.

Fellowes, M. and Wolf, P. (2004). Funding mechanisms and policy instruments: how business campaign contributions influence Congressional votes. *Political Research Quarterly*, 57/2: 315–24.

Foley, M. (2007). *American Credo: The Place of Ideas in US Politics*. Oxford: Oxford University Press.

Folkman, P., Froud, J., Johal, S., and Williams, K. (2007). 'Working for themselves?' Capital market intermediaries and present day capitalism. *Business History*, 49/4: 552–72.

Foote, S. (1992). *Managing the Medical Arms Race: Public Policy and Medical Device Innovation*. Berkeley, CA: University of California Press.

Froud, J., Johal, S., Williams, K., and Leaver, A. (2006). *Financialization and Strategy*. London: Routledge.

Galambos, L. (1975). *The Public Image of Big Business in America*. Baltimore, MD: The Johns Hopkins University Press.

Galbraith, J.K. (1967/1972). *The New Industrial State*, 2nd edition. London: Deutsch.

Gamble, A. (1994). *The Free Economy and the Strong State: The Politics of Thatcherism*. London: Macmillan.

—— (2003). *Between Europe and America: The Future of British Politics*. Basingstoke: Palgrave Macmillan.

—— and Kelly, G. (2001). Shareholder value and the stakeholder debate in the UK. *Corporate Governance*, 9/2: 110–17.

Garrett, G. (1998*a*). *Partisan Politics in the Global Economy*. Cambridge: Cambridge University Press.

—— (1998*b*). Global markets and national politics: collision course or virtuous circle? *International Organization*, 52: 767–824.

Glover, J. (2006). A nation of reluctant supermarket shoppers revealed. *Guardian*, 23 November.

Glyn, A. (2006). *Capitalism Unleashed: Finance, Globalization and Welfare*. Oxford: Oxford University Press.

Gramsci, A. (1971). *Selections from the Prison Notebooks*, G. Hoare and G. Nowell Smith (eds. and trs.). London: Lawrence and Wishart.

Grant, A. (2005). Party and election finance in Britain and America: a comparative analysis. *Parliamentary Affairs*, 58/1: 71–88.

Grant, W. (1984). Large firms and public policy in Britain. *Journal of Public Policy*, 4/1: 1–17.

—— (2000). *Globalization, Big Business and the Blair Government*. Working Paper 58/00. Warwick: Centre of the Study of Globalization and Regionalization, University of Warwick.

—— and Marsh, D. (1977). *The Confederation of British Industry*. London: Hodder and Stoughton.

—— and Sargent, J. (1987). *Business and Politics in Britain*. Basingstoke: Macmillan.

Gray, V., Lowery, D., Fellowes, M., and McAtee, A. (2004). Public opinion, public policy, and organized interests in the American states. *Political Research Quarterly*, 57/3: 411–20.

Graz, J-C. (2003). How powerful are transnational elite clubs? The social myth of the World Economic Forum. *New Political Economy*, 8/3: 321–40.

Greater London Authority (2006). *Retail in London: Working Paper G: Small Retailers*. London: Greater London Authority.

Green, J. (2002). Still functional after all these years: parties in the United States, 1960–2000, in P. Webb, D. Farrell, and I. Holliday (eds.), *Political Parties in Advanced Industrial Democracies*. Oxford: Oxford University Press, pp. 310–42.

Greenwood, J. and Traxler, F. (2007). Associations of SMEs: the United Kingdom, in F. Traxler and G. Huemer (eds.), *National Preparations for EU Social Partnership*. London: Routledge, pp. 315–48.

Gribben, R. (2005). Lobby groups accused of inflating figures: critics suggest membership numbers are puffed up in an effort to carry more weight in Whitehall. *Daily Telegraph*, 29 November, http://galegroup.com/itx/start.do?prodId=SPN.SP00 accessed 13 June 2008.

Grieves, K. (1989). *Sir Eric Geddes: Business and Government in War and Peace*. Manchester: Manchester University Press.

Griffiths, D. (2009). The social networks of the public elite. PhD thesis, School of Social Sciences, University of Manchester.

Guttsman, W. (1963). *The British Political Elite*. London: Macgibbon and Kee.

Hall, P. and Soskice, D. (eds.) (2001). *Varieties of Capitalism: The Institutional Foundations of Comparative Advantage*. Oxford: Oxford University Press.

Hammond, B. (1957). *Banks and Politics in America from the Revolution to the Civil War*. Princeton, NJ: Princeton University Press.

Hannah, L. (1983). *The Rise of the Corporate Economy*, 2nd edition. London: Methuen.

Hansen, W., Mitchell N., and Drope, J. (2004). Collective action, pluralism, and the legitimacy tariff: corporate activity or inactivity in politics. *Political Research Quarterly*, 57/3: 421–9.

Hanson, P. and Teague, E. (2005). Big business and the state in Russia. *Europe-Asia Studies*, 57/5: 657–80.

Harris, N. (1973). *Competition and the Corporate Society: British Conservatives, the State and Industry, 1945–1964*. London: Methuen.

Hart, D. (2001). Why do some firms give? Why do some give a lot? High-tech PACs, 1977–96. *Journal of Politics*, 83/4: 1230–49.

—— (2002). High-tech learns to play the Washington game, in A. Cigler and B. Loomis (eds.), *Interest Group Politics*, 6th edition. Washington, DC: CQ Press, pp. 293–312.

—— (2004). Business is not an interest group: on the study of companies in American national politics. *American Review of Political Science*, 7: 47–69.

—— (2007). Red, white and 'big blue': IBM and the business–government interface in the US, 1956–2000. *Enterprise and Society*, 8/1: 1–34.

Harvey, C. and Maclean, M. (2008). Capital theory and the dynamics of elite business networks in Britain and France, in M. Savage and K. Williams (eds.), *Remembering Elites*. Oxford: Blackwell, pp. 105–20.

Hawley, E. (1978). The discovery and study of a corporate liberalism. *Business History Review*, 52/3: 309–20.

Haxey, S. (1942). *Tory MP*. London: Gollancz.

Heinz, J., Laumann, E., Nelson, R., and Salisbury, R. (1993). *The Hollow Core: Private Interests in National Policy Making*. Cambridge, MA: Harvard University Press.

Hilferding. R. (1910/1985). *Finance Capital: A Study in the Latest Phase of Capitalist Development*, M. Watnick and S. Gordon (trs.). London: Routledge.

Hilts, P. (2003). *Protecting America's Health: The FDA, Business, and One Hundred Years of Regulation*. New York: Alfred E. Knopf.

Hirst, P. and Thompson, G. (1999). *Globalization in Question*, 2nd edition. Cambridge, MA: Polity Press.

Hix, S., Noury, A., and Roland, G. (2006). Dimensions of politics in the European Parliament. *American Journal of Political Science*, 50/2: 494–511.

Hofstadter, R. (1955/1972). *The Age of Reform: From Bryan to FDR*. New York: Alfred E. Knopf.

Holden, L. (2005). Fording the Atlantic: Ford and Fordism in Europe. *Business History*, 47/1: 122–7.

Hope, C. and Hall, J. (2008). Wall-Mart did lobby Blair over ASDA. *Daily Telegraph*, 28 January.

Hopkin, J. (2005). Towards a chequebook democracy? Business, parties and the funding of politics in Italy and the United States. *Journal of Modern Italian Studies*, 10/1: 43–58.

Hoppe, R. and Banker, D. (2006). *Structure and Financing of US Farms 2005: Family Farm Report*. Washington, DC: United States Department of Agriculture Economic Research Service.

House of Commons Public Administration Select Committee (2008). Lobbying: written evidence unapproved, http://www.publications.parliament.uk/pa/cm/cmpubadm.htm accessed 20 June 2008.

House of Commons Treasury Select Committee (2007). *Private Equity. Tenth Report of Session 2006–07 Volume I Report, Together with Formal Minutes*. HC 567–1. London: The Stationery Office.

Hunter, F. (1953). *Community Power Structure: A Study of Decision Makers*. Chapel Hill, NC: University of North Carolina Press.

Hutton, W. (1995). *The State We're in: Why Britain Is in Crisis and How to Overcome It*. London: Jonathan Cape.

Ingham, G. (1984). *Capitalism Divided: The City and Industry in British Social Development*. Basingstoke: Macmillan.

Inman, P. (2008). OFT raids Barclays and RBS over alleged collusion. *Guardian*, 3 June.

International Association of Business and Parliament (2007). *European Business and Parliament Scheme*. Brussels: European Parliament.

Jacobs, D. (1999). *Business Lobbies and the Power Structure in America*. Westport, CT: Quorum Books.

Jayasuriya, K. (2001). Globalization and the changing architecture of the state: the regulatory state and the politics of negative coordination. *Journal of European Public Policy*, 8/1: 101–23.

—— (2005). Beyond institutional fetishism: from the developmental to the regulatory state. *New Political Economy*, 10/3: 381–7.

Jeffery, C. and Wincott, D. (2006). Devolution in the United Kingdom: statehood and citizenship in transition. *Publius*, 36/1: 3–18.

Johnson, C. (1982). *MITI and the Japanese Miracle*. Stanford, CA: Stanford University Press.

Jones, G. (1969). *Borough Politics: A Study of Wolverhampton Town Council*. London: Macmillan.

Jones, S. (2006). *Antonio Gramsci*. London: Routledge.

Jordan, G. and Halpin, D. (2003). Cultivating small business influence in the UK: the Federation of Small Businesses' journey from outsider to insider. *Journal of Public Affairs*, 3/4: 313–25.

—— (2004). Olson triumphant? Recruitment strategies and the growth of a small business organisation. *Political Studies*, 52/3: 431–49.

Josephson, M. (1962). *The Robber Barons: The Great American Capitalists 1861–1901*. London: Eyre and Spottiswoode.

Kagan, R. (2001). *Adversarial Legalism: the American Way of Law*. Cambridge, MA: Harvard University Press.

Katz, R. and Kolodny, R. (1994). Party organization as an empty vessel: parties in American politics, in R. Katz and P. Mair (eds.), *How Parties Organize: Change and Adaptation in Party Organizations in Western Democracies.* London: Sage, pp. 23–50.

—— and Mair, P. (1995). Changing models of party organization and party democracy: the emergence of the cartel party. *Party Politics*, 1/1: 5–28.

Kelly, D. (2005). The International Chamber of Commerce. *New Political Economy*, 10/2: 259–71.

Kerwer, D. (2005). Rules that many use: standards and global regulation. *Governance*, 18/4: 611–32.

King, A. (1981). The rise of the career politician in Britain – and its consequences. *British Journal of Political Science*, 11/3: 249–85.

King, R. and Kendall, G. (2004). *The State, Democracy and Globalization.* Basingstoke: Palgrave Macmillan.

Kynaston, D. (1995). *The City of London: Volume I. A World on its Own 1815–1890.* London: Pimlico.

—— (2000). *The City of London: Volume III. Illusions of Gold 1914–1945.* London: Pimlico.

Lazonick, W. (1991). *Business Organization and the Myth of the Market Economy.* Cambridge: Cambridge University Press.

Lees-Marshment, J. (2001). *Political Marketing and British Political Parties.* Manchester: Manchester University Press.

Lehne, R. (2006). *Government and Business: American Political Economy in Comparative Perspective*, 2nd edition. Washington: CQ Press.

Lenin, V. (1917/1975). *Imperialism: The Highest Stage of Capitalism: A Popular Outline.* Moscow: Progress Publishers.

Levitan, S. and Cooper, R. (1984). *Business Lobbies: The Public Good and the Bottom Line.* Baltimore, MD: Johns Hopkins University Press.

Lindblom, C. (1977). *Politics and Markets: The World's Political-Economic Systems.* New York: Basic Books.

—— (2002). *The Market System: What It Is, How It Works, and What to Make of It.* New Haven, CT: Yale University Press.

Lipset, S.M. (1964). *The First New Nation: The United States in Historical and Comparative Perspective.* London: Heinemann.

—— (1996). *American Exceptionalism: A Double-Edged Sword.* New York: Norton.

Lisle-Williams, M. (1984). Merchant banking dynasties in the English class structure: ownership, solidarity and kinship in the City of London, 1850–90. *British Journal of Sociology*, XXXV/3: 333–62.

Lockwood, G. (2005). Trade Union governance: the development of British conservative thought. *Journal of Political Ideologies*, 10/3: 355–71.

Logan, J. and Molotch, H. (1987). *Urban Fortunes: The Political Economy of Place.* Berkeley, CA: University of California Press.

Lukes, S. (2005). *Power: A Radical View*, 2nd edition. Basingstoke: Palgrave Macmillan.

Luo, M. and Drew, M. (2008). Obama picks up fund-raising pace, *New York Times*, 3 July, http://www.nytimes.com/2008/07/03/us/politics/03donate.html accessed 22 July 2008.

Lupton, T. and Wilson, S. (1959). The social background and connections of top decision makers. *The Manchester School*, XXVII/1: 30–52.

MacDonald, A. (2001). *The Business of Representation: The Modern Trade Association.* London: Trade Association Forum.

Maclean, M., Harvey, C., and Press, J. (2006). *Business Elites and Corporate Governance in France and the UK.* Basingstoke: Palgrave Macmillan.

Mair, P. and Van Biezen, I. (2001). Party membership in 20 European democracies, 1980–2000. *Party Politics,* 7/1: 5–21.

Maloney, W., Smith, G., and Stoker, G. (2000). Social capital and urban governance: adding a more contextualised 'top down' perspective. *Political Studies,* 48/4: 802–20.

Marchand, R. (1998). *Creating the Corporate Soul: The Rise of Public Relations and Corporate Imagery in American Big Business.* Berkeley, CA: University of California Press.

Marsh, D. (1992). *The New Politics of British Trade Unionism.* Basingstoke: Macmillan.

Martin, C. (2000.) *Stuck in Neutral: Business and the Politics of Human Capital Investment Policy.* Princeton, NJ: Princeton University Press.

May, T. and McHugh, J. (2002). Small business policy: a political consensus. *Political Quarterly,* 73/1: 76–85.

—— McHugh, J., and Taylor, T. (1998). Business representation in the UK since 1979: the case of Trade Associations. *Political Studies,* XLVI/2: 260–75.

McCartney, L. (2008). *The Teapot Dome Scandal.* New York: Random House.

McConnell, G. (1966). *Private Power and American Democracy.* New York: Alfred E. Knopf.

McCraw, T. (1984). *Prophets of Regulation: Charles Francis Adams, Louis D. Brandeis, James M. Landis and Alfred E. Kahn.* Cambridge, MA: Belknap Press of Harvard University Press.

—— (1997). American capitalism, in T. McCraw (ed.), *Creating Modern Capitalism: How Entrepreneurs, Companies, and Countries Triumphed in Three Industrial Revolutions.* Cambridge, MA: Harvard University Press, pp. 303–48.

McGrath, C. (2005). *Lobbying in Washington, London and Brussels: The Persuasive Communication of Political Issues.* Lampeter: Edwin Mellen Press.

McKibbin, R. (1974). *The Evolution of the Labour Party 1910–1924.* Oxford: Oxford University Press.

McLean, B. and Elkind, P. (2003). *The Smartest Guys in the Room: The Amazing Rise and Scandalous Fall of Enron.* New York: Portfolio.

McQuaid, K. (1982). *Big Business and Presidential Power: From FDR to Reagan.* New York: William Morrow.

—— (1994). *Uneasy Partners: Big Business in American Politics 1945–90.* Baltimore, MD: Johns Hopkins University Press.

Melman, S. (1970). *Pentagon Capitalism: The Political Economy of War.* New York: McGraw Hill.

Mercer, H. (1994). The state and British business since 1945, in M. Kirby and M. Rose (eds.), *Business Enterprise in Modern Britain: From the Eighteenth to the Twentieth Century.* London: Routledge, pp. 287–314.

Mereu, F. (2007). A Russian house cleaning that wasn't. *International Herald Tribune,* 1 November, http://www.iht.com/articles/2007/11/01/europe/russia.php accessed 23 September 2008.

Merle, R. (2003). US: defense firms consolidate as war goes high tech. *Washington Post,* 27 May, http://www.corpwatch.org/article.plup?id=7868 accessed 21 October 2008.

Metcalfe, J.S. (2006). Entrepreneurship: an evolutionary perspective, in M. Casson, B. Yeung, A. Basu, and N. Wadeson (eds.), *The Oxford Handbook of Entrepreneurship*. Oxford: Oxford University Press, pp. 59–90.

Middlemas, K. (1979). *Politics in Industrial Society: The Experience of the British System since 1911*. London: Deutsch.

Miller, D. and Dinan, W. (2000). The rise of the PR industry in Britain, 1979–98. *European Journal of Communication*, 15/1: 5–35.

Milward, A. (2000). *The European Reconstruction of the Nation State*, 2nd edition. London: Routledge.

Milward, N., Stevens, M., Smart, D., and Hawes, W. (1992). *Workplace Industrial Relations in Transition*. Aldershot: Dartmouth.

Milyo, J., Primo, D., and Groseclose, T. (2000). Corporate PAC campaign contributions in perspective. *Business and Politics*, 2/1: 75–88.

Mitchell, C. (2008). New sheriff in town: the new gifts and travel rules. *Presentation to All American League of Lobbyists*, 19 May, http://www.alldc.org/publicresources/newlobbylaw. cfm accessed 13 October 2008.

Mitchell, J. (2006). Evolution and devolution: citizenship, institutions and public policy. *Publius*, 36/1: 153–68.

Mitchell, N. (1997). *The Conspicuous Corporation: Business, Public Policy and Representative Democracy*. Ann Arbor, MI: University of Michigan Press.

Molotch, H. (1976). The city as a growth machine: towards a political economy of place. *American Journal of Sociology*, 86/2: 309–17.

Moran, M. (1984). Politics, banks and markets: an Anglo-American comparison. *Political Studies*, XXXII/1: 173–89.

—— (1986). *The Politics of Banking: The Strange Case of Competition and Credit Control*, 2nd edition. London: Macmillan.

—— (1991). *The Politics of the Financial Services Revolution: the USA, UK and Japan*. Basingstoke: Palgrave Macmillan.

—— (2006). The company of strangers: defending the power of business in Britain, 1975–2005. *New Political Economy*, 11/4: 453–78.

—— (2007). *The British Regulatory State: High Modernism and Hyper-Innovation*. Oxford: Oxford University Press.

Morgan, K. (2006). Devolution and development: territorial justice and the North–South divide. *Publius*, 36/1: 189–206.

Moriarty, M. (2006). *Report of the Tribunal of Inquiry into Payments to Politicians and Related Matters, Part 1*. Dublin: The Stationery Office, http://www.moriarty-tribunal.ie/images/ sitecontent_26.pdf accessed 11 September 2008.

Mosk, M. (2008). Internet donors fuel Obama. *Washington Post*, 7 February, http://blog. washingtonpost.com/the-trail/2008/02/07/obama_fundraising_strength_com.html accessed 22 July 2008.

Mügge, D. (2006). Private–public puzzles: inter-firm competition and transnational private regulation. *New Political Economy*, 11/2: 177–200.

Mulgan, A.G. (2005). Where tradition meets change: Japan's agricultural politics in transition. *Journal of Japanese Studies*, 31/2: 261–98.

Namier, L. (1929). *The Structure of Politics at the Accession of George III*. London: Macmillan.

National Association of Manufacturers (2007*a*). Why manufacturing is essential, http://www.nam.org/s_nam accessed. 12 March 2007.

—— (2007*b*). *The NAM: Investing in America. 2007 Annual Report*. Washington, DC: National Association of Manufacturers.

National Federation of Independent Business (2005). *National Small Business Poll: Political Participation*. Washington, DC: National Federation of Independent Business Research Foundation.

—— (2007). *Small Business Resource Guide for the 110th Congress*. Washington, DC: National Federation of Independent Business.

—— (2008). National political news items, http://www.nfib.com/object/polNewsFD?fedStartPos=1&fedEndPos=20&stateStartPos=1&stateEndPos=20 accessed 13 November 2008.

National Small Business Association (2007). Frequently asked questions, http://www.nsba.biz/FAQs/ accessed 19 June 2007.

Nettl, J.P. (1965). Consensus or elite domination: the case of business. *Political Studies*, 13/1: 22–44.

Nilsson, A. (2009). Analysts, journalists, firms and the stock market: a thesis on narratives and numbers. PhD thesis, ESRC Centre for Research on Socio-Cultural Change, University of Manchester, in progress.

Ogus, A. (1992). Regulatory law: lessons from the past. *Legal Studies*, 12/1: 1–19.

Olson, M. (1965). *The Logic of Collective Action: Public Goods and the Theory of Groups*. Cambridge, MA: Harvard University Press.

—— (1982). *The Rise and Decline of Nations: Economic Growth, Stagflation and Social Rigidities*. New Haven, CT: Yale University Press.

Paine, T. (1982). Obituary: Sir Paul Chambers, 1904–1981. *Journal of the Royal Statistical Society*, 145/3: 374–5.

Parkinson, J. (1994). *Corporate Power and Responsibility: Issues in the Theory of Company Law*. Oxford: Clarendon Press.

Parmar, I. (2004). *Think Tanks and Power in Foreign Policy: A Comparative Study of the Role and Influence of the Council on Foreign Relations and the Royal Institute of International Affairs, 1939–1945*. Basingstoke: Palgrave Macmillan.

—— (2005). Catalysing events, think tanks and American foreign policy. *Government and Opposition*, 40/1: 1–25.

Parry, G. (1969/2005). *Political Elites*. Colchester: ECPR Press.

Paul, D. (2005). The local politics of 'Going Global': making and unmaking Minneapolis-St Paul as a world city. *Urban Studies*, 42/1: 2103–22.

Pearson, R. (2002). Shareholder democracies? English stock companies and the politics of corporate governance during the Industrial Revolution. *The English Historical Review*, 117: 840–66.

Peck, J. (1995). Moving and shaking: business elites, state localism and urban privatism. *Progress in Human Geography*. 19/1: 16–46.

—— (2006). Liberating the city: between New York and New Orleans. *Urban Geography*, 27/8: 681–713.

Peck, J. and Tickell, A. (1994). Too many partners: the future for regeneration partnerships. *Local Economy*, 9: 251–65.

Phelps. N., Parsons, N., Bollas, D., and Dowling, A. (2006). Business at the margins: business interests in edge urban politics. *International Journal of Urban and Regional Research*, 30/2: 362–83.

Phillips. H. (2007). *Strengthening Democracy: Fair and Sustainable Funding of Political Parties. The Review of the Funding of Political Parties.* Norwich: The Stationery Office.

Pilling, D. 2006. March of the mini-multinationals, *Financial Times*, 4 May.

Pinkham, D. (2005). Public Affairs Council, in C. McGrath (ed.), *Lobbying in Washington, London, and Brussels: The Persuasive Communication of Political Issues.* Lampeter: Edwin Mellens Press, pp. 266–71.

Pinto-Duschinsky, M. (1981). *British Political Finance 1830–1980.* Washington, DC: American Enterprise Institute for Public Policy Research.

Pirie, I. (2005). Better by design: Korea's neoliberal economy. *Pacific Review*, 18/3:1–20.

—— (2007). *The Korean Developmental State: From Dirigisme to Neo-Liberalism.* London: Routledge.

Pollard, S. (1992). *The Development of the British Economy 1914–1990.* London: Arnold.

Polsby, N. (1980). *Community Power and Political Theory: A Further Look at Problems of Evidence and Inference.* New Haven, CT: Yale University Press.

Porter, T. (1995). *Trust in Numbers: The Pursuit of Objectivity in Science and Public Life.* Princeton, NJ: Princeton University Press.

Power, M. (2007). *Organized Uncertainty: Designing a World of Risk Management.* Oxford: Oxford University Press.

Putnam, R. (2000). *Bowling Alone: The Collapse and Revival of American Community.* New York: Simon and Schuster.

Radcliffe, L. (1960). *Committee on the Working of the Monetary System: Principal Memoranda of Evidence. Volume 1.* London: HMSO.

Rast, J. (2001). Manufacturing industrial decline: the politics of economic change in Chicago, 1955–88. *Journal of Urban Affairs*, 23/2: 175–90.

Rauch, J. (2005). Here's a new campaign finance reform: just stop. *National Journal*, 7 May.

Rhodes, R. (1997). *Understanding Governance: Policy Networks, Governance, Reflexivity and Accountability.* Buckingham: Open University Press.

Ricci, D. (1993). *The Transformation of American Politics.* New Haven, CT: Yale University Press.

Ringe, A. and Rollings, N. (2000). Responding to relative economic decline: the creation of the National Economic Development Council. *Economic History Review*, LIII/2: 331–53.

Robinson, W. and Harris, J. (2000). Towards a global ruling class: globalization and the transnational capitalist class. *Science and Society*, 64/1: 11–54.

Roe, M. (1994). *Strong Managers, Weak Owners: The Political Roots of American Corporate Finance.* Princeton, NJ: Princeton University Press.

—— (2003). *Political Determinants of Corporate Governance: Political Context, Corporate Impact.* Oxford: Oxford University Press.

Rowell, A. (2003). Wall-Mart's inexhaustible march to conquer the globe, *Multinational Monitor Magazine*, October, http://www.thirdworldtraveler.com/Corporations/Welcome_Wal_World. html accessed 17 November 2008.

Roy, W. (1997). *Socializing Capital: The Rise of the Large Industrial Corporation in America.* Princeton, NJ: Princeton University Press.

Rush, L. (2007). Influence: a booming business: record $1.3 billion spent to lobby state government, http://www.publicintegrity.org/hiredguns/report.aspx?aid=957 accessed 4 July 2008.

Sampson, A. (1965). *The Anatomy of Britain Today.* London: Hodder and Stoughton.

Samuels, R. (1987). *The Business of the Japanese State: Energy Markets in Comparative and Historical Perspective.* Ithaca, NY: Cornell University Press.

Saunders, P. (1979). *Urban Politics: A Sociological Interpretation.* London: Hutchinson.

Savage, M. and Williams, K. (2008.) Elites: remembered in capitalism and forgotten by social sciences, in M. Savage and K. Williams (eds.), *Remembering Elites.* Oxford: Blackwell, pp. 1–24.

Schlozman, K. and Tierney, J. (1986). *Organized Interests and American Democracy.* New York: Harper and Row.

Schmidt, S., Grimaldi, J., and Smith, R. (2006). Investigating Abramoff. *Washington Post*, http://www.washingtonpost.com/wp-dyn/content/linkset/2005/06/22/LI2005062200936.html accessed 18 September 2007.

Schofield, R. (1994). British population change, 1700–1871, in R. Floud and D. McCloskey (eds.), *The Economic History of Britain since 1700*, Vol. 1, 2nd edition. Cambridge: Cambridge University Press, pp. 60–95.

Scholte, J. (2005). *Globalization: A Critical Introduction*, 2nd edition. Basingstoke: Palgrave Macmillan.

Schumpeter, J. (1943/1976). *Capitalism, Socialism and Democracy.* London: Allen and Unwin.

Scott, J. (1997). *Corporate Business and Capitalist Classes.* Oxford: Oxford University Press.

—— (2003). Transformations in the British economic elite. *Comparative Sociology*, 2/1: 155–73.

Seligman, J. (2003). *The Transformation of Wall Street: A History of the Securities and Exchange Commission and Modern Corporate Finance.* New York: Aspen.

Shonfield, A. (1965). *Modern Capitalism: The Changing Balance of Public and Private Power.* Oxford: Oxford University Press.

Sinclair, T. (2005). *The New Masters of Capital: American Bond Rating Agencies and the Politics of Creditworthiness.* Ithaca, NY: Cornell University Press.

Sklair, L. (2001). *The Transnational Capitalist Class.* Oxford: Blackwell.

Skocpol, T. (2003). *Diminished Democracy: From Membership to Management in American Civic Life.* Norman, OK: University of Oklahoma Press.

Small Business Administration (2006*a*). *Frequently Asked Questions.* Washington, DC: Small Business Administration.

—— (2006*b*). *The Small Business Economy.* Washington, DC: Small Business Administration.

Smith. M. (2000). *American Business and Political Power: Public Opinion, Elections, and Democracy.* Chicago, IL: University of Chicago Press.

Sobel, R. (1965). *The Big Board: A History of the New York Stock Market.* London: Collier Macmillan.

Speth, J.G. (2008). *The Bridge at the Edge of the World: Capitalism, the Environment, and Crossing the Crisis to Sustainability.* New Haven, CT: Yale University Press.

Stewart, R. (1988). Regulation and the crisis of legalisation in the United States, in T. Daintith (ed.), *Law as an Instrument of Economic Policy*. Berlin: de Gruyter, pp. 97–133.

Stone, C. (1989). *Regime Politics: Governing Atlanta, 1946–1988*. Lawrence, KS: University Press of Kansas.

Stone, R. (1991). *The Interstate Commerce Commission and the Railroad Industry: A History of Regulatory Policy*. New York: Praeger.

Strange, S. (1971). *Sterling and British Policy: A Political Study of an International Currency in Decline*. London: Oxford University Press for the Royal Institute of International Affairs.

Supple, B. (1970). *The Royal Exchange Insurance: A History of British Insurance, 1720–1970*. Cambridge: Cambridge University Press.

—— (ed.) (1992). *The Rise of Big Business*. Aldershot: Elgar.

Thompson, J. (2000). *Political Scandal: Power and Visibility in the Media Age*. Cambridge, MA: Polity Press.

Thornley, A., Rydin, Y., Scanlon, K., and West, K. (2005). Business privilege and the strategic planning agenda of the Greater London Authority. *Urban Studies*, 42/11: 1947–68.

Trajtenberg, M. (1990). *Economic Analysis of Product Innovation: The Case of CT Scanners*. Cambridge, MA: Harvard University Press.

Tren, M. (2005). Branded, *Guardian Unlimited*, 1 September, http://blogs.guardian.co.uk/businessinsight/archives/2005/09/01/branded.html accessed 26 September 2008.

UNCTAD (United Nations Conference on Trade and Development) (2006). *World Development Report*. New York and Geneva: United Nations.

US Census Bureau (2008). *Selected Historical Decennial Census Population and Housing Counts*, http://www.census.gov/population/www/censusdata/hiscendata.html accessed 10 June 2008.

Useem, M. (1984). *The Inner Circle: Large Corporations and the Rise of Business Political Activity in the US and the UK*. New York: Oxford University Press.

Van Apeldorn, B. (2000). Transnational class agency and European governance: the case of the European Round Table of Industrialists. *New Political Economy*, 5/2: 157–81.

Van der Pijl, K. (1998). *Transnational Classes and International Relations*. London: Routledge.

Vidich, A. and Bensman, J. (1960). *Small Town in Mass Society: Class, Power and Religion in a Rural Community*. New York: Anchor Books.

Vogel, D. (1978). *Lobbying the Corporation: Citizen Challenges to Business Authority*. New York: Basic Books 1978.

—— (1986). *National Styles of Regulation: Environmental Policy in Great Britain and the United States*. Ithaca, NY: Cornell University Press.

—— (1989). *Fluctuating Fortunes: The Political Power of Business in America*. New York: Basic Books.

—— (1996). *Kindred Strangers: The Uneasy Relationship between Politics and Business in America*. Princeton, NJ: Princeton University Press.

Vogel, S. (1996). *Freer Markets, More Rules: Regulatory Reform in Advanced Industrial Countries*. Ithaca, NY: Cornell University Press.

Webb, P., Farrell, D., and. Holliday, I. (eds.) (2002). *Political Parties in Advanced Industrial Democracies*. Oxford: Oxford University Press.

Weber, M. (1919/1970). Politics as a vocation, in H.H. Gerth and C. Wright Mills (trs. and eds.), *From Max Weber: Essays in Sociology*. London: Routledge, pp. 77–128.

Welch, J. and Welch, S. (2005). *Winning*. New York: HarperCollins.

Whitaker, L. (2004). *Campaign Finance: Constitutional and Legal Issues of Soft Money*, 21 July, http://fpc.state.gov/documents/organization/34815.pdf accessed 12 October 2008.

Wiener, M. (1981/1998). *English Culture and the Decline of the Industrial Spirit 1850–1980*. Cambridge: Cambridge University Press.

Wigham, E. (1973). *The Power to Manage: A History of the Engineering Employers' Federation*. London: Macmillan.

Wilks, S. (1999). *In the Public Interest: Competition Policy and the Monopolies and Mergers Commission*. Manchester: Manchester University Press.

—— and Bartle, I. (2002). The unanticipated consequences of creating independent competition agencies. *West European Politics*, 25/1: 148–72.

—— and McGowan, L. (1996). Competition policy in the European Union: creating a federal agency, in G. Doern and S. Wilks (eds.), *Comparative Competition Policy*. Oxford: Clarendon, pp. 225–67.

Wincott, D. (2006). Social policy and social citizenship: Britain's welfare states. *Publius*, 36/1: 169–88.

Winstanley, M. (1995). Concentration and competition in the retail sector 1880–1990, in M. Kirby and M. Rose (eds.), *Business Enterprise in Modern Britain: From the Eighteenth to the Twentieth Century*. London: Routledge, pp. 246–72.

Wolfe, A. (1977). *The Limits of Legitimacy: Political Contradictions of Contemporary Capitalism*. New York: Free Press.

Woll, C. (2006). Lobbying in the European Union: from *sui generis* to a comparative perspective. *Journal of European Public Policy*, 13/3: 456–69.

Wood, A., Valler, D., Phelps, N., Raco, M., and Shirlow, P. (2005). Devolution and the political representation of business in the UK. *Political Geography*, 24/3: 293–315.

Wood, Z. (2008). Tesco rivals to get say on stores test, *Observer*, 3 August.

Wray, R. (2006). The search for influence: Google becomes a political player, *Guardian*, 24 October.

Wright Mills, C. (1956/2000). *The Power Elite*. New York: Oxford University Press.

Yandle, B. (1983). Bootleggers and Baptists: the education of a regulatory economist. *Regulation*, 7/May–June: 12–16.

Young, A. (2001). *The Politics of Regulation: Privatised Utilities in Britain*. Basingstoke: Palgrave.

INDEX

Aberdeenshire County Council 92–3
Abramoff, Jack 59, 123
academic research institutes 137
accountability 115, 135, 152
accounting practices 46, 68–9
acquisitions 76
advanced capitalism 1, 3, 17, 69, 153, 154, 159
    converging in dominant cultural traits 130
    famous characterization
        of 151
    fundamental changes in the character of 36
    one of the weakest economies 133
    opposition to key features of 143
adversarial legalism 141, 142, 146, 170
advertising 112, 113, 119, 124
advocacy coalitions 75
aggressive discounting 99
agriculture 20, 28, 88, 91
    free trade in 108
    numbers employed in decline 94
aircraft makers 100
airlines 146
Albert, M. vii, 10
allocation of resources 8–9, 17, 150, 165
ALTER-EU (Alliance for Lobbying
        Transparency and Ethics
        Regulation) 131
amalgamations 87
Amazon 164
American Civil War (1861–5) 29, 140
American Enterprise Institute 147
American Tobacco Company 148
Americanization 170
Andersen (Arthur) 67
Anglo-American capitalism vii, 10–11, 18,
        27, 168, 169–71
animals in experiments 137
anti-big business messages 146
anti-business culture thesis 134
anti-discrimination programmes 142
anti-globalization protests/alliances 137, 143,
        155
anti-market orthodoxy 150
anti-Semitism 36
antitrust regulation 13, 99, 100–1, 136
Apple Computer 160, 164

Arab-Israeli War (1973) 133
aristocracy 20, 23, 132
Arts Council 111
Asda 63, 76
assembly-line working 36
Association of Convenience Stores 76
Association of Foreign Banks 78
Astra Zeneca 66
Atlanta 35
ATMs (automatic teller machines) 101
audiotapes 50
Austro-Hungarian monarchy 24
autocracy 27
automobile industry 34, 36, 162
    leading association for 78

Babb, J. 27, 94
baby milk campaigns 139
Bache, I. 19
Bank of England 28, 44, 109, 111, 133
    foundation of 21
    lobbying channelled through 43
    role of 21, 25
Banker, D. 99
bankruptcy 12
banks:
    collapse of 64
    crises 111, 166, 167
    cross-state networks 101
    failing 168
    federally chartered 98–9
    partial nationalization of 135, 167
    plan to underwrite untradeable debts 168
    rescue packages for 15, 25
    small deposits safeguarded 33
Bankwatch Network 131
Barclays 136
Barker, A. 111
Bassett, K. 89
BAT (British American Tobacco) 107, 148
Baumgartner, F. 54, 57, 120, 122
Bean, J. 98
Beer, Samuel 64–5
Béland, D. 147
Bensel, R. 29
Bensman, J. 102

Berezovsky, Boris 69
Berle, A. 8, 162
BERR (UK Department of Business
    Enterprise and Regulatory Reform) 61,
    84, 88
Berry, J. 35, 143, 145, 147, 149, 155
BEUC (Bureau Européen des Unions de
    Consommateurs) 131
big business 34, 35, 36, 65, 70, 97, 98, 146,
    147, 152, 157, 164, 171
  ambitions against anti-competitive
      protections 101
  close connection between state agencies
      and 27
  coalitions substantially controlled by 54
  connection between Conservatives and 87
  criticism of 144, 145, 158
  cultural context 146
  cultural expectations hostile to 38
  devolution may have strengthened 92–3
  domination by 90
  enforced partnership between big
      government and 60
  films that expose allegedly antisocial
      activities of 145
  global expansion of 140
  golden age for legitimacy 35
  hostility to 32
  ideology that unites small business to 96
  integration of state and 69
  most important institution of collective
      action for 75
  national survey (2004) 95
  new challenges to the power of 30
  perception increasingly unfavourable 68
  politics and 69
  popular view of 159
  public relations disaster for one section
      of 100
  suspicion of 114
  tendency to dominate 102
big government 28, 29, 60, 140
Bilderberg Group 78, 81, 158
Bipartisan Campaign Reform Act (US
    2002) 122
Birch, A. 87
Birdlife International 131
Blackaby, F. 42
Blair, Tony 76
Blank, S. 25, 26, 109
blind people 50
Bloomberg, Michael 125
Boddewyn, J. 73

Bolton Inquiry on Small Firms
    (UK 1971) 87, 88
bond rating agencies 80
bonuses 15
booms 10, 36, 116, 133, 147
'boosterism' 149
Bootlegger–Baptist coalitions 57
Bowman, S. 12, 31, 100, 101
boycotts 139, 154, 155
BP 46, 66, 68, 69, 78, 107
Braithwaite, J. 3, 12, 79
brand management 74, 167
brands 46, 68, 148
  boycotted 139
Branson, Richard 68
Brent Spar oilrig 67, 68
Bretton Woods 159, 160
bribery 59, 121, 123
British Airways 66, 136, 138
British Chambers of Commerce 44,
    89, 90
British Employers' Confederation 109
British Private Equity and Venture Capital
    Association 117
Brown, Gordon 88, 111
Brussels 41, 48, 50, 58, 131, 152
  UK Federation of Small Businesses in 85
Bryson, J. 88
Buffet, Warren 127
Bundesverband der Deutschen Industrie 152
Bush, George (Sen.) 146
Bush, George W. 56, 124, 146
business class 5, 9
Business Councils 53, 71, 75, 88, 111, 115,
    147
  see also World Business Council
Business Europe 152
business finance 37, 113, 120–1, 125
  circumventing regulatory limits to 124
  dependence/reliance of politicians on 128,
      156
business institutions 21, 38, 110, 129
  adversarial criticism of 31
  central place to state in steering 9
  constraints on 33
  development of 18, 20
  important 8
  legitimacy of 14, 32, 130
  ownership and control of economic
      resources 6
  perceived power of 95
  popular hostility towards, or support for 4
  setting of rules 23

business interests 48, 59, 61, 82, 84, 86, 91–2, 95, 99, 103, 133, 136
  cultural weakness of 132
  hegemony deferential to 138
  important source of division between 161
  informal coordination of 43
  instrument for uniting military adventures and 21
  introduction into the public sector 134
  lobbying by 41, 107, 127
  mobilization at local level 89
  new democracy critical for 26
  old and new 20, 23, 108
  organizing 40, 42, 51, 55, 100
  political parties and 16, 105, 106, 108, 109, 111, 114, 117, 118, 120, 127, 128, 156
  problematic tool of 28
  representation of 26, 44, 158–9, 161
  sectional 26, 87, 118, 123
  selfish 75
  strategic 56
  well-established 22
business politics 22, 25, 95–6, 129
  comparing 1–3
  devolved systems 92
  history of 20, 30, 59
  party politics and 106–28
  reshaped 26
  restless capitalism and 159–63
  restless democracy and 153–9
  watershed in 37
business power 16–17, 86
  and campaign financing 124
  critical accounts of 4, 31, 131
  democratic politics and 2, 3–7, 106
  foundations of 94
  models of 7–11, 169–71
  most influential academic study of 5–6
  policy issues and 11–16
  significance of 53
  structural account of 5
business representation 43, 44, 47, 50, 53, 57, 59, 60, 88, 89, 90, 108, 162
  consequences for stability and continuity of 161
  economic change and politics of 151–3
  fundamental problems of 95
  organization of 51, 55
  practical politics of 49
  round table format for 58, 62
  sectional domains of 56

Business Roundtable (US) 52–3, 56, 72, 75, 152
  impressive resources and professionalism 147
business solidarity 81
business unionism 34

cable news channels 146
Cain, P. G. 21
Calder, K. 94
California 34, 118
Cambridge University 49
campaigning groups 91, 104
Canada 74
cancer 73, 148
capital accumulation 99
capitalism 82, 108
  critics of 146
  democracy and 3, 5, 16–17, 36
  development of 8
  diversity of 7
  first industrial society based on principles of 132
  founding period of 69
  harshnesses of 1
  highest stage of 8
  incompatible with environmental sustainability 145
  industrial 140
  influential accounts of 167
  legitimacy of the institutions of 130
  models of 2, 7–11, 17, 168, 169–71
  modernizing 98
  opposition offered by socialist movements 31
  plutocratic 120
  regulated 33–4
  restless 151, 153, 159–63
  saved 32
  small-scale agrarian 99
  spectacular economic success 27
  stock-exchange dominated 2
  success of 130
  see also advanced capitalism; varieties of capitalism
Cardiff 48
Carnegie, Andrew 29, 120
Carosso, V. 30, 31
Carroll, W. 80, 158
Carson, C. 80, 158
cartels 127, 128, 146
Cater, D. 35
Catholic Church 116, 137

Cato Institute 56, 147
CBI (Confederation of British Industry) ix–x,
  28, 44–5, 47, 52, 69, 104, 152
  assigned central role 43
  dominant role 42
CEN (European Parliament Committee for
  Standardization) 85
Center for Public Integrity (US) 118, 123
central banks 27, 168
  see also Bank of England
centralization 43, 53, 59, 64
CEOs (Chief Executive Officers) 58, 73, 76,
  80, 111, 149
  dominant/leading 70, 71, 72, 78, 79
  politics and 53, 72, 74–5
Chamber of Shipping (US) 64–5
Chambers, Sir Paul 65
Chambers of Commerce, see British
  Chambers of Commerce; International
  Chamber of Commerce; US Chamber of
  Commerce
Chandler, A. 8–9, 13, 17, 29, 32, 70, 73, 99,
  165
change 143, 162
  cultural 24, 135, 137, 138
  historical 7, 9
  institutional 135, 153
  legislative 134
  market-driven 159
  political 87, 112
  procedural 24
  regulatory 161
  structural 44, 94, 159
  see also economic change; social change
charities 137
Chartered Institute of Public Relations 47
chemicals and fibres 65
Chicago 102, 146
China 16
Christian Aid 148
Christian Right 96
churches 72, 137, 143
CIFE (*Conseil des Fédérations Industrielles
  d'Europe*) 152
Cincinnati 52
citizen activist groups 149
citizenship 17
City of London 2, 23, 25, 28, 43, 48, 65, 109
  anti-globalization protests 137
  celebrated as emblem of British economic
    success 168
  development as key centre of financial
    activity 37

global orientation 22, 77, 78
  self-regulation 132, 135
  well-developed web of interests 21
civil servants 49, 64–5, 90, 113, 133
civil society 17, 72, 105, 137, 142, 164
  attempt by state actively to redesign 135
  campaigns against multinationals 139, 148
  critical institutions in 82
  critics of big business 158
  global 82
  lobbying groups in 131, 150
  parties declined in significance as
    institutions in 119
  parties in decline as institutions in 127
  political parties and 108, 119, 127
Clapham, J. H. 21
Clark, G. 138
Clarke, M. 14
class coalitions 117
class interest 5
Clay, H. 26
clientelism 116
Clinton, Bill 74
coal and steel 19
Coates, D. 10, 110, 130
Coca Cola 139
Coen, D. 41, 50, 64, 66, 79, 93, 95
cohesion 48, 51, 152, 155
  problems of maintaining 152
  strategic 53, 77–82
cold war economy 34
collaborative relationships 34
collective action 41, 46, 85, 89, 93, 104, 147
  coordinating amongst large numbers of
    firms 62
  limitations of 77
  long-term problems involved in organizing
    business for 60
  most important institution for big
    business 75
  multinational corporate elites 80
  participation through trade
    associations 78
  political institutions concerned
    with 154
  strategies for 152
collective bargaining 26, 45, 72
collusive relationships 13
colonization 21, 22, 38
commercial insurance services 21
commercial services 21
Committee on Standards in Public Life
  (UK) 115, 126

Common Market 19, 41
communication 91, 140
Communist functionaries 69
competition 14, 15, 79
  combating attempts by business to rig 141
  democratic 156
  economic 153
  electoral 26
  foreign 87, 108
  globalized 101
  legislation governing 136
  political 153
  price 76
  protection from 94
  regulated 8
  regulatory restrictions on 100–1
  restrictions on 161
Competition Appeals Tribunal (UK) 76
Competition Commission (UK) 76
competition policy 136
competitive advantage 64, 79, 122
competitive markets 1, 76, 92
  profit generation in 17
competitiveness 140
  export 133
  national 135
computing industry 118
Confederation of British Business 42
Conference Board (US) 51, 55
conglomerates 30, 100, 124
Conservative Party (UK) 16, 24, 43, 90
  business and 26, 28, 38, 87, 108–14, 117
  precipitous fall in membership 153
  radical economic policies 45
consumer protection 141, 142
consumerism 143
consumption 36
contracts:
  enforcement of 12
  lucrative 35
  temporary 163
  terms of 12
convergence 170
convertibility 159
Cooper, R. 95–6, 97
Coordinated Market Economies 10
copyright piracy 58
core values 141
CORE (Corporate Responsibility
    Coalition) 148
Corporate Crime Reporter (US 2007) 124
corporate governance 10, 12–13, 14
  key problems of 15

corporate power 37
  hostility to 31, 32
Corporate Watch 89, 91
corporatist capitalism 10, 17
corruption 30, 32, 145
  deterring from 123–4
  exchange of money and favours 116
  limited by morality and fear of being
      caught 123
  periodic scandals 127
  state-level 124
  US states that topped the league 124
Council of Ministers (EU) 41
Council on Foreign Relations (US) 51
County Antrim 93
Courtaulds 65
Cowling, M. 25, 109
creative destruction 7, 130, 151, 159, 160, 161
credit 30, 94
credit-card consortia 101
credit-rating agencies 80
criminality 136, 145
crop production 118
Croydon 90, 102
cultural setting 129–30
Curran, J. 89
currencies 19

Dahl, Robert 3–4, 144
Daily Telegraph 76
damage limitation 46
Dannreuther, C. 95
Davenport-Hines, R. T. P. 26
Davignon, Etienne 62
Davis, A. 47
Davos 81, 158
decentralization 50–9, 103
decision-making 11, 67, 74
  polyarchal 6
  regulatory 6, 41
defence sector 34, 35, 100
Delaware 118
Deloitte Touche Tohmatsu 58
Delors, Jacques 78
demand 3, 36
Demark 19
democracy 18
  Anglo-American 153
  capitalism and 2, 3, 16–17, 36, 60
  changing character of 156
  competitive 27
  oligarchies and 20–8
  parties and 106–8

democracy (*cont.*)
  populism and 28–37
  restless 151, 153–9, 163
  varieties of 37–9
democratic capitalism 15
democratic institutions 23
  construction of 19
  development of 18, 22
Democratic Party (US) 16, 35, 71, 118, 119,
    124, 125, 127
democratic politics 103
  agenda of 111
  business power and 2, 3–7, 106
  competitive character of interest-group
    politics in 100
  connection between business and 153
  construction of institutions 19
  conversion to 16
  defending 16
  development of 18, 20
  markets and 168
  parties are central to 106
  privileged section of business
    manipulating 5
  public workings of 5
  rise of 23, 37, 38
  signs of difficulty or crisis in
    functioning 154
  understanding of the character of 11
  wider issues for 16
demonstrations and marches 154, 155
Dennis, W. 95, 144
Department of Trade and Industry (UK) 88
deregulation 14, 110, 111, 147, 163
  academic advocates of 146
  cheerleaders for 138
  powerful advocates of 146
  widespread employment of rhetoric of 170
Derthick, M. 73, 74, 100, 120
developing countries 139
development agencies 89
developmental state 27
Devlin Commission on Business
    Representation (UK 1972) 42
devolution 48, 92–3, 103, 114
Diet (Japanese Parliament) 94
Dimitrakopoulos, D. 115
Dinan, W. 47
direct foreign investment 2, 65
disclosure rules 59
division of labour 136
  elaborate 73, 80, 162
  Fordist 36

Docker, Dudley 26
Drahos, P. 3, 12, 79
Dublin 116
Duke, James 148
Duma (Russian Parliament) 69
DuPont 74, 118

East Asian financial crisis (1997) 27
EBPS (European Business and Parliament
    Scheme) 107
economic activity 2, 12
  means of coordinating 1
  productive 20
  share of 88
Economic and Social Research Council
    (UK) 92
economic change 32, 66, 87, 151–3
  accelerated 29
  extraordinary 30
  long-term 20
  massive 140
economic crises 3, 81, 152
economic growth 9, 71, 166
  sustained 140, 159
economic interests 80, 108
  dominant 28
  promotion of 50
economic liberalism 10
economic miracle (1950s) 27
economic performance 9
economic planning 42, 89
economic policy 45, 136
  broader 134
  damaging 133
  EU 152
  foreign 51
economic resources 129, 165
  ownership and control of 6
economic union 19
economies of scale 87
ECSC (European Coal and Steel
    Community) 19
Edinburgh 48, 93
EEA (European Economic Area) 131
egalitarianism 140
Eisenhower, Dwight D. 35, 56, 141
Eisner, M. 57, 141, 143, 144, 161
Elections and Political Parties Act (UK
    2000) 113, 126
Electoral Commission (UK) 126, 128
electronic campaigning 155
elites 25, 51, 62, 70, 82, 143, 163
  commercial 21, 22, 23

educational 49, 132
enrichment of 149, 150, 163
financial 23
global 158
governing 4, 44, 48, 49, 72, 132, 133, 134, 138, 165
hostility to business concerns 145
industrial 38
intellectual 138, 147, 149
metropolitan 43
multinational 65, 77, 80, 81
plutocratic 171
policy 10, 64, 95, 101
power 3, 4, 5, 6, 35
reward for 15, 134, 165
state 21, 22
strategic 81
see also political elites
employers' associations 42, 45, 69, 152
Employers' Confederation of Latvia 152
employment:
  boosted 36
  competitive market pressures on 1
  criticism of practices 138
  discrimination in 141
  rising 166
  temporary 85
enfranchisement 24
Engineering Employers' Federation (UK) 42, 44, 45
Enhanced Supply Chain Security 85
Enron Corporation 14, 67, 124, 145
entrepreneurs 68, 100, 118
  belief in the primacy of 96
  creative 30
  individual 22, 96
  political 91
  small 8, 30, 99
  successful 91
environmental groups 93, 131, 155
  long-established 143
environmentalism 143, 156
equality 17
Ericsson 107
ERT (European Round Table of Industrialists) 62, 66, 78, 152
Erturk, I. 15, 163
ESBA (European Small Business Alliance) 85
ethical behaviour standards 14
EU (European Union) viii, 19, 48, 107, 136
  case against Microsoft 140
  cumulative impact of procurement policies 115

direct foreign investment in 2, 65
economic government of 60
growing influence of 170
lobbying in 41, 62, 92
policy process 93
regulation of business lobbyists 131
representing business in 152
small-business representation 95
transfer of locus of policy making to 114
EU Civil Society Contact Group 131
EU–US summit (2008) 58
Euro (currency) 19
European Commission 19, 41, 48, 58, 62, 66, 78, 93
  DGIV 136
  forums for targeted sectors and industries 95
  joint initiative of US State Department and 79
  proposal for Small Business Act 85
European Court of Justice 136
European Economic Community 19
European Parliament 41, 107
  Committee for Standardization 85
Europeanization 65, 66, 93
extractive industries 20, 29, 72
extreme right wing views 36

family dynasties 49
Fannie Mae (Federal National Mortgage Association) 168
fare fixing 136
farmers 94
FBI (Federation of British Industries) 25, 26, 44, 90–1, 109
FEC (US Federal Election Commission) 121, 122, 126, 128
Federal Deposit Insurance Corporation 33
Federal Election Campaign Act (US 1971) 120, 126
Federation of German Industries 58
feminism 143
Fennema, M. 80
Fiat 62
film industry 138, 145–6
finance capitalism 7–8, 29
financial crises 11, 15, 27, 101, 111, 135, 159, 168
financial engineering 163
financial institutions:
  excessive exercise of power 33
  global 27
  profound crisis of 60

financial institutions: (*cont.*)
  regulation of 80
  revelations surrounding collapse of 144
financial intermediaries 161, 162
financial markets 23, 30, 33, 55, 138
  emergence of 4
  global 27
  governing 25
  highly-developed 11
  intermediation in 161
  lightly regulated 168
  outrageous business abuse 32
  pressures in 161
  regulation in 141, 168
  rewards to the super-rich 15
financial services 15, 28, 44
Financial Services Authority (UK) 135
financial speculation 34
financialization 161, 162
Fine Gael party 78
fines 136
firm autonomy 22, 28
  fragmentation and 42–50
  history of 26
First World War (1914–18) 23–4, 25, 31, 36,
    38, 51, 86, 108–9, 110
  economic consequences of 29
  economic differences between business
    arising out of 81
  'maturing' of the giant corporation during
    and after 32
  surge in state intervention during 42–3
fixed exchange rates 159
focus groups 155
Foley, M. 30, 32
Folkman, P. 125, 163
food 31, 94
  cheaper 108
Food and Drug Administration (US) 31
Ford Motor Corporation 36
Fordism 34, 36
foreign multinationals 65, 69, 78–9
foreign policy 133
Fortune 500 companies 52–3
Fox News Channel 146
France 19, 49
franchises 69
fraud 32, 33, 124
  critical legislation designed to control 22–3
Freddie Mac (Federal Home Mortgage
    Corporation) 168
free-market forces 10
  triumphalism 168

free trade 108
  see also NAFTA
Freedom of Information Act (UK 2000) 76
Friends of the Earth 131, 137, 148
Froud, J. 161, 162
FSB (UK Federation of Small Businesses) 85,
    89, 91, 103
  Scottish policy unit 92
FTSE-100 companies 161
fuel protests 88

Galambos, L. 35
Galbraith, J. K. 8, 162, 167
Gamble, A. 22, 135, 169
Garrett, G. 11
Gates, Bill 73
Gazprom 69
General Elections (UK) 24, 108
  spending on campaigns 112–13
General Electric 149
General Motors Corporation 141
general store myth 99
George, S. 19
German monarchy 24
Germany viii, 17, 19, 36, 76, 139
  success of economy 10
giant firms 3, 8, 29
  first 4
  lobbies surrounding 141
  maturing of 32
  politics and 61–82
  problems in managing reputations 124
  rise of 13, 30
  see also multinational corporations
Gibraltar 85
Glass–Steagall Act (US 1935) 33
global economy 27, 63
  dominant power in 71
  large strategic questions facing 81
  one of the nerve centres of 77
  opening up of 21
  powerful structural forces in 104
  strategic issues of management 80
global power 8, 51
globalization 65, 94
  acceleration of 63, 160
  challenges of 54
  consequences of the great burst
    of 66
  financial 27
  new waves of 11
gold 159
Goldman Sachs 78

Google 160, 161, 163
  Political Action Committee 73
government 5, 6
  aristocrats prominent in 23, 132
  authority of 29
  centralized, metropolis-dominated 91
  devolved 60, 114
  electoral fate 15
  exclusion of business from key policy-
    making processes 133
  federal 35
  multi-level 59–60
  retreat in scale of control 24
  scepticism of 96
  suspicion of 28
  weaknesses of systems of 30
government relations function 46, 47, 57, 64,
    65, 68, 73–4
Gramsci, Antonio 36, 129–30, 133, 134, 135,
    137, 138, 147, 149–50
Grandes écoles 49
Grant, W. x, 28, 44, 46, 64, 65, 79
Gray, V. 57
Graz, J.-C. 81, 158
Great Crash/Depression (1929) 32, 33, 71, 168
Great War, *see* First World War
Greater London Authority 89–90
greed 14
Green, J. 119, 154
Green representation 114
Greenpeace International 131
Grieves, K. 26
Griffiths, D. 111
grocery trade 63, 88, 99, 164
Guttsman, W. 20, 87
Gyllenhammar, Pehr 62

Hall, P. vii, 10
Halpin, D. 89, 91
Hammond, B. 29
Hannah, L. 1, 43
Hanson, P. 69
hard technology 91
Harding, Warren 32
Harris, J. 158
Hart, D. 70, 72, 73, 77, 123
Harvey, C. 49
Haughey, Charles 116
Haxey, S. 113
health and safety 13, 38, 65, 132, 135, 141,
    142
Hearst newspaper empire 145
Heath, Edward 43

hegemony 27, 129–30, 132–5, 137, 138, 147,
    149–50
Heinz, J. 54, 56, 74
Heritage Foundation 56, 147
Héritier, A. 93
hierarchy 8, 140, 165
  deference to 132
  moral right to exercise authority 17
higher education 144
Hilferding, R. 7
Hofstadter, R. 28, 29
Hollywood 145
Hopkin, J. 121
Hopkins, A. G. 21
Hoppe, R. 99
House of Commons (UK) 50, 87, 113
  Select Committees 47, 115
House of Lords (UK) 115
Hunter, F. 35, 53
Hurricane Katrina (2005) 98
Hutton, W. vii

IBM 70–1, 72, 79, 161
Iceland 131
ICI 65
IKEA 69
illicit payments 123
image management 78
Imperial Tobacco Company 148
imperialism 8, 9, 22
  links between commerce and 21
incentives 149, 156
  profits and 8
income 127
  attempt to manage by law 43
  huge increase in gap 163
  inequality 162
  unequal distributions of 15
Indian tribes 123
individualization 50, 157
industrial policy 65
industrial relations 110, 134
Industrial Reorganization Corporation
    (UK) 65, 86
Industrial Revolution 20, 22, 37–8, 72
industrialism 26
  consequences of 13
  destructive and humanity-threatening 143
  global pioneer of transition to 20
  new interests of 22, 108
  problems created by 23
  take-off to 21
  see also ERT

inequality 14–15, 147–9, 166
  new age of 160, 162–3, 167, 171
INFACT (Infant Formula Action
    Coalition) 139
inflation 159
Ingham, G. 22
innovation 7, 9, 29, 161
  enterprise and 134
  institutional 21, 27, 64, 152
  market 100, 101
  policy 156
  political 83–4, 104–5
  technical/technological 88, 101, 159, 160
insolvency 12
Institute of Directors (UK) 45
insurance:
  deposit 33
  health 103
  maritime 21
intellectual property rights 58
intellectuals 130, 150, 166
interest groups 41, 88, 100, 123
intermarriage 23
International Association of Business and
    Parliament 107
International Baby Food Action Network 139
International Chamber of Commerce 81
International Code of Marketing Breast-Milk
    Substitutes 139
International Organization of Securities
    Commissions 80
Internet 125, 127
Interstate Commerce Commission (US) 31
investment banking 33, 78
invisible hand 8
inward investment 77
Ireland, Republic of 19, 78
  clientelism and party-business
    relations 116
  see also Northern Ireland
Israel–Arab War (1973) 159
IT (information technology) 88
ITGA (International Tobacco Growers'
    Association) 148

Jacobs, D. 52, 53
Japan viii, 9, 10, 27, 94, 164
Jayasuriya, K. 27
Jeffery, C. 48
Jews 36
Johnson, C. 27
Joint Stock Companies Act (UK 1844) 22
joint ventures 69, 146, 148

Jones, G. 87
Jordan, G. 89, 91
Joseph, Sir Keith 134
Josephson, M. 29, 120
judicial tribunals 116

Kagan, R. 126, 142
Kahn, Alfred 146
Kansas 118
Katz, R. 118, 127
Kearton, Sir Frank 65
Kelly, G. 22
Kendall, G. 5
Kennedy, John F. 35–7
Kennedy, Joseph 34, 35–7
Kentucky 124
Kerwer, D. 80
Keynesianism 36
Khodorkovsky, Mikhail 69
King, R. 5
Kipping, Norman 90–1
Koizumi, Junichiro 94
Kolodny, R. 118
Komsomol 69
Kynaston, D. 21, 26

labour markets 134, 163, 165
  government of 169
Labour Movement 138
Labour Party (UK) 24, 25, 108–9, 111–12,
    114, 118, 156
  'cash for peerages' scandal 115
  membership fall 153
  reforms (after 1997) 48, 90
  revolutionary socialism abandoned 26
  rise after First World War 86
  transformation in policies towards
    business 110
  see also New Labour; Old Labour
Labour Representation Committee (UK) 24
labour unions, see trade unions
law 12, 13, 126, 135
  competition 170
  dominance of 33
  electoral 94
  industrial relations 134
  planning 91
law firms 41, 47
  multinational 48
  prestigious 57
Lawler, P. 110, 130
Lazonick, W. 9, 10
LDP (Japanese Liberal Democratic Party) 94

Leech, B. 54, 57, 120, 122
Lees-Marshment, J. 112
legal culture 33
legal reforms 45
legitimacy 15, 16–17, 137
  business institutions 14, 32, 130
  democracy and 164–7
  golden age for 35
  sectional activities 85
  tax and criminal convictions 69
Lehne, R. 72, 73, 120
leisure and cultural organizations 155
Lenin, V. I. 8
Levitan, S. 95–6, 97
libel action 139
liberal capitalism 2, 10
Liberal Market Economies 10
Liberal Party (UK) 24, 26, 108, 109
liberalization 27
libertarians 149
Lichtenstein 131
Lighthouse Projects 58
Lindblom, Charles 5–6, 7, 144, 146
Lions Clubs 87
Lipset, S. M. 29, 70
liquidity 168
Lisle-Williams, M. 23
literacy 139
Lloyd, Edward 21
Lloyd George, David 108
Lloyds Corporation 21, 23
lobbying 16, 24, 37, 39, 42, 44, 45, 64, 65, 69,
    70, 72, 73, 85, 88, 93, 97, 100, 106, 123,
    124, 140, 142–3
  channelled through Bank of England 43
  competitive systems of 92
  corporate interests dominate the
    system 127
  crisis of the business system 59
  'do it yourself' 50
  effective 62
  evolution in the EU 41
  explicitly disavowed 107
  formally organized groups 55
  full-time 47
  global economic 77–82
  growing sophistication and resources of 60
  individual/individualization of 41, 157
  informal, by senior executives 46
  institutions of 90
  marketing practices in the developing
    world 139
  mass 91

national 38
open 75
operational 67
organizational shape of 51
professional 48, 50, 54, 57, 60, 66, 71, 74,
    75, 104, 156, 157
regulation of 59, 131
resources put into 46, 56–7
rise in 141
small-business 98, 103
special-interest 107
specialized function 47, 60, 66
surge in level and intensity of 48
third world activities 148
transformation in sophistication of 146
well-resourced organization 89
Lobbying Disclosure Acts (US 1995/2007) 59
local authorities 86, 89
London 51, 84, 90, 93, 107
  elite gentlemen's clubs 115
  see also City of London; Greater London
    Authority
Louisiana 124

Maastricht Treaty (1992) 107
McConnell, G. 30, 31, 59
McCraw, T. 28, 33, 146
MacDonald, A. 46, 79
McDonald's 69, 139, 145
McFadden Act (US 1927) 97, 98, 101, 102
McGrath, C. 50, 57
McHugh, J. x, 87–8
McKibbin, R. 25
McKinley, William 120
Maclean, M. 49
McQuaid, K. 35, 53, 71, 75
Mafia 145
'mainstreaming' 138
Mair, P. 127
Major, John 134
manufacturing industry 20, 29, 72, 94, 96,
    133
  CBI dominated by 44
  export competitiveness 133
  share of output 43
Marchand, R. 70, 141
marginal costs 146
maritime trading enterprises 21
market competition manipulation 13, 31
market economy ix, 3, 6, 7
  core institutional structures 5
market failure 141, 142
market-making 19

market order 159, 167
  effectively functioning 163
  intellectual critics of 150
market power 98, 99
market research 112
market share 76, 83, 148
market strategy 68, 76
marketing 107, 148
  lobbying a corporation about its
    practices 139
  mass 36, 119
  political networking and 68
  marketing power of giants 76
  retail 76
  unscrupulous practices 139
markets:
  captured 29
  change in structures noticeable in 160–1
  commercial 23
  cross-state 101
  deregulation of 147
  global 78, 102
  interlocked 168
  international 29
  liberalization of 27
  loss of control over 99
  niche 95
  protected 94
  regulation of 27, 29
  securities 80
  variety of 74
  see also financial markets
Marks and Spencer 46, 76, 164
Marsh, D. 28, 44
Martin, C. 57, 74, 157, 158–9
Marx, Karl 7, 10
Marxism/Marxists 5, 8, 129, 130, 138
mass media 119, 145, 149, 150, 155
mass prosperity 140
May, T. x, 46, 87–8
Means, G. 8, 162
means of production 5, 110
media 138
  campaigns managed through 119, 121
  change in tone of 145
  controlling reporting 117
  treatment of business 35, 145
Medvedev, Dmitry 69
MEPs (Members of the European
    Parliament) 85, 107
mergers 87, 136, 168
Metropolitan Police 126
Mexico 74, 76

Microsoft 61, 73, 136, 146, 160, 161, 163, 164
  EU case against 140
Middlemas, K. 26, 42, 109
military-fiscal state 21
Miller, D. 47
millionaires 29
Milward, A. 19
Milward, N. 45
Ministry of Agriculture
    (Japan) 94
Mississippi 124
Mitchell, J. 48
Mitchell, N. 96
mobilization 91
Model-T car (Ford) 36
money 116, 119
  soft 121, 122, 124
Money Trust 30, 31
Monnet, Jean 19
Monopolies and Restrictive Practices
    (Inquiry and Control) Act
    (UK 1948) 136
monopoly 8, 15, 136
Moody's 80
moral authority 14
Moran, M. 26, 43, 98, 101, 135, 137
Morgan, J. Pierrepoint 30, 31
Morgan, K. 48
Moriarty, M. 116
mortgages 168
Moscow 69
Motion Picture Association of America 79
movies, see film industry
MSNBC 146
Mulgan, A. G. 94
Mulhall scandals (US 1913) 59
multinationals:
  branches of 41
  campaigns against 139, 148
  corporate law 48
  giant 11, 107, 164
  one of the longest established 139
  pioneer of 99
  politics and 61–82

NAFTA (North American Free Trade
    Agreement) 74
NAM (US National Association of
    Manufacturers) 96–7
narcissistic celebrities 158
National Association of Manufacturers
    (US) 52
national champions 65, 86

National Economic Development Council
  (UK) 43, 45
  Economic Development Committees 42
national interest 71
National Small Business Association (US) 97
National Union of Manufacturers (UK) 26,
  87, 109
nationalization 168
  large-scale 111
  partial 135, 167
natural resources 69
NBC 146
neo-liberalism 138
  powerful advocates of 146
  rise of 149, 162
Nestlé 139
networks 43–4, 82, 155
  global 3, 102
  informal 114
  inter-corporate 80, 81
  long-lasting 161
  political 68
  social 80
New Deal (US 1933–9) 32–3, 34, 35, 37, 118,
  140, 141, 168
New Labour (UK) 90, 110, 111
  historically established policies
    abandoned 137
  none of key Thatcherite reforms
    reversed 134
  reinvented as business-friendly 156
  scandals 113
New Orleans 98
new technologies 31, 160, 163
New York 2, 4, 30, 120, 125
  financial system 29
New York Stock Exchange 55
NFIB (US National Federation of
  Independent Business) 52, 96,
  97, 103
NGOs (nongovernmental organizations) 81,
  158
niche markets 95
Nigeria 68
Nilsson, A. 46, 67, 70
Nixon, Richard M. 120
nomenklatura 69
Norman, Montagu 25
North Sea 67, 68
Northern Ireland 92, 93
Northern Rock 135, 168
Norway 131
Norwich 87

Obama, Barack 125–7, 154
obedience 17, 165
obligations 12, 17
OFT (UK Office of Fair Trading) 136, 138
Ogus, A. 13
oil 69, 70, 118
  price rises 133, 159
Old Labour (UK) 114
oligarchies 20–8, 69, 132
Olson, M. 84, 89, 104
one-party systems 86
OPEC oil cartel 159
opinion polls 68, 71, 143
opportunism 68, 76, 77, 81, 89, 92, 104
organized labour 10, 36
Ortoli, François-Xavier 62
outsourcing 74, 110
overseas expansion 76
Oxford University 49

pacifism 143
PACs (US Political Action
  Committees) 121–2, 123, 124
Paris 62, 152
Paris, Treaty of (1951) 19
Parkinson, J. 22
Parmar, I. x, 52, 147
party systems 26, 51, 86, 87, 119, 122, 154, 156
  business-friendly 24, 108–17, 128
  historical relations between business
    interests and 127
  increasingly distinctive 114
  single most historically important feature
    of 118
patronage 30
Paulson, Henry 168
peak associations 26, 43, 52, 53, 96, 104, 106,
  109, 152
  best-known 44
Peck, J. 90, 147
Peel, Sir Robert 108
penalties 136
Pentagon capitalism 34
Perot, Ross 215
personal contacts 46
pharmaceutical industry 31, 75
  sustained campaign against leading
    companies 137
Phelps, N. 90, 102
Phillips Report (UK 2007) 113, 115
Pilling, D. 63
Pinkham, D. 56
Pinto-Duschinsky, M. 112

pioneering enterprises 22
Plaid Cymru 114
pluralism 3–4, 6, 16, 129, 130, 144, 146, 149
  persistence of 150
plutocracy 29–30, 120, 125, 128
policy issues 11–16
political asylum 69
political control 69, 168
political elites 23, 68, 114, 133, 137, 165, 166, 171
  business-friendly 117
  concentration of power well connected to 37
  critical relationships forged with 60
  important parts of 38
  peak of 53
political engagement 15–16
political funding 121
political institutions 15, 40, 67
  changes in 94
  comparatively simple 71
  concerned with collective action 154
  democratic 17, 19
  leaders of 35
  varying role of 9
political parties 5, 87, 107
  business-friendly 16, 24, 28, 39, 56, 103, 108–17, 127–8
  business interests and 106, 120, 124
  changed character of 156
  flow of finance from business sector to 122
  newly successful competitors to 157
  plutocratic colonization resisted 171
  relative decline as agents of representation 88
  see also Conservative Party; Democratic Party; Fine Gael; Labour Party; LDP; Liberal Party; Plaid Cymru; Republican Party
political power:
  business as an organized system of 49
  reshaped nature of 29
  threats from the exercise of 99
  US Chamber of Commerce 123
political strategy 74, 76, 139
  highly personal 68
pollution 13, 132, 135
Polsby, N. 53
polyarchy 6
populism 4, 5, 38, 95, 98, 99, 145
  democracy and 28–37
  development of 140
  revival of 144

rise of 102
Porter, T. 23
Power, M. 67
Presidential elections (US) 103, 125
  turnout in 154
pressure group politics 155
Press, J. 49
prestige 17, 57, 132, 140, 141
  cultural 165
price collusion 136
price-fixing 138–40
price stability 27
prices:
  attempt to manage by law 43
  oil, rises in 133, 159
  ruthless competition 76
private equity firms 111, 115–16
privatization 63, 111, 137, 168
  ambitious policy of 134
  massive wave of 69
privilege 38, 164
  autonomy and 132
  gained in return for observing obligations 12
production methods 36
productivity 36
professionalism/professionalization 73, 74, 75, 156, 157–8
professions 30, 132
profits 69
  and incentives 8
  pursuit of empire and 21
  unequal 15
progressivism 30
propaganda 146
property ix, 23, 44, 132, 162
  productive 69
  right to appropriate 129
  rules of 5, 6, 7
property rights:
  redistributed 163
  regulation of 79
  trading of 161
  see also intellectual property rights
prosecutions 69, 138
public affairs 41, 57
Public Affairs Council (US) 56
public control 64
public opinion 143–9
  long-term shifts in 141, 147
  professional probing of 155
public ownership 168
public policy 42, 67, 71, 72, 153, 168

critical issues 74
  influences on 55, 65, 146
  monitoring the stream of 47
  privileged position in making and
    delivery of 54
public relations 47, 60, 74
  disasters 66, 68, 73, 100
  fiascos 46
  huge free material 68
public utilities 63–4
Pujo hearings 31
Pure Food and Drug Act (US 1906) 31
Putin, Vladimir 69
Putnam, R. 155

Qualified Majority Voting 41
quasi-government bodies 111
Quigley, James 58

Radcliffe, L. 44
radicalism 45, 114, 142
  agrarian 30
rail 29, 30
Rast, J. 54, 102
recession 99, 159
Reform Act (UK 1832) 23
regulation 6, 8, 13, 22, 146, 171
  adversarial 31, 122, 123, 126, 168
  big business shaping jurisprudence
    of 100
  business-friendly 135, 170
  changing character of 141–2
  contrasting national styles 126
  cooperative 23, 32, 38
  economic 80
  economically sensitive professions 135
  environmental 135
  failures of 14
  federal 31, 32–3
  global financial 27
  key area of 136
  key institutions in 121
  legal/legalistic 23, 122, 126, 138
  lobbying and 48–50, 59
  new age of 128
  party-business connection 117–27
  public 15
  scandal connected with 120
  social 120, 142, 144
  terms of 79
  see also self-regulation
reinsurance 21
religious observance 116

Representation of the People Act (UK
    1918) 24
Republican Party (US) 16, 35, 59, 71, 118,
    119, 124, 125
reputation 46, 65
  building 57
  damaged 67, 68
  highly vulnerable 70
  means of promoting 67
  problems in managing 124
reputation management 67, 68, 74, 148
Retail Consortium (London) 93
retail sector 44, 76, 84, 98
  alliances in 88–9
  banking 33, 168
  giants in 61, 76, 99
rewards 14–15, 104, 124, 134, 149
  enormous 163
  golden age of 165
  maximizing 161
Rhee, Syngman 27
Rhodes, R. 48
Ricci, D. 147
rice production 94
Riegle-Neal Act (US 1994) 101–2
right-wing politics 36
Rio Tinto 66
Ritz–Carlton Hotel chain 69
RNIB (Royal National Institute for the
    Blind) 50
road haulage 88, 91
robber barons 29, 30, 120, 163
Robinson, W. 158
Robinson–Patman Act (US 1936) 98, 99, 101
Rockefeller, John D. 29, 120
Roe, M. 10
Rome, Treaty of (1957) 19, 41, 152
Roosevelt, Franklin D. 32, 168
Rotary/Round Table 87
Roy, W. 30, 100
Royal Bank of Scotland 136
Royal Society for the Protection of Birds 93,
    155
RUIE (Russian Union of Industrialists and
    Entrepreneurs) 69
ruling class 5
rural areas 29, 30
Russian Revolution (1917) 24

Sainsbury 63
Sampson, A. 115
Samuels, R. 27
Sargent, J. 45

Saunders, P. 87, 90
Savage, M. 161
scandals 14, 15, 31, 34, 59, 67, 113
　corruption 123, 127
　exposure of 145
　new age of 128
　party financing 115, 120, 128
　trust recouped after revelations 167
Schlozman, K. 57, 120
Schmidt, S. 123
Schofield, R. 20
Scholte, J. 11, 63, 77, 160
Schuman, Robert 19
Schumpeter, J. A. 7, 8, 130, 138, 144, 147, 150,
　151, 159, 160, 161, 162, 166–7
Scotland viii, 48, 92, 103, 114
Scott, J. 44
Scottish Executive 93
Scottish Retail Consortium 93
Second World War 94, 140
Securities and Exchange Commission
　(US) 33, 34, 141
securities markets 10
self-employed people 89
self-interest 50
self-regulation 26, 34, 132, 136, 170
　historical preference for 169
　licensed 55
　notions systematized in ideologies of 38
　persistent corrosion of the structures
　　of 135
　privileged 138
　publicly overseen institutions 54
selfishness 14
Seligman, J. 34
service sector 90
share ownership 8
shareholder capitalism 2
shareholder value 147
　maximizing 162
Shell 46, 62, 66–7, 68–70
Sherman Act (US 1890) 31
shipping 21, 64–5
Shonfield, A. 9, 49, 162
Siemens 62
Sierra Club 72, 143, 155
Sinclair, T. 80
Singapore 27
single-issue politics 89
Single Market Act (1986) 48
Sklair, L. 46, 74, 139
Skocpol, T. 143
small business 26, 44, 52, 53, 93

　politics and 83–105
　　see also ESBA; FSB
Small Business Administration (US) 83, 98, 99
Small Business Legislative Council (US) 97
Small Business Service (UK) 88
Smith, Adam 8
Smith, M. 52, 96, 97, 123
smoking 73, 100
Sobel, R. 32
social change:
　accelerated 29
　extraordinary 30
　fundamental 112
　massive 140
social cohesion 48
social integration 49
social mobility 162
social policy 152
social resources 129
socialism 159
　extreme command forms 166
　gravely weakened 165
　radicalism of 114
　revolutionary 24, 26
　traditional policies of 111
Society of Motor Manufacturers and Traders
　(UK) 78
soft-money campaigns 121, 122, 124
soft technology 91
software 61, 164
Sommer, Tina 85
Soskice, D. vii, 10
South Korea 27
Soviet Union/Soviet bloc (former) 16, 19, 69
specialized information 93
Speth, James Gustave 144, 145, 146
SSFs (separate segregated funds) 121–2
state-dominated capitalism 10
state intervention 23, 42–3, 169
　protection against 38
state power/controls 10, 135
　bailouts 15
　surveillance 12
steel 29, 30
sterling 133
Sterne, Laurence 49
Stewart, R. 142
stock exchanges/markets 10, 12, 23, 33, 34
stockholder activism groups 143
structural reforms 32
Super Size Me (film) 145, 146
supermarket chains 63, 76, 88
　　see also Asda; Sainsbury; Tesco; Wal-Mart

Supple, B. 21, 43, 86, 88
Sutherland, Peter 78

TABD (Transatlantic Business Dialogue) 58, 79, 80
tactical-missile manufacturers 100
takeovers 76, 168
  hostile 161
tariffs 94
taxation 69, 115, 134, 149
Teague, E. 69
TEC (Transatlantic Economic Council) 58
technologies 99
  see also new technologies
telecommunications 80, 93
television 69, 138, 145, 146
temporary contracts 163
Tesco 63, 76, 111, 164
Texas 118, 125
Thatcher, Margaret 45, 65, 134
Thatcherism/Thatcherites 133–4, 135, 137
think-tanks 147, 149
Thompson, J. 14
Thornley, A. 89–90
Thumann, Jürgen 58
Tickell, A. 90
Tierney, J. 57, 120
Tiger economies 27
Time-Warner 80
tobacco industry 73, 100, 107, 148
Tokyo 2
Toshiba 61, 164
Toyota 78, 164
trade associations 43, 44, 64–5, 106, 111, 117, 157
  'capturing' or founding 152
  collective action through 78
  introspective and largely ineffectual 148
  manipulation of 148
  national 79
  poorly resourced and poorly organized 46
  producers in 42
  sectoral-level 41, 45
  specialist-representative 95
trade liberalization 94
trade unions 10, 27, 108–9, 111, 112, 154
  bargaining with 26, 42, 43
  brutal suppression of 32
  corporations and business relationships with 35
  entrenched power of 76
  membership decline 165
  parliamentary faction operating as lobby for 24
  power greatly reduced 134
  powerful sections of 34
  powerful sections of the movement 34
  weakening of 31, 45, 110, 137
  well-organized 72
Trades Union Congress (UK) 45
trading practices 138
transparency 27, 115, 121, 123, 131
Treasury (UK) 25, 133, 168
Trilateral Commission 56, 78, 81
Trump, Donald 93
trust 143, 165–6
  building 167
  destroyed 67
trust-based capitalism 10
Turkey 62
tycoons 69

UNCTAD (UN Conference on Trade and Development) 65
unemployment 32, 159
UNICE (Union des Industries de la Communauté Européenne) 152
Unilever 66
United Seniors Association 75
universal suffrage 17, 24
universities 144, 149, 150
  critiques of business order 146
  elite 132
University of Chicago 146
urban growth coalitions 102
US Census Bureau 29
US Chamber of Commerce ix–x, 52, 96–7, 104
  political power of 123
US Congress 53, 103, 118, 121, 122, 123
  Congressional Committees 72–3, 98
  election costs 119–20
  Enron efforts to lobby senior figures 124
  leading figures in 31, 35
  regulatory programmes 141, 142
US Department of Commerce 58
US Justice Department 101, 124, 136
US State Department 79
US Treasury 168
Useem, M. 80

values 140, 141
Van der Pijl, K. 81
Vanderbilt, Cornelius 29
varieties of capitalism vii, 37–9, 169
  systems central to viii

VAT (value-added tax) 85
Vatican 78
Verheugen, Günter 85
Versailles Peace Conference (1919) 51
vetoes 41
Vidich, A. 102
Virgin enterprises 68, 138
visible hand 9, 17, 73, 142, 165
vocational education 132, 133
Vogel, D. 4, 35, 126, 142, 144
Vogel, S. 161
voluntarism 136
voluntary associations 87
Volvo 62
voting rights 23, 24

Waddan, A. 147
wages 1, 36
Waitrose 76
Wales viii, 92, 103, 114
Wall Street 4, 30, 140
    collapse of financial institutions 144
    hostility to 32, 168
Wall Street Journal, The 147
Wal-Mart 76, 99
Walters, Bob 76
Washington DC 51, 54, 56, 57, 72
    professional lobbyists 73
Watergate 120
Watson, Thomas 70–1
wealth 15, 29, 69, 112, 140
    family 37
    incentives for creation of 149
    land 20
    personal 125
Webb, P. 127

Weber, Max 16–17
WEF (World Economic Forum) 56, 58, 81–2,
    158
Welch, Jack 149
Welch, S. 149
welfare state 163
Westminster Parliament 103, 108, 110,
    111, 114
    civil service and political elite 133
    dominant parties 112, 113
    see also House of Commons
Whitaker, L. 121–2
Whitehall 64, 67, 90
WHO (World Health Organization) 148
Wigham, E. 26
Wilcox, C. 145, 155
Wilks, S. 136
Williams, K. 161
Wilson Governments (UK 1964/1970) 65
Wilson, Charles 141
Wilson, Woodrow 52
Wincott, D. 48
Winstanley, M. 86
Wolfe, A. 54
women 24, 155
working class 34, 109
'working rich' stratum 163
Working Time Directive (EU) 85
World Business Council for Sustainable
    Development 56, 81
World Trade Organization 78, 94
Worldcom 14
Wright Mills, C. 4, 6, 35

Yale 144, 146
Yukos 69